Goodbye, Dearest Holly

KEVIN WELLS

Goodbye, Dearest Holly

HODDER

First published in Great Britain in 2005 by Psychology News Press

This edition published in 2005 by Hodder
A division of Hodder Headline

A Hodder paperback

2

A CIP catalogue record for this title is
available from the British Library

ISBN 0 340 89791 0

Typeset in Sabon MT by Palimpsest Book Production Limited,
Polmont, Stirlingshire

Printed and bound by
Mackays of Chatham Ltd, Chatham, Kent

Hodder Headline's policy is to use papers that are natural,
renewable and recyclable products and made from wood grown in
sustainable forests. The logging and manufacturing processes are expected
to conform to the environmental regulations of the country of origin.

Hodder and Stoughton Ltd
A division of Hodder Headline
338 Euston Road
London NW1 3BH

Contents

Message to Nicola

At no stage in my lifetime will I be able to give you what you desire the most – the chance to walk and talk again with Holly – and that hurts very much. Having witnessed your selfless devotion to two children for so many years, I know how deeply you felt and still feel the loss of your precious daughter, friend and soul-mate every day. There is no loss quite like a mother's loss.

I hope that this book will allow others to realise what an incredible daughter Holly was and the impact she made on all who knew her – she really was so amazing. You should be very proud of the loving, nurturing role that you played in Holly's young life.

Over the last couple of years, your strength of character, fortitude and resolve have been truly inspirational to all who walked beside you during those times of adversity – especially me.

Together, we do have many wonderful memories of Holly to share and recount, but more importantly now, many more to create with our son, Oliver. Behind closed doors, your quiet unassuming personal focus and impassioned interaction with our son allows our family to move forward and this book to draw a line under our personal tragedy.

You have my love and respect.

Kevin

Prologue 2001

Margaret Bryden has been a positive part of my life since I was a pupil at Soham Village College. She was one of my teachers for two years, and my form teacher for one. During that year, Margaret asked me to be her form captain. My fellow pupils teased me mercilessly but I proudly accepted the role. It proved to be a perpetual bond between Margaret and me. When we bump into each other in Soham, 21 years later, we always stop and chat.

I was surprised to get a call from Margaret in the summer of 2001. There were chronic caretaking difficulties at the school, she said, and that wouldn't have been easy for her to admit because the school has been her life. Just before the autumn term, my small team of staff and I completed the high-level cleaning, floor cleaning and window cleaning for the school site, much to the relief of Mrs B. Scott Day, my business partner, and I also accepted Margaret's invitation to close down and lock up the Lodeside part of the school, late at night when evening classes had finished. We took on that role for many months.

During that time, Margaret told me interviews were taking place to find a full-time caretaker. In the end a successful candidate emerged by the name of Ian Kevin Huntley. He was not the first choice, and he came with his live-in girlfriend, Maxine Carr. They spoke of settling down, marrying and having children when they first came to see the school. Margaret gave them a chance.

From the start, Margaret was not too happy with her new caretaker. Huntley took a great deal of time to understand his duties and was poor at supervising his support staff. Margaret's very 'matter of fact' approach did not suit him. Often, when she criticised Huntley because he was not doing the job well, he would leave the meetings in tears. Late into the evening Huntley would then return to apologise. Often when this happened, Huntley was accompanied by Maxine Carr, who made it very clear by her aggressive demeanour that she was far from happy about seeing him so upset.

Margaret was also bothered because Maxine Carr consistently helped Huntley complete his duties. She wanted to improve her boyfriend's chances of keeping his new job. Actually not being an employee of the school seemed to make little difference to Maxine Carr. Margaret told me Huntley was 'simply the best of a bad bunch', but, quite rightly, she wanted to give him time to settle into the job; so she asked me to continue with the night-time care-taking duties a little longer while Huntley 'found his feet'. I agreed. Not only would it give Huntley a little breathing space and a chance to improve, but also it meant I could help Margaret. If she didn't get help, I knew she would close and lock up the College herself at the end of every day. I did not want my former teacher to have to do that.

By the spring of 2002, Scott and I stopped our part-time care-taking. Ian Huntley seemed capable of managing his full range of duties. We were happy to have helped. The next time Scott and I saw Ian Huntley it would be in rather different circumstances.

Sunday 4 August

Holly and her friend Natalie eventually pull themselves from the warmth of their beds and go outside to play, which reduces the decibel level in the house. But not for very long. While I schedule next week's work in my tiny office, the girls run in and out all the time. Their attention spans are so short that it's a miracle if they concentrate on any project for half an hour.

Sometime in the morning Holly gets a phone call from Jessica, who has just returned from holiday. She has a present for Holly and wants to come round and play. Oliver also has a friend visiting. Two boys, three girls, kid city, more decibels. Does that mean Dad in the office is left to get on with his vital admin duties? Fat chance, as the three girls dash in and out, ask to play on my computer, giggle, laugh, and chat. I don't find it charming.

Mid-morning, Natalie goes home. Jessica stays for a lunch of egg sandwiches as we're having a barbecue in the afternoon. The weather isn't playing fair, as it can't make up its mind; it's sunny and then it rains. Jessica is meant to be home for tea but late in the afternoon, she rings her mother to ask if she can stay for the barbecue. When Sharon says yes, Holly and Jessica change clothes. Holly pops on her Manchester United top and Jessica borrows Oliver's shirt as it is very cool to look the same. Holly is wearing her new necklace, which Jessica gave her. Jessica is also wearing a necklace and the girls are now convinced they're the trendiest of all young ladies. All is well in a small town in middle England.

Our guests for this Sunday's barbecue are Robert and Trudie Wright, old friends, great company. Nicola and Trudie have been particularly close for many years, going back to pre-Rob days.

Trudie is pregnant, very pregnant. She is so large that Nicola makes her best friend pose for a shot in profile. Holly and Jessica also want to be a picture in their matching Manchester United shirts. The time is 5.04 p.m. Click, click, and off they go again.

It was to be the last photograph of either girl.

As with all the best barbecues, the men do the cooking! Rob and I cook a great deal anyway and we speak about family, business, horse racing and cricket, though being men we don't discuss recipes. The weather still can't decide whether to pour sunshine or rain, so we move the barbecue from the garden to the front of the house, just inside the garage. Holly and Jessica continue to yo-yo round us and help take food in and out of the house. Eventually the feast is ready.

We get the children to sit down with us but they're far too busy and restless to eat for long. As soon as they can, they ask if they can get up and go. They're happy when we give them permission to get up. They run up to Holly's room to play music.

We can't escape the sound of Holly and Jessica jumping and dancing – the ceiling doesn't quite shake but it bounces. Nicola and Trudie retreat to the relative quiet of the living room. Rob and I play dominoes. I establish an unassailable 2–0 lead and decide to tell Trudie how useless her husband is – at dominoes. We talk and don't notice that the ceiling is no longer bouncing up and down.

Around 8.20 Rob and Trudie are ready to go. As we walk them to the front door, it is open. That's very unusual. Nicola shouts up to Holly and Jessica to pop down to say goodbye to our guests, but there is no reply. The girls have gone out. None of us adults can recall the girls leaving or asking permission to go. That too is unusual. Our children are well behaved. Jessica rang her mum to ask if she could stay, the kids ask if they can leave the table, the children know there are rules.

But it is only 8.20. We have just extended Holly's evening return time to 8.30 as these are the school holidays. She has ten more minutes. From 8.30 to 9 she's allowed to play in the garden or in the cul-de-sac. She has to be indoors for 9 o'clock. Holly also has very clear boundaries about where she can go.

Rob and Trudie leave. Trudie says something like they'll wave to the girls from the car, if they spot them.

Neither Nicola nor I can remember Holly saying anything about going somewhere. The 8.30 deadline passes and there is still no sign of Holly or Jessica. Nicola rings Holly's mobile. To our surprise it rings in the house. Holly has not taken it with her. Part of the front display is broken.

We start to worry. It is not like Holly to miss her deadline. It has not happened before and it's totally out of character. She's a girl who asks permission. Nicola telephones Jessica's mother, Sharon, to see if the girls are with her, but they're not. Sharon has tried ringing Jessica, but Jessica does not answer her mobile.

It's time to do something. I jump on my bike and do a quick lap of the immediate area. No sign of the girls. It is now past 9 o'clock and we're beginning to be really concerned. So are the Chapmans.

We check with Oliver. He has not seen Holly or Jessica for some time. We send him out to look and tell him to complete a large circle to the south of Red House Gardens. I go the opposite way. Jessica's father, Les, is out in his car too, looking for the girls. Intermittently we cross one another's paths – and every time we have bad news for each other. Neither of us has found the girls.

The journey from being irritated at your daughter breaking the rules, to starting to worry, to feeling real fear takes about an hour. Sharon Chapman arrives at Red House Gardens and says it is time to ring the police. Nicola is too upset to do it so Sharon makes the call.

Holly is allowed to walk with a friend no more than a few hundred yards from her home. I cycle round these boundaries a number of times. I ride to St Andrew's School, shouting out for Holly and Jessica. I repeat their names every ten to fifteen seconds, then pause. I expect an answer back. We're here, Dad. But there's only silence. Well, that's not quite true, as I'm now aware of the sound of my heart thumping. I'm feeling sick, sick with worry, sick with fear.

The light's gone now. I stand alone in the middle of the school playing fields, very confused and very frightened. I'm desperately trying to think where Holly might have gone. My hands have started to shake.

I bike on, do a full 360 degrees and make for the Village College grounds. I keep on shouting. I take the path which leads to College Close, past the caretaker's house and through to the Village College and Sports Centre. Holly knows this route. We've walked here, collecting 'conkers' from this very corner of the field.

It is too dark to ride safely. I am now in the vicinity of people's homes and, rather oddly, I feel embarrassed about making such a noise on a Sunday night, but I still shout for Holly and Jessica. At the far corner of the College grounds, where Ian Huntley's house is, there are street lights again. I get back on the bike. I tell myself that when I make it home, miraculously, Holly and Jessica will be there.

But they're not. Instead, the house is now filling up with friends and family. Nicola has been telephoning for help. So have the Chapmans. Soham is a small community but a real community. Nicola's relatives are turning up to assist in the search.

The police are already in my living room. Nicola and Sharon are very upset. I've no time to talk to the police. I must carry on searching for the girls. I contact my business partner, Scott, to see if he is fit to drive. Scott is at my door in minutes.

We have no specific plan but it seems to make sense to drive out from Soham. Our theory is that if some young lads have picked the girls up, they could have dropped them off somewhere remote, as a practical joke. Scott and I return to Soham at about 11 p.m. We search around the town, shouting out of the van window for the girls. I was a postman in Soham for five years and I know every street, play area, 'cubby hole', dodgy nook and dodgy cranny. No result.

I am becoming quieter and withdrawn in the passenger seat. The seriousness of the situation frightens me.

And then I feel something strange in the midst of my fear. I have an urge to return to the school areas. I can't explain it, but the feeling is very strong. Scott drives into the Village College (Beechurst) car park. We're using the car headlights to illuminate the sports fields next to it. As we swing round, we both see the school caretaker, Ian Huntley, walking his dog. He is coming from the direction of a rubbish skip in the corner of the car park.

I think we should explain our presence. He might wonder what the hell an unauthorised car is doing on the school grounds. I'll explain or apologise later, I decide. We can't stop looking for Holly and Jessica.

I don't analyse the situation coolly. Ian Huntley is the residential caretaker. If he sees a car driving all around the school grounds, late on a Sunday night, surely he would either intervene himself or contact the police. But I'm in no mood to be too rational.

Scott and I drive over the school fields. We stop, get out, and both shout and listen. The fields are silent. We drive back to the car park area and head for home. Ian Huntley and his dog are nowhere to be seen. I don't think about them for a second. My aim is to go back home, get an update, see where others are searching and talk to my wife. Because of the panic and urgency, I give no thought to the school caretaker disappearing.

When I get home, Nicola is crying.

'Have you found the girls?'

'No. I would have telephoned you if I had.'

'Where are they, Kev?'

'I don't know.'

'What's happened to them?'

'I don't know.'

'What are we going to do?'

'I don't fucking know.'

Nicola deserves better from me. She is under pressure from the

7

local police whose assumption is that these are silly girls up to something naughty. Standard police practice seems to be to treat the fact that the girls have gone missing as something initially not too serious. Most children are back home in 24 to 48 hours. So in all the early questioning, the police are trying to find out whether Holly has rowed with her parents. Would she feel frightened to come home if this were so?

I tell the police that is not our Holly. 'Nicola obviously knows her own daughter. Please listen. This is totally out of character for both Holly and Jessica,' I say. But the police stick to their set line of questioning. Have the girls got any money with them? Have they been involved in pranks before? And then there is the reassurance. Don't worry – this type of incident normally ends happily as the child or the children return safely and are rather embarrassed.

I'm not reassured and I insist. 'Is no one listening? Something has happened to Holly and Jessica. Something bad. Please, please listen. Something needs to be done as a matter of urgency, please.'

I don't want to stay in the house arguing the odds. I must keep on searching. It is now totally dark. Scott and I take torches and march over fields and along paths that Holly has been taken for walks on. All kinds of explanations buzz round my mind. It's been raining and we've had lightning. It may just be that one of the girls could have been struck. Maybe part of a tree has been hit and trapped one or both of the girls. One of the girls may be hurt and her friend does not feel she can leave her alone. Consciously, or maybe unconsciously – I'm not a shrink – I avoid thinking about the grimmer alternatives.

It turns midnight, then 1 a.m. Scott and I keep on shouting out for Holly and Jessica. As we walk together into Brook Street, we see Coral and Ray Paxton – their daughter is Holly's godmother. They have both been out searching, too. Coral asks if there is any news. I simply cannot speak. I make sounds but they don't make sense. This must be what it's like to break down.

I do recover myself. Scott and I continue searching and march into the fields behind the hotel, torches in hand. Our throats are slightly sore and we feel the cold. The summer night has turned freezing. We are soaked through.

We decide to try Lofties Bridge at the edge of Soham. We look and shout along the river, we check the water, we check the banks, we check a very large soft clay area where the river has been dredged recently. If I'm feeling cold, wet and confused, what must Holly and Jessica be feeling right now? In my mind I see their two little faces, waiting to be found. It spurs me on.

We press along the riverbank through to East Fen Common and through to Brook Dam Lane but there is no sign of the girls. In the end, we go back to our house.

The police are still there but they have no news. Nicola is sitting with Trudie who has returned with Rob from Newmarket. The mobile rings and rings as people touch base to see if they can help. After a few minutes, I decide it's time to go again.

Rob drives us round. We know we are covering the same ground as before but we might have missed something. We drive in and around the main roads of Soham. Then we head for Isleham, Fordham, Wicken and Upware. We used to live in Upware for two and a half very happy years, so Holly may head this way. I know I'm clinging to straws.

We drive through to Swaffham Prior, Reach, Burwell and back through to Fordham and Soham. There is a fog descending, a fog the lights of Rob's car can't pierce, so we get out and search on foot. Round 4 a.m. we head back to Red House Gardens.

I talk to Nicola who looks completely numb. Trudie is comforting her. I don't talk to anyone else. It occurs to me that I have not searched the Village College buildings thoroughly. The gates are locked and of course the school closed for the summer holidays. The girls could have climbed inside and now they could be trapped. Something tells me to return to the school.

Even though it is very nearly 4.30 in the morning, I feel it would be polite to wake the caretaker up to let him know our intentions. Both Scott and I know Ian Huntley and, in such an emergency, getting him out of bed is something we can justify.

As we come out of Gidney Lane, the caretaker's house is directly ahead. We walk towards it, I notice a light coming from one of the rooms at Lodeside. Scott and I know this to be the caretaker's office.

We go through the door into the building where the office is and I shout out a loud, 'Hello'. Before anyone answers, a big black dog runs towards us aggressively. We close the door and get back outside as fast as we can; this is not a dog to argue with. We stand outside hoping that someone will turn up and deal with the dog. Ian Huntley walks out with the dog, which is calmer with him around.

Surprisingly, Huntley doesn't seem to recognise us. The man is obviously not thinking clearly, as he asks how we know which room was the caretaker's office. I remind him that we've been cleaning the school and helping to lock up at night. Huntley seems quite normal and shows no signs of panic. He tells us we don't need to look around as the police have just finished a search inside the College.

The police and their sniffer dogs found nothing. Bugger . . . I had hoped.

As we are about to leave, Huntley starts to explain why he was in the caretaker's office before dawn. He was writing a note to one of his colleagues explaining he'd be late into work as he had been helping the police.

But I don't think about any of that because I have a strong feeling in my guts. I can't explain it, or justify it rationally, but as I walk back to Red House Gardens, I know that I will not be seeing Holly alive again. Jessica will not be going home either. I have butterflies in my stomach and severe feelings of nausea. A long spell on and over the toilet does nothing to help.

Soon, if this were a normal day, it would be time to go to work. Scott takes on the practicalities of organising work and leaves at about 5.30 a.m. Ironically, as the sun eventually scatters the fog, it's a fine day. Nicola and I try to rest a little and gather our thoughts. The stark reality is that Holly and Jessica are both still missing. Our frantic search has failed. I have failed to protect the daughter I love so much.

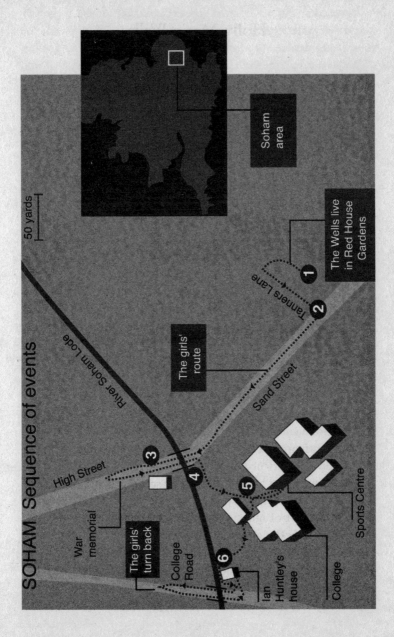

SOHAM Sequence of events

50 yards

Soham area

The Wells live in Red House Gardens

1

Tanners Lane

2

River Soham Lode

The girls' route

Sand Street

High Street

3

War memorial

4

The girls' turn back

College Road

5

6

Ian Huntley's house

College

Sports Centre

II

Holly Marie Wells

Our daughter who disappeared on 4 August was the light of our lives.

Allow me to tell you a little about Holly.

By the time she was 6, my wife and I realised we had a very talented daughter. Holly was keen and eager to learn. As parents, Nicola and I marvelled at her expressive reading, her ability to retain facts and her positive approach to all school work. Holly had made the perfect start to school life – the kind of start that meant going to a Parent's Evening was a pleasure, not a chore.

At home, Holly was fiercely proud of her work – and she was good at many kinds. She wrote poems, she made cakes with her mum or grandmother, she drew and painted countless pictures as gifts to family members and friends, all accompanied by the message 'Love from Holly' somewhere on the front. It was not just her academic abilities that made us proud. Holly showed an artistic side, which led us to devise a 5-year personal and business plan. Its aim was to fund Holly so she could study in the best environment possible – King's School, Ely.

By her 10th birthday, Holly was a confident, outgoing, and vivacious child who enriched everyone's life she touched. She was naturally inquisitive and hard-working. Her school work was of a very high quality – and that impressed us. We were sure she would be the first member of our family to go to university. Holly was also reading music and playing the recorder and the cornet. Her music teacher, Derek Bullman, felt she had a natural gift and that she would be invited to join the youth band – something Holly was actually quite nervous about!

The very things which Holly was beginning to excel at, music and art, she had managed without any guidance or tuition from her parents. But though she was strong and confident, she also had a certain shyness and caution. Until Holly learned to know and trust someone, she was always distant. It took encouragement from someone in the family for her to become less distant. Once comfortable with that person there would be no holding back, but it was not inevitable that Holly would accept someone just because they were around. Far from it.

Holly was an active member of the Soham Brownies and also squeezed in midweek practice for the Fenlander Majorettes, so she often performed at local fetes and functions. Oh how she looked forward to meeting and performing with her fellow troupe members.

As a family, we would sometimes visit the local 'children welcome' Free House in Upware to enjoy an evening of karaoke. Often Holly would take a friend along and they would fill in many request slips to sing something together. 'Angels', by Robbie Williams was always on Holly's list. Then, before handing the list over, Holly would sneakily add my name to hers, so that we had to go on stage and sing together. Every time Nicola and I would feign surprise when the compere announced the duet, and, every time, Holly would laugh out loud believing she had tricked her dad once more.

Yet, it was young Holly's character, above all, which will stay in the memory of all who knew her. An extremely caring girl, Holly would naturally warm to any young children who visited our home. She had grace and purpose. Nothing was too much trouble as she entertained her young charges. Holly's 3-year-old cousin, Emily, lived just opposite our house. Holly asked to see Emily every day, because, in her own words, she 'loved her cousin'. Holly enjoyed the role she chose for herself – to love, play with and teach her only girl cousin. The images of them together remain indelibly implanted in my mind.

Holly had a keen sense of humour, which was simply the best. She was wonderfully observant, understood 'adult observational comedy', understood irony and was sweet enough to laugh at all of my jokes. Life was a ball for her and for those of us who were with her. She lit up a room wherever she went, with her blue eyes and long blonde hair, long before a word could be spoken; those who engaged with Holly adored her. She was intensely loyal to her friends and delightfully familiar with the playground politics of the day. When she got home, two bemused parents would always find themselves being updated about the very same!

Throughout her life, people she loved and trusted surrounded Holly. Her intelligence and the fact that she wore her heart on her sleeve, at times brought her into conflict with parents and grandparents. But the rows never lasted long, because Holly was always approachable and always listened to reason. Despite 'putting on' her sour face, she never held a grudge, although she and her older brother, 'Olls', often argued incessantly. Occasionally, Oliver would get the better of her. Then we'd hear each door on the way to Holly's bedroom sanctuary slam shut, almost off its hinges. Her parting words – 'don't bother' – would always be the same. Just the same in a bit, she would come back, be reasonable and offer to make up the row. It was delightful.

The busyness, the noise, the laughter, the love, the friendship and her ability to appreciate life made Holly the person she was. What happened on 4 August was the beginning of a nightmare, which continued for 18 months – and will affect the rest of our lives.

We have had to deal with our sense of loss as well as bitter feelings of unfairness and injustice. The system often did not help. Our world was turned upside down – and darker and bleaker than you could imagine. Our focus became survival and salvation.

This book will take you through the repercussions of a paedophile's vile intrusion into an ordinary family's life, beginning on the day after Holly never came home.

Monday 5 August

At 9 a.m., the police issue a public appeal, voicing their increasing concern for the girls' safety. The statement suggests the girls have run away from home. Both Nicola and I are unhappy at this, as we know it's just not true.

We are about to discover, in more detail than I ever wanted, how the police work and that it is not easy to be processed by their procedures. As Holly is a much-loved daughter, it does not occur to us that standard practice at first is to assume that someone in the family has done it. It might have been better if the police had explained that to us.

We desperately need information but the police have very little – and give us even less. We have no confirmation of any clear search plans. We are getting very frustrated, as are many of our friends and family who are out searching. Many local people decide not to start their working week, but make themselves available to search instead.

We are told a press conference is to take place at 3.30 p.m. The idea behind this is explained to us – to promote public awareness of Holly and Jessica and their dreadful situation. I am sure that any parent would feel uncomfortable about appearing on television in such circumstances.

I have no clear memory of that press conference but I remember thinking we would do anything to help find Holly and Jessica. Feeling ill at ease in front of the media doesn't matter. I also remember thinking – 'we are about to be judged by the general public'.

I'm not completely naïve and I suspect that this press conference will also give the police a chance to study the four parents, to analyse the words we use and our body language. They'll be watching to see if we're hiding something.

It rains as we walk from Ely Police Station to the Council offices. We have no umbrella or coats. The press conference is short, sharp and less harrowing than expected. All four of us just want our daughters back. It is not difficult to present a united front, as it's genuine. The Chapmans feel as lost, frightened and bewildered as we do. Not by choice, we are now intrinsically linked.

I can't stay at home for long as it feels like admitting defeat in the search for Holly. I eat. The body is bizarre. I can't sleep but I can eat. After lunch, I find myself sitting in the living room. Truth is I want to avoid the noise and melee in the kitchen. It has now been 17 straight hours without sleep, searching is physically demanding and I am completely shattered. As I try to think where to search next, I become enveloped by a sense of loss. My head tingles and this sensation moves down my body. I hate this feeling and it seems a very negative sign.

I need to be as close to Holly as possible. I walk upstairs, shut myself in her bedroom and lie on the bottom bunk. I start to sob. I feel the need to touch and smell Holly as best I can. The sobbing becomes so intense that at times I struggle to breathe. I slump to the floor and bury my head in Holly's quilt.

I can't believe someone could hurt her. Not Holly. She is simply too caring and friendly to upset anyone. How can any bastard hurt her? I start to punch Holly's quilt and mattress. I sob, and in between gasps, I shout out every swear word I know.

Nicola notices I have 'disappeared' and comes upstairs to see what is going on. I'm so wrapped up in my grief I do not hear or see her in the room. Scared, Nicola gets Aunt Sheena, Aunt Reliable who always knows what to do. Sheena comes up. As I realise someone is sitting next to me on the floor, I feel very foolish. Sheena is an incredible lady. Upset as she is, she still manages to get me talking, to cajole me back to reality.

It takes a while but we both agree something terrible has happened to Holly. We agree then and there, that until we know for sure that Holly is dead, we will not give in to despair. We'll try and be strong for everyone else. Sheena leaves me to reflect for a little while longer, alone.

As ever, she is right. *Stop wallowing in your sadness, Kevin, get out there and do something.* As I tell myself this, I begin to punch the bed again, to get the adrenalin going. Kneeling on the floor, with my eyes closed and head and chest lying on Holly's quilt, I eventually feel strong enough to start the search again. To pump myself up, I announce it out loud. I will carry on searching.

So now I spring up from the bed, Mr Strong. But I've completely forgotten that I am on the bottom bunk of Holly's bed. I smash my head into the underside of the wooden railing and find myself lying flat out in the middle of the bedroom floor. The heroic dad has to check there is no blood, make sure he hasn't broken his thick skull and try to compose himself. It will be weeks before I admit to Nicola or anyone else the embarrassing fact that I almost knocked myself out.

Downstairs the house is full of family and friends, all desperately trying to do something. People are crying. I feel, however, that I have cried enough for the moment. It is time to coordinate more searching and go out myself, independently of the police. I can't think what else to do. Surely a father has the right to search for his daughter even if that is not best practice as defined in the police manuals.

At teatime, we finally find out the police have a plan. They will coordinate the search from a mobile station, based at St Andrew's School. Now we can at least tell people to meet at St Andrew's and wait for instructions.

The police ring to tell us that 'sniffer' dogs have been deployed from another force and will be at the house later tonight. They need items of Holly's so the dogs can get her scent. Can we please make sure that no one interferes with Holly's bedding, as this is usually the best area for quality? Nicola knows I have just spent a considerable amount of time on the bed, I know and Sheena knows. What have I done? This is the first specific police request and I have just messed things up by sobbing all over Holly's bed clothes.

Nicola and I go into Holly's bedroom. We find Holly's night time soft toy, 'Snoozums', and her hairbrush. I work out that I did not actually lay my head directly on Holly's pillow, so we remove the pillowcase and this completes the package for the dog team officers. On our own, we cuddle in the bedroom. We don't exchange words of encouragement. We both know they would be hollow. Nicola agrees to hold the fort downstairs and I will go to St Andrew's School to join the public in searching.

As I drive from Red House Gardens I am surprised to see that Tanners Lane, normally quiet, is full of parked cars, and many more are double-parked in Sand Street. Where the pavement is wide enough, cars are on that too. So many people are walking in between the cars that it feels like a football crowd. A lump comes to my throat as I realise all these people are here to help. Local companies have also allowed their work force time off to take part in the searching. I must join them immediately.

I park my car by the Sports Centre and walk down the private road in the direction of St Andrew's School. As I get near the school, I hear a strange clamour. Slowly I make out the sound: crowd noise. As I walk past the tennis courts, I see just how many people have come to help. I have to stop as I'm overwhelmed. My eyes well up with tears; I can't really see. But I feel tremendous. If 500 to 600 local people are helping the police effort, then we have a chance. I recognise so many people. Friends, family, customers, staff, cricket and football team mates, parents, children, local community and acquaintances alike.

And then, I suddenly realise I am standing exactly where Scott and I last saw Ian Huntley. But, of course, at that moment I think nothing of that.

The 500 volunteers are not pleased, though. Everyone is complaining about the lack of police organisation. Many volunteers were told to return for formal instructions in the evening. Well they are here now, chomping at the bit, but no plans are in place, no communication is in place. People are getting angry, they're desperate to help. I feel just the same. Many hundreds of search hours have already been lost. We risk losing more. We'll be losing the light soon.

I rub my eyes, compose myself and walk into the mobile control room. I know one of the two senior officers inside, Inspector Darren Alderson. Darren lives in Soham, and has come up to assist voluntarily. He used to be a window-cleaning customer of mine and I ask what is causing these delays.

Darren assures me they are sorting out the problems. But I can't help overhearing the other inspector's phone calls. His main concerns are to do with health and safety issues dealing with the crowd! It almost beggars belief. Two girls are missing and they're fretting about how to protect the police's position in case any volunteers injure themselves or become lost. No local person will get 'lost' in their own town. These are not the Yorkshire Moors, we're in Soham.

I soon discover the police don't even seem to have maps to co-ordinate a plan. I feel very let down, angry and confused. I ask myself 'Is there a hidden agenda?' Has something happened to Holly and Jessica that the police don't want to reveal to their families, let alone the public? Have the girls been found, dead? My head hurts with questions I cannot answer.

Enough is enough. I tell Darren something needs to be done immediately. I know the area, and will therefore simply divide people into rough geographical groups. It is not rocket science.

Just then, Robert Palmer enters the control room with maps. Specifically maps of the local waterways. He is allowed to take as many people as he needs to go with him. He acts as a catalyst. Quickly, people who have travelled from Upware, Wicken, Fordham and Isleham are asked to return to search their own villages. Villages they were all familiar with. At long last things are moving. Those that remain are split into groups, 50 strong and asked to go East, West, North and South. Bureaucracy still rules though. People are asked to return to the control room at dark, to sign themselves back in. I know many people did not return. Their view was – you can stick this red tape crap where the sun don't shine.

I have missed a number of calls from Nicola and I'm worried about her. It turns out she's been trying to get me to say I don't have to worry about having interfered with the scent of Holly on the bed linen. The dog handling team have bagged up the stuff which we collected from Holly's bedroom and feel these items are sufficient to obtain a strong scent. I am relieved.

When I get home, I find a different police officer in the house. This time, it isn't someone from the local station who will disappear the moment their shift finishes, but a designated Family Liaison Officer (or FLO) – Sergeant Trudie Skeels.

I'm glad Nicola will have a policewoman to stay with her. Trudie's priority is to get as many details as possible from Nicola, so my wife is asked about Holly's likes and dislikes. What groups and clubs did Holly go to? Is anything missing from Holly's bedroom? Has she taken any money with her? Had an argument with anyone? Would Holly have any fear of coming home if she had been naughty? The list of pointless questions continues.

Then, our computer is seized and taken away. Routine, we're told.

Trudie goes on to explain that as a matter of procedure, at some stage, a team will also visit our home to complete a detailed search. This seems completely inappropriate. Trudie is calm and pleasant, but we still feel that the police priority is as much to judge us, as it is to find Holly and Jessica.

I decide to go out. With my close friends, I search across from the Soham bypass, in the fields along the single-track road to the village of Isleham. Strung out across the fields we look like the largest pheasant beating team ever assembled. We constantly call out for Holly and Jessica. We look in sheds, behind discarded farming equipment, in crops, thickets, ditches and dykes. But we find nothing. We're losing the light, and I'm losing heart.

At 10 p.m., we head back. Tired, frustrated, but, above all, frightened, I arrive home with no positive news for Nicola.

We are now in what would be the unfamiliar, the frightening and the unexpected for any family. I have not been interested in the paranormal before but a friend of my sister-in-law arranged to see a medium recently. She had what she calls 'a good reading' with him. When Holly disappeared, she spoke to him. He has offered to visit us tomorrow. This does not impress Trudie, who tells us that any major police enquiry receives many calls from mediums. They often give conflicting messages.

After Trudie goes, Nicola and I ask all family and friends to leave immediately. We have to face the fact that this is the second night Holly is not at home. But Nicola and I can hardly speak. Our eyes reflect our anxiety. We both look drawn and harrowed and need some rest. Nicola decides to take a sleeping tablet. I do not, just in case there is a development and I need to drive. As we head upstairs, we walk past ten framed photographs of Holly. Her smiling, beautiful face makes us feel our loss very intensely. We lie together and cry.

Eventually we sit up on the bed, facing one another, gently wiping each other's tears. Our foreheads come together and Nicola asks:

'Where is she, Kev?'

'I don't know, Nic.'

'Is she coming home?'

'Let's try and get some sleep, Nic.'

The sleeping pill helps Nicola drift, exhausted, to sleep, a little before 11 p.m. I watch her for a while before lying down. I don't even get the chance to sleep fitfully because the front doorbell rings. I go downstairs, open the door and see a posse of police officers. To add to the weird effect, they're dressed all in black. They tell me that they are here to search the house and that the visit has been formally agreed.

No, that is not the case, I point out. I add that we have not had any sleep for two days. Could they at least come back at a more convenient time? The answer is no.

I wake Nicola, who is drowsy from the sleeping tablet, but she does her best to re-focus and joins me downstairs. Then our phone rings. It is Trudie Skeels, the FLO.

'Nicola, I am just ringing to let you know that a search team will be turning up late tonight.'

'Yes, I know.'

Nicola is polite, not cutting, but bloody brief and to the point. The conversation ends there.

It is not the best of starts for Trudie. It is a bit late to inform us our home is to be invaded by men in black.

Nicola and I sit in the living room and have a grandstand view of every conceivable item being searched. From the loft to the downstairs toilet, things are picked up, opened and examined. Books are feathered through, CDs, tape cassettes and drawers opened. Every piece of furniture is lifted off the ground with military precision. We are asked to get up from the settee, which is then lifted up. Revealing . . . a bare wooden floor. I wonder what they imagined they might find.

The officers are polite but we don't say much, because we don't like being made to feel like suspects. It is the best part of three hours before the search is completed. Finally, in the early hours of the morning, we get our home back. We try to sleep but we're too stressed. We're angry at the intrusion, livid at being thought of as suspects and, above all, furious with whoever has put Holly and us in this traumatic situation.

The police have also given us a list to complete of family and friends – who might be involved in the disappearance of Holly and Jessica.

We love this town and we don't enjoy facing the fact that someone, somewhere, here in Soham, knows where the girls are. We briefly talk about our family and friends who might appear on the 'to be completed list' for the police. We decide their list is a complete waste of time. Like the police search of our house was.

Tuesday 6 August

W e have no way of immediately contacting our FLO. All we do know is that a briefing is taking place at Police HQ. We wait, wait for news, wait for any positive developments.

This morning's papers lead with the missing girls. The *Daily Mail* headline reads, 'How did they just vanish?' We are asking the same question.

I am about to carry on searching at the school when suddenly a newsflash on the television says the girls have been seen. In a tiny village called Little Thetford, of all places, about 8 or 9 miles from Soham. There's euphoria in the house. The girls are alive. Then, we do a very quick reality check – why haven't the police told us? That's not acceptable. The situation is desperate enough without having to hear information on television first.

Before doing anything, we must speak with our FLO, but the only way we can get the police is by dialling 999. We are really at a loss as to what to do. The phone starts ringing. Is the good news true, girls found, happy ending? It's surreal and embarrassing to have to say we have no idea as we have heard nothing from the police.

I want to go to Little Thetford immediately. I know the village, as it was part of my old window-cleaning round. It's close to the very busy A10 from Ely to Cambridge, so someone could have dropped the girls off there.

Then we hear from Trudie. A lady who lives on the Ely Road has called the police and given a statement. Search teams are being sent to Little Thetford. Trudie insists there is nothing we can do to help, so could we please stay in Soham?

By now it's clear Cambridgeshire Police do not see us as the ideal parents of a missing daughter. We have been designated 'difficult' because we actually want to do something and insist on searching for Holly and Jessica with our friends. We won't leave it to the professionals. Parents should be more pliable and sit by the phone praying while the great Cambridge constabulary sorts it out. They can't have us flapping around out of control. So they have decided to assign a more senior officer, Detective Sergeant Chris Mead, to liaise with us. I don't know it at the time but the police are afraid that we might actually find the girls. We don't understand the procedures and could create problems of site and evidence contamination. Fortunately, here in Soham, we are all blissfully unaware of these problems and carry on searching regardless.

I return to the Lodeside part of the Village College once more. A few metres away from the caretaker's house in College Close runs the river Lode. I walk the bank, up to the bridge and search in a small copse area on the other side of the water. I am just about to move down-river when my phone goes.

Nicola tells me Chris Mead has arrived and has asked me to stop searching and go home to meet him. I start the short walk home which means I go past the caretaker's house, past Lodeside gym and past the Sports Centre, completely unaware I am walking the same route Holly and Jessica took on Sunday – but in reverse.

I walk into my home. Nicola is there 'alone', which means that there are just the Family Liaison Officers – always called FLOs – in the house. Everyone else has gone to Little Thetford. We sit in the dining room and Chris introduces himself and explains what FLOs do. I've never met the man before so I have nothing against him, but I'm not impressed at having been asked to stop searching for Holly so I can be treated to an introductory lecture on procedure.

But Chris speaks plainly and to the point. He wants to establish what the police need from our family, and what they will do for us.

We immediately agree that the best chance of finding Holly and

Jessica is to work together. Nicola and I explain some of the problems we've had and Chris gives us his mobile telephone number. We can ring any time. He promises to update us personally on any developments and on the way the enquiry is progressing. Both Nicola and I are pleased. We seem to have a police officer blessed with common sense, a man we feel is really on our side.

The phone rings again. It's a close friend, Tracy. She lives in Little Thetford and is aware of the sighting. She warns me that the lady in question is a local character and that her 'observations' are not likely to be accurate. We shouldn't build up our hopes. We are now back to square one. I know the police have to consider, take statements and be diplomatic but a local character is a local character. We know in our hearts that the sightings are false. We still have no leads.

We are also about to learn to deal with the media. I have never featured much even in the local press, although 8 weeks ago I was photographed throwing a wet sponge at the local vicar. The picture did not make the nationals. Again, we have to cope with things we never expected to be part of our lives.

All day reporters and photographers come to the door. We even have the television cameras in Red House Gardens. The press want up to date photographs of Holly. Reporters say this will help find the girls, as the public needs to see recent images. We offer anything we have that may help. The house feels like a pressure cooker – family and friends coming and going, phones ringing continuously, police talking into mobiles. The worst of it is our emotional distress and panic, panic we have to strap in and buckle down. If we give in to fear, we won't be able to keep going.

And we must keep going.

Our one lifeline is that the girls are together. Hopefully, they will be able to comfort and support one another until we find them.

Nicola and I begin to see how complex police procedures are. Chris and Trudie take us through their agenda and we have to deal with:

- *The structure of the police enquiry.*
- *How much control of the family computer did we have as parents?*
- *We are asked to agree to the home computer being taken away for analysis.*
- *We are asked to describe the girls' clothing. We confirm that Holly was wearing black trousers and a Manchester United top.*
- *We describe the clothes Nicola and I wore on Sunday 4 August.*
- *We give full details of all family movements for Saturday 3 August.*
- *The police request video footage of Holly.*
- *We give them all of our phone numbers and previous addresses.*
- *We give them Holly's bank account details.*
- *We are asked if any money/savings have been taken from elsewhere.*
- *Does Holly have a boyfriend?*
- *The police repeat the promise that our family will be kept up to date with developments at all times.*

The police also tell us they are setting up a Major Operations Room. Cambridgeshire Police have requested help from other forces, including staff at the American airbase. We're told some details about the police search capabilities and that Ely Police Station will be used as the centre for search teams.

The police also want to discuss 'media strategy' and how we are going to work with their press office. We say we are unhappy at the way the police keep presenting this as a missing persons investigation. Neither Holly nor Jessica is the kind of girl who leaves for a prank, and neither was unhappy at home.

Chris and Trudie go back to Police HQ for a briefing at about 6.30 p.m. Chris promises to update us as soon as it is finished.

Our home is once again filling up with friends and relatives. John Stannard is organising the boys from Ely and Haddenham Cricket Club to search all the villages in and around Little Thetford. Scott Day is organising the search of villages around Soham.

Nicola and I want to get out of our house and so we drive out towards Little Thetford. We motor aimlessly for about an hour and drive through Haddenham, Witcham, Witchford, Sutton, Wilburton, Grunty Fen and Wentworth. We pray we'll catch a glimpse of something red. We're getting used to the rather daunting sight of black uniformed search teams in fields and ditches. Normal life is on hold in Soham.

As the story has become 'bigger', reporters ask more and more locals to record their thoughts. Happily, no one close to either family does so. On TV, we find some of the contributions from 'locals' quite painful. We know everyone here, but we don't recognise many of these people offering their thoughts. Some of them can hardly utter a coherent sentence. The rest of Britain must see the inhabitants of Soham as moronic rustics. In the general scheme of things this is utterly insignificant, but it still annoys me.

I feel a horrible tug of hopelessness in my guts. It gets worse by the hour.

Then, we get an unexpected lift. David Beckham has issued a statement on behalf of all Manchester United players appealing to Holly and Jessica to return home. 'Please go home. You are not in any kind of trouble. Your parents love you deeply and desperately want you back.' We are both flabbergasted, as well as very grateful. It is another sign that the coverage is becoming huge and taking on a life of its own. However, if this helps find Holly and Jessica, then so be it.

This statement has a big effect on us. It means more because I am a lifelong United supporter. I feel so emotional that I'm reduced to tears. But not for long, as we know time is very much against us and we must do something.

Nicola and I go over the little we know. We both believe that no one from Soham can be guilty of such evil so we focus on addresses whose occupants are not from, or known in, our community – 'stranger danger' if you like. We narrow that down to addresses that fall within the area Holly had permission to walk in. This is Brook Street, Sand Street, Gidney Lane, Clay Street and the beginning of the High Street.

I ask a former Royal Mail colleague to help put a new plan in place. It takes less than 20 minutes to identify 25 properties which have been let to people we do not know.

We confirm their landlords. We now have a plan of action. It involves the assistance of two CORGI-registered plumbers – Rob and his colleague, Keith. After about an hour, we are ready to inspect these worrying addresses and we have a reason for entering the properties. Our official reason is that we are investigating reports of a gas leak.

Nicola is worried by the plan. With so many journalists around, do we want to have headlines saying we are behaving like vigilantes? I don't really care. Holly and Jessica need to be found. Although I understand Nicola's concerns, I feel I can justify my actions.

My wife asks me to contact the police first before we do anything rash. We did promise to work together with them and, in light of that, she's right. But Chris is not here. I leave a message on his mobile. Then I wait.

I wait and watch television. I see the images of Holly, of Jessica, of Soham, of Nicola and myself. I watch the speculation about the Little Thetford 'sighting'. By the time Chris rings back at 22.37, I am hardly in the best frame of mind. I'd expected, perhaps unreasonably, to have heard from him earlier and I'm bitter because it is too late to search these 25 properties tonight. I'm about to explode to Chris when he stops me dead in my tracks.

'Sorry I am so late in getting back to you. There has been a development.'

The dread – what if it's bad news? Caught on this emotional see-saw, I try to sound calm as I ask the question that has to be asked:

'That's okay, Chris. What is the development?'

The police have been told of a travellers' site following reports of a white van behaving suspiciously in Soham on Sunday. Some young girls from Soham have also told the police that two young travellers tried to pick them up on Sunday. We are not told where the site is but it is going to be raided tomorrow morning. This information must not leak. The police want to make sure no one on the travellers' site has any inkling of the impending search. Chris promises to tell us what they find first thing tomorrow.

As I put the telephone down, and tell Nicola what he said, I feel a mix of emotions again. Clearly there is a chance that Holly and Jessica may have been picked up and held against their will somewhere by two young lads. Odd as it may be, I see this as something positive, for it means the girls are likely to still be alive. It is a thought which I hold on to with a clenched fist. I know that if boys have picked them up, the girls may be involved in a sexual incident. In my despair, I accept that my ten-year-old daughter may have been raped. The overriding priority is to get her home alive. If Holly needs hundreds of hours of counselling afterwards, it doesn't matter. We'll cope. We'll cope with anything once she's back.

Again I'm hopeful. Travellers are guilty of many petty crimes, but I have never in my life heard of a sexual crime being committed by the local travelling community. After asking everyone to leave, Nicola and I go to bed, without much faith or hope that we'll sleep.

Tomorrow is going to be a busy day. First, we are going to search these 25 properties. Then, we have agreed to meet with the medium to see if he can offer any help. The medium simply calls himself Dennis and the appointment has been arranged for lunchtime. Little did we know the impact Dennis was going to have on our lives.

Wednesday 7 August

A call from Chris at 6.30 in the morning. There are no traces of the girls on the travellers' site in Grunty Fen. We go to the newsagents to buy the morning papers. The images of ourselves and the Chapmans, looking distraught and at a complete loss, say it all.

I call Rob and Keith. We are ready to go and search the 25 houses.

Chris arrives at 9 a.m. Fifteen minutes later, Trudie joins us. Chris's focus is to get us to this morning's press conference for 10 a.m. at Lodeside. Although exhausted, we will do as asked. We're told Det. Supt David Hankins will read a short statement before allowing questions to both families.

We are shown a copy of his statement. A couple of sentences hit us. They suggest the police are turning from a missing persons enquiry into an investigation of a possible abduction. Detectives from Sussex who were involved in the Sarah Payne case are arriving today. We are about to face the press and here, in black and white, is frightening news. The Cambridgeshire Police think it appropriate to seek help from officers who have worked on the highest profile paedophile murder case of recent times. We can't get that thought out of our minds.

We know the Lodeside gymnasium hall will be full of media. But we're still stunned when we're greeted by an explosion of camera flashes – an army of reporters, photographers and TV cameras in front of us in a crescent-moon shape. Throughout the press conference, if Nicola and I look at each other or wipe a tear to try and gain composure, it triggers a cacophony of camera clicks and flashbulbs.

No one really chairs the conference. The media have no microphones and there is no procedure in place to take questions in an orderly fashion. People shout at us throughout. It feels like total chaos, the most testing of times.

We finish the press conference and wait outside to be driven straight home. As Chris and I stand in the sunshine, I suddenly feel someone standing very close to my left shoulder. It is Ian Huntley. He is so near to me that I have to take a step back before speaking to him. At the time, the oddness of his words did not strike me as suspicious.

'Kev, I just wanted to say, I did not realise it was your daughter.'

I took him to mean he had not made the connection when Scott, Rob and I talked to him in the early hours of Monday morning. He must be under a great deal of pressure; he looks bloody shattered. His eyes are so dark that he reminds me of a panda bear. Huntley tells me he would like to speak with Chris to arrange a formal change to his previous statement. Apparently he has given the wrong time, which may or may not be significant, but it is best to be on the safe side. I call Chris over and introduce him to Huntley.

On the journey back, in College Road, Nicola's sister flags our car over. She has had the photographs Nicola took on Sunday developed. Lesley was trying to get them to the police during the press conference. We immediately take them back to Lodeside. The photograph which is handed over was taken at 5.04 p.m. and shows two happy little ten-year-old girls, dressed in Manchester United football shirts. This picture is about to become the symbol of Britain's biggest-ever murder hunt.

It's been a busy morning and I need to get my plan in action to search the 25 addresses.

Chris and Trudie have a few things to discuss first. The police have told the general public not to continue with any searching. This is hard to accept, but I understand the reasons behind their decision. The incident room has received approximately 2,000 calls from the general public. We have still got a shout. Someone knows where Holly and Jessica are, let us hope they see sense and release the girls. And we clutch at straws. It could be argued that, in their sick way, paedophiles care for children. The two girls are together; that must help them survive.

Our focus is simple. Completely forget about the worst-case scenario. Continue to search for Holly. Continue to support family and friends who are equally distraught and confused. We feel so adrenalin-pumped that I announce to most people I see:

'It's okay, we are all cried out at the moment. Let's continue searching.' I say it because I believe it, and it might just motivate the person who will find the girls.

Chris is more than aware of my increasing state of agitation and suggests that we leave to search together.

As we are about to go, the vicar turns up. Tim Alban Jones looks apprehensive. But he has come to say that a vigil service is planned for tonight.

Eventually, Chris and I head off. There is no simple way of telling the police that you have arranged to search 25 houses and it is going to happen soon. I blurt it out the moment we are alone together. Chris is absolutely stunned. His first objection is that, from a police viewpoint, you need valid reasons to search houses. I argue that no one really knows the history of any of these tenants. Most of them are foreigners and the rest are not from Soham. That is a valid enough reason for me under the circumstances. I explain how we will search.

Chris tells me that if he takes my request further up the line, it simply will not get official backing. I point out that our plans did not involve the police anyway. I was just telling him to be polite. He gets his mobile out. He is trying desperately to get an official okay.

I watch him and wonder – is he really going to try, or is he going to be the officious policeman? Will this man I've only known for 48 hours perform for me?

Chris argues that making the search official is vital if the family are to be kept onside. There are also other issues, he stresses to his superiors:

What if Kevin, Rob and Keith actually find the girls?

What if a fight breaks out with a disgruntled tenant?

What if entry has to be forced into any of the properties?

What if the press find out about the search plan?

Can vigilante-type action be seen to be taking place?

For an hour, we wait. The police obviously don't want to go in but they are even less keen on me and my friends acting as vigilantes. For the first time, I feel the police realise they have to give us something. After a nail-biting hour, I get an undertaking the police will go into the 25 properties this afternoon. I can inform Rob and Keith that their services are not required.

Chris has performed, and we have established a level of trust that could never have been created sitting at home waiting for news.

I tell Nicola that all of the 25 houses are to be searched by the police. She is so relieved. And she needs to be calm because we are meeting the medium. Our house is so frantic that we decide to meet Dennis Mackenzie in Lesley's living room. Nicola is clutching a number of Holly's personal items. I'm very sceptical and expect nothing from our contact with the medium.

Dennis is waiting outside Lesley's house with Lorraine, another medium. He explains that they sometimes work together and that Lorraine assisted in the Sarah Payne case. I have no idea if this is true, but we shake hands, hug – this seems to be the etiquette for the occasion – and disappear into the house.

Dennis is a huge man and a very eccentric one. He explains that he often lies on the floor when he works. Lying on the floor seems utterly melodramatic but Dennis asks sensible questions. The most crucial is how would Nicola and I like to hear any information. We're slightly confused by his words, so he explains there are two options. He can be completely truthful and to the point, or, if the message is negative, he can interpret it in the most hopeful light.

There is no time to mess about with getting consumer-friendly messages from the other side, we decide. Nicola and I need the truth, however awful.

As we sit holding hands on the sofa, Dennis begins, 'I am really sorry but both the girls are dead.'

We are completely stunned. I feel as if someone has just punched me in the stomach. Nicola starts crying. Eventually after swallowing hard many times, I offer the feeble question:

'Are you sure?'

Dennis gives a tiny nod of confirmation.

We don't know what to do. We try not to break down totally. Dennis continues:

'There are three people involved. Two men and one woman. One man is dark-haired and looks to be in his thirties. The second man is much older. The woman has mouse-like features and looks quite young.

'They are not from this area. They have northern accents and possibly come from York or Manchester.

'There is a red car involved. It is an older car and therefore an older shape. It is a small car and quite square at the back.

'There is water next to their house and it is a straight piece of water. There is a very tall building, possibly a windmill, but without sails, in the background. Ducks figure prominently on this piece of water.

'The girls were wrapped in something, possibly bubble wrap, but likely carpet.

'The girls have been moved away from Soham.

'The letter J features. Possibly the beginning of a Christian name, but it was not John.'

Dennis describes a road the girls have been taken down. He is uncertain about the area, as there is grass on both sides of the road. He adds:

'The letters C and O are in the address of the property.

'Kevin, you've walked past this house when you were searching.

'Looking out from inside one of the rooms in the house, I can see the number 18.

'Does the word *Prickwillow* mean anything to you?

'Kevin, the police are withholding information from you.'

Towards the end of the session Lorraine says something which completely takes our legs away.

'I am able to see Jessica on the other side, but there is no Holly.'

Lorraine keeps on trying to reach Holly on the other side but can't.

What does this mean? Have the girls been separated? Or can she not reach Holly because our daughter is still alive?

We're unsure what to do next, though I feel I am in the presence of a very talented medium. I ask him if he will come with me on a drive around Soham. I also ask if I can take him to the 25 properties to see if he can sense something. Will he walk through the town with me to see if anything feels unusual to him?

I also have a theory involving the grass road which Dennis described. I think it is East Fen Common. East Fen Common, once you have travelled over the bypass becomes East Fen Drive, which leads to Isleham. Turn left and you reach Prickwillow, the village Dennis mentioned. Obviously that's where we need to search. Long, deep-water drains line the straight road into Prickwillow. I also remember there is a drainage museum in the village and it's run by someone whose name starts with J – Joan. We must get organised and over to Prickwillow.

Dennis agrees to come with me. Before the drive, we go home. The moment Nicola and I get back into our house, everyone wants to hear the news. Trying my very best to avoid any eye contact, I tell them that we have been told the girls are dead. There are gasps, groans and disbelieving mutterings. People start crying and I wonder if I should have been so blunt.

Almost without thinking, we immediately write down everything Dennis said to avoid any false interpretation of his observations later on. I also decide not to tell Dennis which three properties out of the 25 I have the most reservations about.

As we walk towards Sand Street from the High Street, Dennis stops dead in his tracks just opposite The Ship and says he has a strong feeling that the spot where he stands has some relevance to Holly. He has actually stopped at the very location where I first met my wife in 1982. Nicola and her close friend often used to sit on the low wall overlooking the river. This is a sign to me that I am in the presence of a genuine psychic talent and, though I am bursting to tell him the relevance of his observation, I choose to remain silent.

We walk the short distance to the bridge. Dennis again stops and he says he feels a mobile telephone has been discarded in the river. I know that the press have said Jessica's mobile is missing, but Dennis feels certain that this part of the river is crucial to locating the mobile telephone. We continue the short walk towards the first property of the 25.

Dennis's method is to touch the front entrance door trying to sense if Holly and Jessica are within. Twenty-two doors draw no response at all. Three properties do, however, trigger a negative reaction. Incredibly, they are the three properties which I felt most unease about. Even though Dennis feels there is something bad within two of the properties, it has nothing to do with Holly or Jessica. But the last property worries Dennis. He feels the girls have been very close to this one and possibly, just possibly, may have been inside. This place looks empty to me. I look through all of the downstairs windows and see nothing. But I will come back – and get inside.

As we get to East Fen Common, I pass my old house and drive for about another 300 yards before pulling over. There are no footpaths on East Fen Common. When I stand next to Dennis outside the car, he becomes sweaty and drained of colour. I think he is going to be physically sick. Dennis says this is definitely the road he saw during the reading and that the girls have been brought through here. But, he also feels that the girls were not alive then.

I'm less stunned than when I first heard they were dead. Dennis obviously needs to go. I thank him from the very bottom of my heart. He declines my offer of money and we have an emotional hug. Before he sits back in his car, Dennis says:

'Kevin, I have never been wrong before when I say someone is dead. I hope and pray that I have got it wrong on this occasion.'

'That makes two of us then.'

Looking at my old house, where we lived when Holly was born, I find myself battling against the desire to cry. My late grand-mother Ivy was born in that house and we named Holly after the traditional English carol, 'The Holly and the Ivy'. And now, according to Dennis, 'Holly' is with 'Ivy'. I stand alone in the hot sunshine unable to stop myself from crying.

Once again I manage to regain some shred of composure and drive home. I need to tell the police about Prickwillow. And I need to speak to Nicola. I tell her that Dennis felt the girls were dead when they were taken through East Fen Common. She cries, of course she cries, but she rallies. Then I tell Chris what Dennis sensed.

To me Dennis's observations are startling, but that is not the perception of the Cambridgeshire Police. I am told that in any major enquiry, hundreds of messages from mediums are received and many of those messages conflict. It is not usual practice to deploy police resources based on a medium's observations. But the police want to 'keep the family onside', so Chris will go with me to Prickwillow and arrange for a police search team to go there too.

I didn't know at the time that Chris's job was also to observe me and how I was reacting. Later, he told me his initial conclu-sions were:

1. Kevin is very task-orientated and needs to be active at all times and satisfied that his actions have a chance of locating his daughter.
2. Kevin has lost control of his house. The place is full of family and friends. He has no private time with Nicola.
3. Kevin requests all information and asks 'nothing' to be with-held.

Chris and I sit in his car. We both watch the police search in virtual silence.

'Chris, why are they not shouting out for Holly and Jessica?'

'I don't know. I will ask.'

As Chris calls to the search advisor, I know the answer. No one feels the girls are alive.

As we wait for the search advisor to come and explain what they are doing, Chris decides to log the points raised by the medium. This may well have been an attempt to placate a desperate father, but I go along with it. It starts to rain heavily. We're in the car, dry; we watch the police search team being drenched and smirk at our good fortune. This is the first moment Chris and I share a little humour in the face of adversity.

A little later Chris turns to me.

'Tell me about your brother.'

'Meaning?'

'Meaning, tell me about your brother.'

'I can tell you there is no way my brother is involved in this situation.'

'I accept that. Are you close?'

I answer these questions which seem a little absurd and, then, I feel it is time to turn the tables. Although I did not believe Dennis when he said the police were withholding information from me, now is the time to ask. I sound apologetic but I do say:

'Chris, Dennis says that you are withholding information from me. Is this true?'

'Yes.'

Then silence. My look of utter surprise and dejection says it all. I cannot understand how information can be withheld from the father of a missing child.

'There is information in relation to this enquiry that I am aware of that I cannot tell you for operational reasons,' Chris adds.

'Okay.'

'I will not lie to you. There will be times when I cannot always tell you everything that is occurring. I will however be honest and truthful to you at all times. If there is a time in the future when I need to withhold information, I will tell you.'

The good thing is that he will not lie to me but it seems mad that we are not to be told what happens.

We watch the search team for a little longer and then decide to go off and search a different part of Prickwillow. Down riverbanks, mud tracks and over fields. Searching yet more sheds, derelict buildings and farm outbuildings. Chris keeps on getting calls on his mobile and I always want to know what information he's getting.

The most dramatic news is that there are a number of rewards being offered. The first is for £10,000 and comes from a local businessman who wants to remain anonymous. This offer brings a lump to my throat and I feel very emotional. I also feel I should match this offer myself. Never mind that I don't have that kind of money. If I sold my business and my home, I could probably raise £40,000. I must make a matching offer myself as soon as possible.

Before I can say a word, Chris and I hear of another anonymous reward of £50,000 from a businessman in Derbyshire. To compound the strange thoughts in my head following the £10,000 offer, I feel a failure. There is no way I can match this offer.

Within hours, two more rewards are offered. The *News of the World* has offered £100,000. This to me is incredible and generous. The figure thuds in my head and I hope and pray that these offers can make a difference in the search for Holly and Jessica. Exhausted, I am not in control of my emotions.

Chris receives another call. As is usual when taking important calls, he takes the mobile from the hands-free position to his ear. Chris's manner shows that the contents of this call are serious. I hope, I dread. What's happened? I will Chris to finish the call and tell me.

He switches off the mobile and car engine. This is serious. We both turn to face one another.

I simply ask, 'Well?'

'The *Express Group* have confirmed they are to offer a reward of one million pounds.'

I can't speak. My throat hurts from trying not to cry. Someone has been so affected by our plight that they've offered this vast reward. I start to cry, as does Chris. Crying in front of another man is uncomfortable and odd. We both soon pull ourselves together – and decide to continue searching.

In the fens, the blackness of the soil is unmistakeable. The land is very wet and, as we are in the middle of summer, the banks, verges and general area are overgrown. Soon, we are both soaked through and covered in mud. I'm dressed for it, but Chris is in a detective-smart shirt and tie and has a once shiny pair of shoes on his feet

We get so involved in the search we lose track of the time. Tonight is the vigil service at St Andrew's Church. It is just after 7 p.m. and when Chris drives us to a dead end in the very heart of Prickwillow Fen, we realise we will be late. It takes us another 40 minutes to reach the church.

As I walk into the church, I could curl up with embarrassment. There is standing room only inside but my place is reserved on the front pew. I join a very agitated Nicola, who is relieved to see me, but she is under enormous strain. She has had a testing day. Trudie plied her with questions ranging from whether Holly had any phobias, to what were her favourite places and pieces of jewellery. The police also asked for Holly's doctor and dentist details to assist with identification. Nicola knows what that implies.

Nicola is quite right to be upset with me. I suddenly think about where she is. Your daughter has disappeared, you have become the centre of a media frenzy and you have to sit at the front of a packed, hushed church waiting for your husband to turn up because he's been out searching; which he has to do. It makes him feel as if he is doing something. But he's kept everyone waiting.

I'm surprised Oliver is not with his mother. Nicola explains that he is at his cousin's playing and she thought it better to let him stay where he was happy. As ever Nicola's judgement is sound. Oliver has been keeping himself busy, spending a lot of time with his friend, Ryan, and his cousins, Paul and Michael. We both feel it is his own way of avoiding the brutal truth that he may never see his sister again.

During the service, I pray for the safe return of Holly and Jessica. I pray for Nicola. I pray for Oliver. Many hundreds of people light a candle of hope. I will never forget our turn. Nicola and I walk up and, with the eyes of the congregation upon me, my hand trembles so much that I'm relieved the candle gets lit and doesn't fall down.

When the service ends, we shake hands with some of our friends and hug others. It's a small comfort. Nicola and I leave by the side exit and manage to avoid the gathering press. We walk through the High Street, towards home, completely untroubled by anyone, before our friends Rob and Trudie stop to pick us up. We need to be left alone. The sense of loss, magnified by the atmosphere inside the church, is too much to bear.

Then we have to become practical, not emotional. We carry on searching. We are looking for any house with the letters C and O in the address, a house that might have a large building or windmill close by.

We have two windmills in Soham. One stands behind a cul-de-sac called Cornmills Road so there is a C and an O in the address. Rob accompanies me. We look and walk round the windmill and the grass playing area round it. We look into the garaging area and into every single house in Cornmills Road. Nothing but a number of old cars – not much to go on for the moment.

We return to Red House Gardens for now, but I intend to come back in the early hours, when people will be in bed, to have a closer look.

Back home and, as usual, the rolling 24-hour *Sky News* is our channel of choice. We are completely taken by surprise when an appeal is made to four individuals who had been using the Ross Peer's Sports Centre to come forward to see if they could help the police. We were completely unaware that this position was in the pipeline and immediately feel let down that important information was not making its way to the parents first. By the end of the appeal there is stunned silence in my home.

And there is anger too. Up and down the country, people with no connection to this case are seeing these images, at the exact same moment as us. For the second time in quick succession, we have learned sensitive information, because we happened to be watching the right channel. This is completely unacceptable. We thought we were working together with the police.

I ring Chris but he is not there. Finally he returns my call at 22.51, explaining that he felt *Sky News* behaved inappropriately by showing the video that evening. Apparently, it had been handed over, off the record, with an informal agreement that it should not have been shown till Thursday morning. This would have allowed time for the families to be shown the video before transmission. Chris accepts what happened was hardly telling the families first. Chris's tone of voice, more than his words, suggests he understands how upset this makes us feel.

Nicola and I sit together. There is no getting away from the bleakness. It has been three days since we last saw Holly and Jessica, three days of wondering where the girls may have been taken to or taken from. Suddenly we may have an answer. The CCTV images show adults getting into a car. These people may be able to help once they have been identified. We pray for their intervention.

It is now around 11 p.m. Chris Mead is back at Police HQ for the evening and, so, unavailable. That means I can continue my search for Holly alone without breaking my pledge to work with the police.

Slightly before midnight Rob and I decide to return to Prickwillow to search a derelict outbuilding on the Isleham road. It is a very dark night with little or no moonlight. We both take baseball bats, just in case we get into a fight. Nicola does not want me to take the bat. I can't blame her for not liking the sight of her husband with a club, but I feel that we will find the girls. There's no point finding them if we can't deal with whoever is holding them. My emotional distress is beginning to take its toll. The large outbuilding is rather decrepit. Once inside we look by torchlight. The place reminds me of my late grandfather's allotment shed. There's nothing but an earth floor, rotting timbers and discarded agricultural equipment. No sign of the girls. I wonder what made me feel so optimistic earlier, made me feel it would be okay, and that Holly would be sitting next to me in the car on the journey home.

It's been the longest day of my life.

Thursday 8 August

FLO Trudie arrives at 8.30 a.m. with the 'elusive' CCTV footage. The images are definitely of Holly and Jessica. Trudie then reads us a statement the police have drafted for us. It says:

'It has been very emotional for us every time a reward has been put up. We are overwhelmed. We would like to thank all parties for the offers and are grateful for continued support.'

In this case, 'overwhelmed' means sitting in a remote field, in the middle of Prickwillow Fen, bawling like a small child, but only those who are very close to me know that. We agree the statement can be issued.

The *Daily Express* headline reads, '£1 Million Reward'. The *Sun* confirms its offer of £150,000. Even though we knew these rewards were in the pipeline, reading these headlines, emblazoned above a photograph of Holly and Jessica, completely knocks us for six.

We're also learning that the police never stop asking questions – often seeking information that seems completely irrelevant and downright obscure. But Nicola is glad to help, and glad to have Trudie around. Everyone knows it has been four days since the girls went missing and the more time passes, the less chance we have of finding our daughter alive. Yet from somewhere very deep within her, Nicola acts the positive mother.

'Until anyone can tell us different we will search for two girls, believing they are alive,' she says and she means it passionately. There is not a trace of bravado in Nicola's tone.

Soham has become a media city in the last 48 hours. There are posters in every shop window. Many have been printed and copied by members of my family. We know we need to maintain this high profile position. It may jog someone's memory, or even inspire someone with suspicions of a neighbour or stranger to contact the police.

Reporters no longer knock at our door. They have been told that all enquiries must go to the press officer for Cambridgeshire Police. The vast majority respect that decision and keep away. Nicola and I are surprised and delighted by this restraint.

Soham has been searched and searched again. This morning we face the fact that the girls must have been taken away from their home town. The only alternative we can bear to think of is that they are in an abductor's house in Soham and still alive. I try hard to form a new search plan based on the medium's observations.

Suddenly, although I have been over most of this area before, I realise Chris Mead stopped me from searching fully behind College Close, back along the river and through to the yards of Clark and Butcher mill. He didn't mean to, but I was in College Close when I had to drop everything and rush back for our first meeting. Now that the CCTV footage places Holly and Jessica nearby at the Sports Centre, I must ransack that area. But, as I promised to work with the police, I have to wait for Chris. Waiting isn't easy.

Trudie tells us there have been some local reports of a car driving erratically on Sunday evening. We hear the sniffer dogs found an initial scent trail to the East of Red House Gardens. This is where I had reservations about the occupants of two particular properties. I have visited both of these properties already under the cover of darkness, but we need to have some official answers.

I am painfully aware that the general search is slowly but surely moving out of my control. That chips away at my soul. Any questions or concerns we raise seem to take an age to be answered or addressed. It makes us feel even more frustrated and we're not being unreasonable.

I know that the police have a huge task – thousands of phone calls to log, follow up and sift through. I know, but do not really understand their problems. Equally, they know but do not *feel* mine – I have a daughter missing.

Chris is still not here. I'm out of patience and need to be out searching those parts of College Close I did not comb before. I'm not interested in why he might be late. I insist Trudie contacts Chris. She rings him and soothes that he should be with us shortly. Angry about losing a whole morning's search time, I ask to speak with him. I can't hide my anger, so my tone, perhaps unjustly, is curt in the extreme. Chris promises to leave Police HQ shortly. It will be about 40 minutes before he gets here. But I stick to the working together deal and wait – I won't say patiently.

After 40 minutes, still no Chris. I tell Trudie I can't wait any longer. If there are police concerns about me compromising a crime scene by finding Holly and Jessica, they can allocate a police officer to escort me – and do it now. God knows there are enough policemen in town. I feel uneasy laying down the law to the law, as it were, but I just can't wait any longer.

I set off into Soham to find a policeman so that I don't do anything rash and compromise police procedure. Luckily before I drag some hapless copper into coming with me, Chris rings. He agrees to re-schedule a meeting and promises he will be with me at two in the afternoon. I agree to wait a little longer.

The waiting doesn't end at two, though. At 2.02 p.m., I ring to find out where Chris is. Finally the man himself arrives 15 minutes later.

We drive down towards College Close. Soham has seen the world's media gather. The specialised transmitting vans are in place and throngs of reporters are standing around. Sky TV has erected a tower lift. Reporters angle for any snippet of information from whatever source.

We find nothing at the rear of College Close. I knock on the door of many houses and ask:

'Sorry to trouble you. Can we just have a look in your garden and sheds for Holly and Jessica?'

'Kevin, you can have access to wherever you like, but we have already searched on your behalf.'

Next we search in Sand Street, which is now under the electronic eye of the Sky tower lift camera. I also want to search the river and bridge areas because Dennis the Medium felt very strongly that the telephone was thrown in the river. We find nothing.

Then we decide to stop because it is felt prudent by Chris not to create an easy photo opportunity for the million or so waiting cameras. Reluctantly, I agree.

We go back to Red House Gardens where we discover the real reason Chris was late. He had to attend meetings with senior officers from the Sarah Payne enquiry. Chris has also met with a child psychologist, Ruth Harrison. Nicola and I are upset. We do not accept the thesis that Holly and Jessica must have been taken by a paedophile. On top of that, bringing in a child psychologist suggests that we're inadequate parents. Neither Nicola nor I have said that Oliver needs 'professional help'. We have not discussed anything of that nature with the police.

Individual officers are trying so hard, though. A number have come back from leave to help. Nicola and I are so grateful for the hard work and dedication of these officers. But the police still have no leads. And so they are doing what their manuals say. Chris tells us that individuals who are on the Sex Offenders list are being asked to account for their whereabouts on Sunday 4 August. Those who can't explain where they were are taken into custody.

Also routine, the police are sifting through house rubbish collections looking for any trace of the girls' clothing. Chris confirms the police now consider the information from Mrs Easy, the lady from Little Thetford who saw the girls 'larking about', to be unreliable. There seems little point in saying 'we told you so', but we do anyway.

The telephones ring incessantly. Each time Chris receives a call, we can't help feeling a glimmer of hope – any call could be the one that gives us a clear lead. But it never happens. Time after time, we feel crushed. And have to pick ourselves up.

In the middle of the afternoon scenes-of-crime officers arrive to examine Holly's bedroom. It is another set of police officers in the house – another intrusion. At least they go upstairs out of the way.

We are asked what we think about doing a televised appeal. 'We will do whatever is best to get the girls back,' Nicola says. Plans have obviously been made without consulting us; the police recommend doing a *Tonight with Trevor McDonald* special. We accept. Les and Sharon Chapman also agree. The filming will be done tomorrow.

Just before the officers complete their work in Holly's bedroom, they explain they need some of her DNA. They take Holly's hairbrush and the mouthpiece of her cornet. When we go back up to Holly's bedroom we find lots of things are covered with a fine powder used to lift fingerprints. It's eerie, as if ghosts have left a mark here.

In the midst of all this activity, Chris springs a tough question. 'How do you want to be told if there is a significant find?'

The police are anxious that the media might get information and release it before Chris or Trudie can arrive in person to tell us. We agree that if there are any significant developments, we want to hear at the earliest opportunity. If possible, we want to be told directly by one of our FLOs in our house. If there is a danger of the media getting hold of something and broadcasting it before this can happen, then a telephone call would be acceptable – as long as it is from Chris or Trudie. We stress the police must make every effort to avoid details going out on radio or television before the families are informed. We also agree the police will provide a mobile phone dedicated only to urgent calls.

We also agree – but I'm not sure we have much choice – that Ruth Harrison can see Oliver. Ruth is a highly regarded specialist in traumatic loss. It seems more acceptable to allow a visit from her now they are not using the term *child psychologist*. We are also offered counselling from Victim Support. We politely tell them we're not interested.

Having now spent the entire afternoon dealing with questions,

I want to resume my own searching. Chris agrees to chaperone me. Together we search, based on the medium's observations. We look in fields, outbuildings, farm sheds and derelict houses, this time on the outskirts of Soham. The fens stretch out, flat, bleak and interminable. The enormity of our task is soul-destroying.

I feel very comfortable in Chris's company and our bond is growing stronger. Chris doesn't shirk hard questions. He feels my intense and acute sense of loss, but still asks the only real question: 'Where do you think Holly and Jessica are, Kevin?'

We look at each other for a long time.

'They are both dead, Chris,' I say finally.

He stares at me. Maybe it's too much for him and he returns to police procedure. I have still not given a formal statement to the police and have preferred to search rather than waste time on paperwork. I realise that the police may wonder why there is so much resistance on my part.

Our house is filling up again. Friends and family drop by to report in on their day's searching; other people set off to scour yet more fields. It all seems quite organised now. Each and every visitor asks the same question – 'Any news?' Unable to offer anything concrete, Nicola and I usually answer with a simple, 'Not yet.'

FLO Trudie is proving to be a star. Nicola feels very comfortable with her. For Nicola these daytime hours drag so slowly. Yet in her anguish, Nicola is able to comfort and support her close friends and family. It is a remarkable display of resilience.

Everyone is stressed and stretched. The police recognise that further help is required. Detective Inspector Gary Goose has been appointed as FLO Coordinator, which will free Chris from the deluge of mobile calls. Each family will get another FLO; for our family this will be Detective Constable Stewart Nicol. Unknown to us, his first task is to get formal statements from Nicola and me, the formal statements we have so far not given. Confrontation looms.

Oliver returns. He is sleeping in our house – for the first time since last Sunday – tonight. We are so pleased to have him home. I have seen very little of him this week. God only knows what effect this is having on him. He seems to be holding up at the moment but that impression may be wrong, just my wishful thinking.

It has been a very long, depressing day. Today's developments suggest that the police fear the worst. They have samples of Holly's DNA and we have agreed a procedure for dealing with 'significant developments'. I can't block out the thought that the next development will be finding the bodies of my daughter and her friend.

We cling to one hope. Tomorrow we are going to record a *Tonight with Trevor McDonald* special. This may just help. The world's media are encamped here in Soham. If someone is holding the girls, then he may already be in a state of panic. If that person hears our very direct pleas, maybe that will persuade him to release the girls. We won't have to work to show how desperate we feel.

Friday 9 August

At 9 a.m. Chris drives us to the Marriott Hotel in Huntingdon where they are recording the interview. Colin Baker, who is to be our interviewer, is a very big man. All four parents stand before him, nervous, exhausted and bewildered. Not one of us has the slightest desire to be here.

We're told that each family will be interviewed separately. This is completely unacceptable to both us and the Chapmans. We are in this together. A compromise needs to be sorted out. We are taken to another room and have a long wait while the TV people and the police talk. Eventually they suggest that all four parents can be in the room all the time. But TV is about illusion and reality, so after the first interview, the room will be changed around for the second set of parents, giving the impression that we were sitting opposite one another all the time.

This compromise adds to the tension and, to his credit, Colin Baker takes time to speak to us all individually and explain that 'we call the shots'. He is calm and that helps. Crucially we are also promised that if we make a mistake or say something we feel unhappy with, it will not be broadcast. We are about to be interviewed by the gentlest of giants.

Nicola and I are first up. We know how important this can be and we are committed to it. The room is small, the lights very bright, and there's what feels like a crowd watching. The questions are very personal. But we cope and keep to our stance that the girls are alive. It is the only agenda we have brought into the room with us.

Then we see how surreal television is. The room has to be changed for the Chapmans. Naïvely we thought this would be simple. Not so. It takes the best part of an hour before we get the nod to return. This wait must have been unbearable for the Chapmans. Nicola and I feel so much respect for Les and Sharon as they brace themselves for this ordeal with strength and dignity. It feels so intense and emotional that at one point Colin Baker has to leave the room to regain his composure. And he's the hard-bitten pro.

We are then told that the programme will be shown a week later. My heart sinks. The only reason for us doing this is to raise awareness and for the police to appeal directly to any potential abductor. It needs to be shown now. As soon as. What is the point of leaving it for a week?

We are taken back to Soham. On the journey home I wonder if I should call Dennis the Medium. When he and Lorraine said that Holly could not be contacted on the 'other side' it felt like a lifeline. That very idea of Holly somehow still being alive has not left my thoughts since. Perhaps they can tell us more.

Dennis is unavailable. It is about 4.45 p.m. and the police are due back at 5 p.m. with Ruth Harrison, the trauma specialist. We have been told she is coming to assess Oliver – and only to assess Oliver. I go into my tiny office and finally reach the elusive Dennis.

'Dennis, it's Kevin Wells from Soham. Can you talk?'

'Hello, Kevin. How are you and Nicola bearing up?'

'We are both very focused at the moment, Dennis. Listen, have you any more thoughts or observations to share with me?'

'Yes, I have. I am so sorry, but contact has been made with Holly on the other side.'

'Oh no, no, no, it can't be . . .'

'I am so sorry, Kevin.'

I listen in stunned silence as Dennis adds some details.

'Kevin, Holly is laying face down somewhere, almost as if she is floating. It is however not in deep water. I really am sorry.'

I can't stop the tears. The back of my throat hurts where I am trying to stop myself from crying out. Dennis has just snuffed out that one tiny flicker of light at the end of the longest of tunnels. We had faith in him; in the last three days we have planned all our searching on his insights. Now he tells us that the minuscule chance of finding Holly alive has gone.

I know what it's like to have your heart broken. This is the end. Holly will never again be part of our lives. Only a memory.

Fuck! The police are due here in minutes. Fuck! I need to speak with Nicola about this telephone call, *now*. Fuck! Oliver is due to be assessed by Dr Trauma. Do I include Oliver in this conversation?

I'm furious that I have to make these decisions immediately. I decide – and hope this is best for my son – that for the first time I am going to deliberately exclude Oliver from a development. I wipe the tears off my face. I must tell Nicola at once. Holly's mum has the right to know what I've been told.

As Nicola enters the office, she realises something's badly wrong. I have devastating news. She starts to cry and that starts me crying.

'Kev, what's happened?'

I cannot speak.

'Kev, have they found Holly?' I still cannot speak but am able to shake my head.

'Kev, what's wrong?' I can't utter a coherent sentence, I write the word 'Dennis' on a piece of paper. Nicola knows exactly what it means. We hold one another and we weep.

Fuck! The police are now outside. We pull ourselves together as best we can and answer the door. Chris Mead sees how distraught we are. It's obvious that something is badly wrong. I give him the news Dennis gave me. Chris knows only too well what impact this news will have. It is another defining moment together.

But we still have to accommodate police procedure. Ruth is here to see Oliver. She and Oliver sit in the living room while Nicola and I forlornly join Chris and Trudie at the dining table. For the next two hours, they try to lift our spirits. Chris asks us to look at things from an 'objective viewpoint'. Together we review the medium's information. We talk about being positive, rational and constructive. Chris argues that just because Dennis says something, does not automatically mean it is true. Yes, yes, but . . . Human beings are resilient and, by the end of those two hours, we feel a little better.

Ruth Harrison joins us for a cup of tea at the table. She explains that she used a laptop during the 'interview'; Oliver was asked to express his moods by selecting different colours. Oliver is very concerned about the level of police searching, Ruth says, but he was more hopeful when he saw the police helicopter and dog teams. Oliver feels Holly has been in an accident and is in a ditch somewhere, Ruth tells us. We are absolutely flabbergasted. We feel guilty. After the first night, we have deliberately excluded Oliver from searching, to protect him. Instead, we may have contributed to his anxiety. And I have just excluded him from Dennis's observations.

Ruth suggests Oliver needs something to look forward to. The simplest of observations, but not something that Nicola and I had considered.

Chris leaps into action on the phone. He rings colleagues to arrange for Oliver to go out with a dog search team. They agree at once. More ambitiously, Chris tells us he is going to request a flight in the police helicopter. Nicola and I just sit there as Chris eloquently presents 'our case' on why it is so important for Oliver to be granted this 'treat'. There are logistical and insurance problems, but by the end of the evening, those obstacles have been overcome. Tomorrow morning Oliver is going to be taken to RAF Wyton. I feel humble seeing how hard Chris is working on my family's behalf.

We didn't know then that Ruth had also been asked to make covert assessments of Nicola and myself. Cat and mouse again, but the mice didn't know that the cat was watching. It would be the best part of a year before we were let in on the 'secret' and allowed to read the report on ourselves.

Then again the mood changes.

Trudie asks me to produce a list of all the people who have worked for me over the last few years. I do that at once and explain that none of those people would be involved in anything of this nature and that it is a bloody waste of time. Trudie takes the list anyway. Nicola, Oliver and I now go to St Andrew's Church, in order to offer up some prayers and have some quiet time.

Back to Red House Gardens. Chris and Trudie are still there. There has been a development. Brother-in-law Graham has found a house that matches some of Dennis's 'vision'. The house is near water, there is an old red car outside and the gentleman inside was rather 'odd'. Chris is keen to jump in the car and go with Graham immediately, but Trudie points out they have hardly slept for 72 hours. It would be more sensible to send other officers. In the event, the police find nothing there.

The telephone keeps ringing. We notice that the main question is no longer, 'Are there any developments?' Instead, people ask how all of us are coping. It's a subtle change but it reflects the truth. Tomorrow we will be introduced to our third FLO, namely Detective Constable Stewart Nicol. Nicola and I are about to be out-numbered in our own home by police.

When everyone has gone, Nicola and I discuss Oliver. We go over what Ruth Harrison said. As things are bad enough already, we do not want to make them worse by asking Oliver to leave the room. We don't want to stop talking the moment our son walks into a room. God knows this is not how we wanted our 12-year-old to enter adolescence, but we decide to hide nothing from Oliver. Our young son is going to have to grow up quicker than we had ever imagined.

Saturday 10 August

Not much sleep and so many questions. It makes no sense that two lively, fit 10-year-old girls, would allow themselves to be pulled into a vehicle without a struggle. Surely someone must have seen something? Heard something?

Chris has really tried for the helicopter trip. Oliver is blissfully unaware that he will be the first non-police employee to fly in the helicopter. We go off, leaving Nicola to meet our new FLO Stewart. Nicola has agreed to complete her statement today: she is not looking forward to it.

Oliver enjoys riding in a police car and the 'blues and twos' experience. Miraculously, we arrive at RAF Wyton in one piece. One of the chopper crew, PC Gareth Williams, is from Soham, and he gives us the guided tour of the helicopter and equipment. Oliver is allowed to touch the thermal imaging equipment and video camera. My son is enthralled. As they get ready to rotor the blades, it is time for a certain father to show his true colours and opt out of the kind offer to join the crew. Oliver and Chris can hardly contain their excitement. Both look as pleased as punch, waiting to take off.

I watch the chopper rise into the air. During the flight, searching techniques are explained and demonstrated to Oliver. He spots 'something red' in a field and the pilot swoops down to check. But the red is not the girls' shirts. Nevertheless, the trip is a huge boost. Oliver feels like the most important boy in the country.

As we head back to Soham, Chris spots a search team in the fields between Soham and Wicken. We pull over. Oliver again gets to see that a great deal is being done to find his sister. It's blistering hot. In their head to toe black uniforms, the police team must be sweltering. We join in and find ourselves near the railway line. I find myself watching Oliver search. He is concentrating hard and seems incredibly focused. Oliver is also beginning to develop a relationship with Chris and I'm glad of it.

Meanwhile, Nicola is taken to Ely to complete her statement. It is an ordeal and she often breaks down and has to stop talking. Then, she gathers her strength and starts again. When she gets back to Red House Gardens, God bless her, she has not an ounce of strength left. Her eyes are red and swollen and she looks as if she's been emotionally battered. The interview lasted five hours. I'm furious at how long it took.

I feel we shouldn't put up with that. I get in Stewart's face, giving him the pointed finger, asking if he feels this behaviour towards my wife is acceptable. I repeat the word 'outrageous' to make myself clear. But Stewart is mainly interested in following police procedure. With alarming insensitivity he chooses this moment to request that I complete my statement on Sunday.

I can't think of any reason why this would not be acceptable but I feel pressured into agreeing. Great start, Stewart. Harass the parents. Nicola is not happy with the confrontational atmosphere and goes over to her sister's house.

We also discover that the police did not tell us they were preparing a reconstruction. Two young actresses have been chosen to play Holly and Jessica. The reconstruction will start soon and, in my agitated state, I retreat to the quiet of my bedroom and close the landing curtains. I subconsciously decide that observing a Holly lookalike may prove too upsetting.

The weather is bad and the reconstruction hasn't started but no one thinks to let the families know when it will begin. We wait, nervous and uncomfortable. The more I think about the reconstruction, the more displeased I am. Why isn't it being done on a Sunday when the girls actually went missing? Why isn't it being done later in the evening, the time the girls were last seen? Isn't the point to reconstruct as much of the reality as possible?

Chris disturbs me with the gentlest of knocks on the bedroom door. Rightly, he reminds me my house is full of friends and family. On my way downstairs, without thinking, I open the landing curtains.

Then, I see the girls. They are dressed in Manchester United shirts, just about to leave Red House Gardens. I know they're two young actresses, but my heart misses a beat. From the back, the resemblance to Holly is uncanny.

Along with my houseguests, I watch the rest of the recon-struction on TV. The young actress playing Holly not only looks but walks like her. The young actress playing Jessica is also a good lookalike.

I'm too thrown, too upset, to speak much to friends and family. Maybe they deserve better, but I am completely shattered. Everyone is asked to leave with the exception of the police. That means I can ask why this 'bloody reconstruction is not being held on Sunday'. Diplomatically, I am informed that tomorrow, Sunday, there will be roadblocks from late afternoon through to evening. The police don't want to advertise this for fear of alerting any individual who may be travelling through at a similar time as last week. So the reconstruction has to be done today.

I feel very foolish. I did not mean to question the police's ability, and I am sure I sounded as if I thought they had no idea what they were doing. The pressure is palpable. And there is another issue. The media insinuate that Holly and Jessica were dabbling in internet chatrooms, which suggests they might have arranged to meet someone. Before the police leave, we remind them how unhappy we are at these rumours. We know Holly has never used a chatroom on the internet and the police also know this perfectly well, as they have checked our computer. Reading headlines such as 'Did weirdo lure girls?' is hurtful. All the police have to do is release a simple statement. At least, our FLOs listen.

Then Stewart says something which helps the brittle state of things with the police. He warns me that tonight's episode of *A Touch of Frost* is about a paedophile kidnapping. 'I thought I'd better let you know, just in case, well you know . . .' I stop him mid-sentence to thank him. We will not be tuning in.

Nicola comes back from her sister's looking calmer, though still jaded. A little later, my business partner Scott drops by looking for an update. Scott, along with the staff, has been coping with our Cambridge contracts. They've been working long, long days, starting very early so that they can finish and then help search in the late afternoon and evening.

Scott reminds me that next week's work needs scheduling and invoices prepared. The staff's wages need calculating. Usually I do that each Sunday and I decide this week will be no different. I ring Chris to let him know I cannot complete my statement tomorrow due to work commitments. It does not go down well.

I didn't know at the time that, behind the scenes, the police were concerned by this development. They went into analysis mode, dissecting the circumstances, potential ramifications and putting my reasons under the microscope to see if I might have a hidden agenda for not completing my statement. The police can spend as much time as they wish in dissection and analysis. I can't let my staff and customers down. It is that simple. (I later discovered that the police accepted the delay because they sensed I needed to regain some control of my home.)

All evening long, the house is just what a Martian would not expect in middle England. Everyone is emotional and shows it – friends and family alike embrace, cuddle and offer much needed moral support. We maintain our positive 're-focused position' established yesterday with Chris and Trudie. Nicola and I try to hang on to the smallest flicker of hope for people to take home with them.

When our last friends go, we're more honest. Our best and only hope is that the girls are still alive and being held by kidnappers. With the intense media presence and pressure the kidnappers are in a state of panic and do not know what to do.

That is what the police seem to think too. DS David Hankins has put out statements directed at the kidnappers, indicating that there is no need to panic and that releasing the girls is very much an option. These statements have been written with the help of criminal psychologists. For Nicola and me that offers a glimmer of hope. Can this have an effect? We pray to the bottom of our boots that it will. There will be plenty of time for more prayers tomorrow. We will go to church for the Communion Service. It's something I've never done before.

Sunday 11 August

There are no overnight developments. Nicola and I have managed to grab a few hours' sleep.

Trudie drives Nicola to the church while Stewart and I collect my sister and mother. There are reporters and cameramen everywhere. If I were feeling my best, it would be daunting to run that gauntlet. Luckily, I spot the small iron cemetery gate, which is media free. We slip through and make it into church with the minimum of fuss. It feels like a small victory.

Inside, the church is once again completely full. Our seats are reserved at the front of the main aisle. The adrenalin ebbs and we are able to relax a little. Or we would be if it were not for the fact that my mother is incoherent and starts to speak out loudly. This does not cease once the service starts. Mother has been under terrible pressure and she loses her battle to remain composed. I feel for her so much.

Mother's mumblings punctuate Tim Alban Jones' sermon. She gets worse and worse, until eventually I can't stop her from falling. Stewart escorts her out of church and takes her home. It is the first time the stress our family is under shows itself embarrassingly. But in the packed church, no one passes judgement. I feel people understand. It is a stark reminder that no one can escape this nightmare.

Thanks to the vicar, however, a photographer is busy at work. Tim Alban Jones had given permission for pictures to be taken during the service – in my view a very misjudged decision.

FLOs are trained to stay cool under fire. But they too are getting involved. Trudie gets caught up in the emotion of the moment and sheds a tear. Stewart says, 'Our training is our armour,' to help her recover her composure and it works. (This phrase would appear later as a source of much ridicule for Trudie, during lighter-hearted moments, outnumbered as she is by two male colleagues.)

At the end of the service we stay inside the church for a cup of tea. Everyone is kind, supportive, encouraging. It is tremendously uplifting. It gives us the strength to take an on the spot decision – to face the media as we leave in a way that we couldn't on the way in. We walk down to the church gates and we stop just a fleeting moment and face the throng of flash lights and questions.

As soon as we get home, our FLOs remind us curtly about media policy and working through the Cambridgeshire Police, if we feel the need to do anything with the press in the future. As no one has taken any time to explain to us what the 'Press Strategies' are, we hide behind that very sentence. It does not cut much ice with Stewart and Trudie who are under pressure from police managers. Yet again the pesky parents have not followed police guidelines.

After our telling off, we return to all our unanswered questions. Many calls from the public are still coming through. We ask why a photograph of Jessica's mobile telephone has not been shown to the media. We learn that the paedophile recently arrested has been released without charge. We ask if the reconstruction has been successful in evoking any memories, in getting new witnesses.

People may be surprised that at this, the worst of the worst of times, there are still moments when life goes on – and we're grateful. Chris is trying hard to do things that will make it easier for Oliver to cope.

At about 11.30 a.m., Stewart and Trudie head to an industrial estate in Ely for a demonstration by the dog handler, PC Jeff Turner. I stay behind to do some paperwork for my business. Much to the group's amusement, the team selects Trudie as the 'criminal' for the dogs to work with. She is not utterly delighted. She dons the protective arm guard and wanders off. Within seconds, evil Trudie is grabbed by the police's answer to Rin Tin Tin and is in the vice-like grip of the Alsatian. Stewart, Nicola and Oliver laugh with delight. The second exercise involves Trudie hiding in a bush. When the dog finds her, it is enthusiastic enough to slobber saliva over all her face. That's proper devotion to duty for you!

When the travelling four return, we get some surprising statistics. By 12.30 p.m. there have been 411 telephone calls to the incident room as a response to the reconstruction. Nicola and I are amazed, as we wouldn't expect 40 people to have been around Soham on a Sunday evening. Many officers are about to descend on Soham for the road checks later in the day and they will hand out questionnaires. We just hope and pray that something positive turns up from this exercise.

Who knows what might matter?

On the Saturday before Holly went missing, mother and daughter went on their usual weekly shopping trip together in Cambridge. Holly was particularly excited as they were going to buy her first bra. This is a rite of passage, women tell me, and it was a wonderful moment for mother and daughter to share. That bra is now on the list of clothing Nicola told the police Holly was wearing when she went missing. As it was purchased so recently, Trudie asks if Nicola still has the receipt. Nicola has it and she's sure the packaging is in our rubbish bins. She eventually finds it. Whatever must be going through her mind? Nicola's steadfastness seems quite extraordinary to me.

Trudie also wants 'extra angles for the press'. The media need new snippets as there are no developments in the enquiry. We are asked if we can supply some of Holly's things to be photographed; we hand over a sample of Holly's homework, along with details of her favourite song, which was S Club 7's 'Automatic High'. One of Nicola's relatives has a video of Holly performing in the Soham Fenlander Majorettes. This can be collected later.

In the midst of this, we get back to the nasty subject of internet and chatroom usage. Nicola and I insist we will release a statement ourselves to clarify that there has been no chatroom activity. We will do that with or without the police, as the continuing speculation is making our family angry and distressed. In the end we never have to do that because the police finally get the press to understand that there was no chatroom activity. It brings an end to the vilest of headlines.

The roadblocks go up just as friends and family start to arrive. Each and every one of them says, 'You'll never guess what's just happened to me.' Somewhere from very deep inside we manage a wry smile and reply, 'I think we have an idea.' Every visitor has been caught in the road check and had to explain they are friends of ours, coming to visit Red House Gardens. It matters not a jot to the police – quite rightly so.

But it's a sad evening again. It is now a week since Holly went missing – a whole week. Late at night Rob and I decide to have a drive around. My thinking is that now the road checks have gone, maybe, just maybe, the kidnapper will drop the girls off somewhere. As before, we take baseball bats. It would be pointless to see the girls in someone's house or vehicle and not be in a position to deal with the abductors.

We drive through the surrounding villages, doing a broad sweep of the main roads. There is nothing. We get back home and Rob and Trudie leave. Nicola is worried about the effect all this is having on her pregnant friend, worries that Trudie brushes away.

We are alone in our sad house. Being alone, without having to keep up appearances, Nicola and I have a mini breakdown. It's been a week. Each day lengthens the odds against Holly coming home. There are no leads and nowhere else we can search. We can only hope that tomorrow's *Tonight with Trevor McDonald* programme will produce something. The programme will conclude with a personal appeal to the abductors from DS David Beck, the senior investigating officer. We have been made aware that as a father of two daughters himself, he feels a strong emotional link with this case. David Beck is a trained hostage negotiator and the wording of his appeal may have an immediate impact.

As we struggle to get some sleep, our hopes are with him.

Monday 12 August

The police are beginning to feel under pressure for results and they take some care to impress us with their efforts. Chris explains the system behind the police search, which is called 'the grid'. Soham has been completely ransacked and there are 400 house to house enquiries in hand. Everyone who lives in 285 of these houses has been spoken to. If anything interesting is said, an officer returns to take a formal statement.

One of the things the police will concentrate on today is the evidence of a taxi driver from Newmarket. He says he saw a dark green metallic four-door saloon driving erratically on the A142 towards Newmarket; two children were inside. One child was in the front passenger seat and the second was in the back. The driver was thrashing his arms about and looked Mediterranean or tanned. That makes sense to us. We believe the girls would not have got into any car without a struggle. The A142 runs right through Soham and close to where the girls were last seen.

But one fact stops me getting too optimistic. If the taxi driver was an accurate observer and followed this green car for the best part of six miles, why didn't he get its registration number? We've already had one hoax sighting and we've learned not to get our hopes up. We have become very cautious.

The FLOs keep suggesting the girls must have known their abductor. Nicola and I refuse to believe it. We've known all our friends for many years and we don't believe they're capable of such evil. The police reply with statistics which show it is usually friends or family who commit such crimes. So it's not surprising when Chris and Trudie ask me to choose just a couple of friends or family members I may have reservations about. Is it my brother, aunt, business partner or the milkman I've known for 17 years that I suspect might be a maniac behind the everyday smile? I feel under real pressure.

I have no one to offer up, I say.

Chris and Trudie's faces make it plain; this is not acceptable. Do I want to help or not? More tension, more silence.

Cleverly, Chris asks me to look at this from a different perspective. He asks me to think about people Holly would get into a car with. Is there any individual I feel less than one hundred per cent happy with? I'm confused and upset, I am totally convinced no one among my friends and family would harm a hair on my daughter's head. I can't concentrate and I don't trust myself to make sound judgements under such pressure. The silence continues.

Finally, reluctantly, I suggest the names of two people I have 'reservations' about. As expected, I am asked why these two? I explain that I'm basing my choices on observations from Dennis the Medium. Potentially, loosely, if you really think about it, just maybe, these two individuals might fit. So I have offered up the names, but I am also aware that the police will not act on 'medium information'. In my soul I feel some comfort because I think my two names are unlikely to get a visit from the police.

My formal interview ends at 14.36. Nicola's was twice as long and, bizarrely, I feel the need to apologise to her for this on my return. I cannot help but feel the majority of my statement is pretty pointless and I can't see the use of putting me under pressure to name people I feel 'reservations' about.

Before we get to Soham, Chris gets a call. The police have decided that an exact model of Jessica's mobile should be made available to the media. This is not very difficult, as my own mobile telephone is the same model. We go to the Village College immediately to hand the telephone in.

The area is awash with reporters and film crews. The police think it's unwise for me to be seen, so I agree to lie down on the back seat of the car. As Chris sends the mobile telephone in to be photographed, I nervously await being discovered flat on my back by an eagle-eyed reporter. Eagle eyes seem to be in short supply, so I escape detection, but it makes for a strange end to a very long morning.

There is one small difference between Jessica's and my mobile telephone. Part of hers was held together with masking tape. The police do not release this detail, as it seems to offer a way of verifying the authenticity of any call from the kidnapper(s).

At 2 p.m. the police hold a press conference. Det. Chief Inspector Andy Hebb announces that the police will devote more numbers, especially admin staff, to deal with the ever-growing number of calls from the public. The police are under scrutiny, and not just from us. The nation's press is watching. A whole week without a single lead!

We're not so much critical as concerned, extremely concerned to be sure that all is being done that possibly can be. To placate Nicola and me, officers suggest we watch *Tonight with Trevor McDonald* at Police HQ. If callers ring in with information, we will be on hand, especially if there are queries about Soham names or locations. Nicola and I both jump at the chance to help.

We are taken into the Major Operations Room and the Control Room. As we are shown round, officers go quiet. Quiet as the grave, but I know it's a mark of respect. Still, it's surreal, and we have to walk through looking composed.

I ask about the logistics. When a telephone call is received, how do they decide what priority to give it? I'm told all operators computerise the details of each call and this information is then sent to a supervisor who makes an on the spot decision on the level of priority. The supervisor decides how relevant the call is to the enquiry.

We are taken to one of the telephone control rooms to see for ourselves. Chris authorises an example of the many calls being received, to be displayed on the screen. It reads, 'The dad did it.'

'Oh, that's nice,' I – the dad – say.

'Sorry about that, let me get another one up.'

'The fathers are in it together.'

'Oh, that's even better,' I say.

'Let me get a different one up,' Chris smiles.

'Try looking in any allotment sheds.'

'Before you ask, Chris, I have not got an allotment shed!'

Black humour, gallows humour, is one of the oldest strategies for coping with real horror.

We are then taken to the tiny, Silver Command Room to watch the *Tonight* programme. Colin Baker has kept his promise and they have cut out those parts we were not happy with.

The programme is hideously difficult to watch and by the end, the hairs on my neck are standing up. Nicola is very tense. David Beck makes a direct appeal to the kidnapper, managing to be both clinical and personal. 'Leave the girls somewhere, somewhere safe where they can be found. Examine your conscience and you will know that it's right to do that. Stop this now.' His words could make all the difference. With the green car lead now being actively worked on, will this appeal take us a step further forward? We believe it will.

We are given a copy of the taxi driver's statement. Nicola and I are both slightly disillusioned. It turns out he tried to contact the police much earlier with this information. That is very worrying. Is information being disseminated quickly enough? The problems the taxi driver had getting through would, in fact, mark a turning point in the media's attitudes. They would examine Cambridgeshire Police's performance ruthlessly, giving no more 'benefit of the doubt'.

Thinking now about the green car sighting and remembering the descriptions given by the driver, I suddenly feel I can offer a name which may well link the two. I am so convinced, my adrenalin surges. I ask the police to action it immediately. To their credit, it is made a priority and the police visit the individual.

Round 10 p.m., Chris agrees to take us back to Soham. I want to get into the Studlands Park Estate the green car was seen turning into it. The estate has many hundreds of houses. It is

mainly occupied by visiting American Forces who rent the properties from local landlords. The estate itself is not easy to
manoeuvre through if you have no local knowledge, as it has
only one entrance and exit junction. So I suspect the driver of
the green car lives on the estate. This is why I ask Chris to drive
round Studlands Park before dropping us back home.

Chris is not eager to do this. I know it will mean trawling
around in the dark, maybe drawing attention to ourselves. I do
not care one jot. Chris accepts there are no operational reasons
not to go, and in police-speak he can justify doing it as he 'would
be demonstrating an open, transparent and responsive approach
to the families'.

We drive round the entire estate. Studlands Park is quiet but,
in the dark, we can't tell which cars are green. I am disappointed.

We get back home. I think back on the day. The taxi driver was
not the only person to 'sight' Holly and Jessica. Earlier in the
afternoon a sighting had been reported at Thetford in Norfolk,
further down the A14. Some friends from Stevenage went to 'have
a proper look', but to no avail. It is worth the effort, for you can
never be sure. Other sightings are simply too far away for us to
become involved with, including some in Ireland. News of each
and every sighting lifts our hearts until the follow-up enquiries
slap us down as it becomes obvious it can't have been the girls.
Hopes raised, hopes dashed. It just makes us feel worse in the
end.

But I'm not happy about being unable to spot any green cars
on the estate. Nicola is in bed. I find a torch. I get in my car. I
drive quietly to Studlands Park. I walk around with the torch.
Now I can see colours. I walk up people's drives, look in parked
cars and around the garaging areas. All to no avail. No new leads.

In the early hours of the morning, I return home.

Rather than disturb a dozing Nicola and as I'm still full of
adrenalin, I cycle down to the church. I go in through the side
vestry door, and can't find any light switches. My next hour is
spent alone in the darkness of St Andrew's. I pray, I pray out loud,

I cry to God for help. I'll do anything to get my daughter back. My promises of unrealistic future commitments to God in exchange for the chance to see Holly alive and well again, they echo through the dark church.

Tuesday 13 August

I don't even try to join Nicola in bed, as I'm really impatient for Chris's morning call. I go round the corner to buy the morning papers, but some customers find my arrival too much to deal with. They say nothing and very deliberately avoid eye contact. Yes, I can understand their behaviour – if I'm being generous. But it hurts to be on the receiving end of small gestures like this.

The *Daily Mirror*'s headline, 'Find Him', refers to the driver of the green four-door saloon. What touches Nicola and I, however, is a short interview with Holly's former teacher, Mrs Pederson. She has been on holiday in Italy and found out about the missing girls much later than most. Her anguish is clear. The story includes a poem that Holly wrote for Mrs Pederson at the end of term:

'Mrs Pederson is so cool
She is the very best in school
She teaches us every day
She must be happy when it's Saturday.'

Holly idolised Mrs Pederson. Nicola and I can remember Holly sitting at the dining table, taking great care to get the card and poem just right for her favourite teacher. When she was done, Holly proudly showed us her finished work.

Today is Oliver's formal interview. We decide not to speak with him about any details of Sunday 4 August. His account must be untainted. As parents we are not allowed to be present. Fortunately, an adult of our choice can be, and Aunt Sheena agrees to be there. That reassures us as we trust and respect Sheena. But, as Oliver is driven off to the interview room, Nicola and I still cry at our son's plight.

71

Oliver's interview lasts for one hour and six minutes. He is absent two hours and five minutes. I know, I counted every second.

When he gets back, Oliver seems remarkably laid back and none the worse for his ordeal. But Sheena tells us he was very quiet, seemed sad and often bowed his head. His answers were very short and Oliver spoke of completely the wrong Sunday as he described a barbecue that took place a week earlier on 28 July. Bless him, he really is very confused at the moment. But he is not showing that right now. He seems quite together and wants to visit his cousin.

The police now tell us something that, at first, seems only technical. The mobile phone company has confirmed that Jessie's handset's last signal contact was at 6.46 p.m. At that time, the mobile was either switched off or powered down. So it seems that the time of the first 'last signal', given in the early hours of Monday morning, was a mistake. I'm upset that we appear to have wasted our time searching in Reach, Upware, Burwell and Swaffham Prior.

We debate the significance of the 6.46 time. If the kidnapper switched the telephone off himself at this point, then the girls were in trouble before we realised they were missing – and almost three hours before people began searching. It's harrowing to think about.

The police have political problems now. The media are criticising them. To counter that, the force has decided to give a televised FLO conference. Chris and DC Amanda Blythe, FLO to the Chapman family, will explain what they do. DCI Hebb has briefed the media off the record, arguing that attacking the police doesn't help to find the girls. No one envies Chris his role. He has to prepare what he says with great care. His statement ends simply:

'The family are well aware of the importance of the media's role in the investigation and I know they are hugely appreciative of the efforts and support they have been offered by the media in this enquiry. We, together with the entire investigation team, remain committed to finding both Holly and Jessica and nothing will give us, as FLOs, greater pleasure than to return Jessica and Holly back home to their families, where they belong and where their families desperately await their return.'

After the conference, Chris makes himself available for interviews.

When the doorbell rings just after 5 o'clock, I mean to tease Chris a little about how he did on TV. But it's obvious that's out of the question. In front of me stands a man whose body language is stark. Chris's eyes are glazed. He looks desperately sad as he steps into the house. He suggests our guests wait in the living room. Chris, Nicola and I go into the kitchen. The seriousness of the moment is clear. You could hear a pin drop.

Chris starts to explain what was going on behind the scenes. He had two interviews still to do after the conference when he got an alarming piece of news. A member of the public, who had reported hearing screams on the Sunday, up on the Warren Hill Gallops, decided to visit the site himself. He found two separate mounds of loose or dug over earth and tyre tracks nearby. He told the Suffolk Police who isolated the area immediately as a potential crime scene.

Chris found himself in a terrible situation when he had to give those last two interviews. He had to maintain absolute secrecy and he knew all too grimly what this latest development might mean. But he couldn't reveal any of this.

The police fear the media will get this information – very easy to imagine since so many reporters are staying in Newmarket – and broadcast it before both families can be informed. Chris outlines the events which have led to the top of Warren Hill now being cordoned off. The final words he says to us are the worst. 'There is no alternative but to treat the find as the shallow graves of Holly and Jessica. I'm really sorry.'

This is the moment we've been dreading, the moment we can no longer have any hope. We've lost our Holly. Nicola and I both start to sob. Then, Oliver comes in through the back door and sees his parents crying. Neither of us can speak, so Nicola stretches out her arms and we hold and cuddle Oliver.

It is Chris who makes the immediate decision not to keep our son in the dark. He starts to tell Oliver what has happened. We wipe the tears off our faces. We know we have to open the living-room door and tell everyone else. Everyone is desperately upset because the truth seems so obvious. The shallow graves are Holly and Jessica's.

Everyone in the house is made aware of the need for complete confidentiality. We have to tell friends and family but this news must not leak out. One of those I tell is my brother Andrew. I have no reason to imagine he will go and do something which will have enormous consequences for our family.

Andrew has been befriended by an attractive female TV reporter. Miss Caring and Charming has given Andrew her personal mobile telephone number. Real friends are hard to find in a crisis, she has purred. She is there for him, 24/7. She's been round traumas and she knows how desperately he may need a friendly voice, a shoulder to cry on. It's personal, not business, nothing to do with her job, of course.

Minutes after I speak to him, Andrew contacts her and gives her the Newmarket mounds details I have just given him.

Fifteen minutes later, the newsflash is on TV.

We're angry about this leak – and terrified. Nicola is scared her mother will have seen it and her mother is having to cope with all this after having heart surgery in 1998.

Nicola can't find her mother anywhere. We don't need this stress on top of everything else.

The police are adamant the leak has not come from their side. It can only have come from us, the Chapmans, or a member of our families. We have no idea my brother is to blame. But the immediate impact is devastating. The police simply cut both families out of the information loop. They don't trust us any more.

So all we know is that they have probably found the place where someone has dumped Holly and Jessica's remains. The house fills up; everyone speaks in hushed voices as a mark of respect. Those who live out of the immediate area and have mobile telephones are sent a text message.

Early evening, the 24-hour television coverage dominates the living room. Among the adults is one 12-year-old boy, our son Oliver. He looks sad and withdrawn and I feel the urge to pick him up, comfort him and try to offer some reassurance. But unless I lie, I cannot make it better. I give him a hug, I can't do anything else.

The news leads to a barrage of phone calls as Stewart and Chris try to get an update from the Newmarket site. There is an obvious problem, though. They are not getting much information and, incredibly, the police officers at the shallow grave seem to have no sense of urgency. Stewart and Chris sound increasingly agitated. They understand how desperately we need to know if the bodies are those of the girls. Their colleagues don't seem to comprehend this, not at all.

The media also sense the end is near. Forget the respectful stand off. Television crews now hover in the cul-de-sac, some even come to our door, chancing it to get a comment. Stewart and Chris, both already under enormous strain, deal with the journalists and are very sharp to those who turn up on the doorstep. Our FLOs then head into Tanners Lane, where, perhaps unfairly, they ask any lingering reporters to move on.

There's a farcical moment in our tragedy. As he heads off a reporter, Stewart manages to turn his ankle over. The burly professional policeman suddenly becomes a poor bloke in pain. He hobbles back to our house – and we get the frozen peas out of the freezer and apply them to his foot!

Suddenly, a piece of news from Newmarket completely stuns everybody. The police have decided to start the search only in the morning. There will be no searching tonight. Chris doesn't believe it and he knows that we won't, either. This is a nonsensical decision. Nicola is completely distraught. We are all beyond furious, livid with rage. We pressure the FLOs to pressure their bosses though we know Chris, Trudie and Stewart totally agree with us.

I can't stand it inside any more. Rob and I decide to sit outside. Stewart and Chris are pacing the lawn, busy on their mobiles –

and Stewart is hobbling. We're now well placed to eavesdrop on the frantic phone calls which our FLOs are making.

At this terrible moment, I'm glad to be with Rob. He's burned out with sadness too. I am resigned to losing this battle and, in my heart, I sense that confirmation of Holly and Jessica's death limps ever closer. The thought of waiting for another ten or twelve hours in a state of nervous suspense before the forensic teams start their work is just too much to bear. I ask Rob to go and buy a bottle of my favourite malt whisky, Laphroig. Rob immediately gets up. Chris comes over.

'Kevin, that won't help.' Chris says. He is now an alcohol expert, it seems. I give him the icy, hostile stare such a comment deserves at a time like this.

Rob is stuck in the middle and looking for a little direction. I make it easy for him, saying, 'Rob, fuck off and get the whisky.'

Before I can consume too much scotch, the cool and consistent higher ranks change their minds and decide the police will search tonight. Was it our suffering, as parents? Forgive me, but I suspect someone said 'the media will massacre you if you delay', so they decided to bring in floodlights and make a start. We're relieved. But with the relief comes a stomach-turning apprehension. We know what they are likely to find.

Now there occurs what can only be a total irony. We get an unexpected phone call from the vice-principal of the college, Margaret Bryden. She is concerned Nicola and I may no longer have any personal time and space in our home. So she has arranged for part of the school to be set aside for us if we need it. She has told the caretaker, Ian Huntley, to expect us at any time of day or night. And our reaction? We know that he has been on television many times during the week and he looks drained enough as it is without having to be on call 24/7 for frantic parents.

I thank Margaret, and then I wonder what Ian Huntley thinks about having to do such things as part of his job.

The decision to search during the night won't bring instant answers. I'm learning more about police work than I ever wanted.

Forensic searching is not quick so it will take many hours to establish the contents of the shallow graves, and we are not likely to know the truth till tomorrow morning. We can't bear the waiting especially with all our friends around. We ask everyone to leave. As the last person walks out of our house Nicola and I share a terrible thought – the next time we see our family and friends, we may be telling them of Holly's death.

Stewart and Chris are also exhausted. Sensibly their coordinator, Gary Goose, orders them to go home. Trudie is left to hold the fort. As soon as we are alone with her, we're overwhelmed by fear of the loss we both feel in our marrow will be confirmed.

'Trudie,' I tell her, 'we are going to bed because we believe this is the end. Under no circumstances are you to come upstairs unless it is with news that the shallow graves are not those of Holly and Jessica. Okay?'

We don't want any discussion and go upstairs. Nicola takes a sleeping pill and within half an hour has drifted off. Although exhausted, I am only able to cat nap. At about 4 a.m. I hear Trudie walking about downstairs. I hear her open the living-room door to go, I assume, to the downstairs toilet. But if she's doing that, why is she walking up the stairs? It's not my imagination. I hear Trudie climbing the stairs. She is professional and very sensitive. I had asked her not to trouble us unless the news is positive. Suddenly the hairs stand up on the back of my neck. I sit up, waiting, waiting in fear, waiting in hope.

Trudie knocks very gently. She doesn't need to ask to come in. She whispers, 'Kevin, the first site is a badgers' set. The second site is thought likely to be the same.'

I shout for joy. It is sublime euphoria. Galvanised by adrenalin, I try to wake Nicola to tell her. Groggy as she is, she understands. Then I race down the stairs. Trudie confirms what details she knows.

Then I'm out of the door. I run off to find people to share the good news with. I am not sure who I expect to be around at 4.30 in the morning in sleepy Soham but I can't stop myself running.

The streets are empty but it doesn't matter. I run round to Nicola's parents. There is a downstairs light on. Dennis and Diane are both up, looking drained and defeated. The fact that I have turned up at this ungodly hour means I have very important news. But I can't speak, I struggle to utter a word. My brain is not controlling my body. I'm sobbing and between small sobs I get out, 'It is not Holly or Jessica. They're fucking badger sets. We've still got a chance.'

It feels like a miracle and I head to the place where you give thanks for miracles.

Wednesday 14 August

I am becoming used to sitting in St Andrew's Church alone. I do not consider myself to be alone, though, as I have Snoozums, Holly's bedtime cuddly toy, in my arms. I can smell Holly on Snoozums and in silence, I offer thanks for the hope that we may see her alive again.

But reality kicks in. The fact that the shallow graves are not those of Holly and Jessica doesn't really mean any progress. We are no nearer to finding them – and I say as much to friends who ring. There are still no leads.

When Stewart and Chris reach us, my early morning adrenalin rush has long been replaced with a harsh dose of reality. We hear there have been 1,500 calls to the incident room. They have put in place 'an additional sifting system', an innovation which will allow officers to fast-track action on these calls. They've doubled the number of officers doing house to house enquiries. No one can complain that the police are not trying.

The BBC programme *Crimewatch* confirms that they are prepared to cancel their summer break and do a 'special' next week. The police inform us that the investigation into the link between the disappearance of young Milly Dowler and Holly and Jessica shows there is no connection.

We are asked, as are the Chapmans, to approve a statement for general release. It seems appropriate and reads:

'The last 24 hours have been tremendously emotional for both families. Both Kevin and Nicola, and Les and Sharon, are desperate to have their daughters back home safe and well, and have spent a very long evening and a very long night until they were told this morning that the mounds of earth were not the graves of Holly and Jessica.

The emotional rollercoaster for them goes on. Having been told of sightings and new information early yesterday and then to be told of the possible discovery in Newmarket, left them feeling numb, frightened and dreading what would be found. Clearly for them to be told that the girls had not been found dead and were therefore still missing has come as a tremendous relief and allows them to continue in their hope and belief that Jessica and Holly are still alive and will be returned home safely, very, very soon.'

The statement is formally released in the afternoon. I give a brief quote to my friend James Fuller, who writes for the local *Cambridge Evening News*. He has never pressured me and I appreciate that so much.

Nicola and I are asked by the police to think about writing a public letter to Holly and the 'abductor'. It could be a way of keeping the story alive over the forthcoming weekend. Of course, we agree, and the police have some carefully thought out guidelines to share with us. These are based on the advice of criminal psychologists and deal with the phrasing of every sentence. For example, we are advised to use the word 'difficult' instead of 'trauma'.

I still need to be doing something to find the girls. The answer to this need is not too far away, for I have been contacted by another two mediums. Their information is not as detailed as that from Dennis. Nonetheless the following points are shared:

- *One house involved.*
- *Three people involved.*
- *The youngest person has 'sharp' features.*
- *A road beginning with C, in a state of disrepair.*
- *The girls are now to the East of Soham.*
- *Feel the girls are about to be separated.*
- *Neither person really knows what to do.*
- *Holly and Jessica will be found, almost by accident.*
- *Can see, East of Soham, 3 villages/towns, beginning with the letters, M, B and W – does this fit in with the local area?*

- *The village beginning with B is the biggest.*
- *The village beginning with W features yet is 'too far'.*
- *Very bad feeling about this position.*
- *Dark-haired person standing outside an Italian Restaurant.*
- *The name of Muggsy, Muttley or Muggly.*
- *Man living with grey-haired mother.*

I share this information with the police. As before, the impact is minimal. I understand their scepticism but it is hardly as if they have any clues. I will pursue these new lines of interest myself.

Trudie Wright and I head over to the offices of East Cambridgeshire District Council, to see if we can find any surnames with any resemblance to Muggsy, Muttley or Muggly. Nothing is very close and we return to Soham to check the telephone directory to see if there is an obvious match.

Our detective skills, or lack of them, are quickly exposed. Nothing fits. There is no address that starts with a C. It is hugely disappointing. Not to be outdone, we conclude that these may be informal nicknames, so we retain them on our sheets for future reference.

There is better news with the three village letters, East of Soham. Following the mediums' observation that the village commencing with B is the largest, it suggests that these villages or towns are Mildenhall, West Row and Bury St Edmunds. Geographically, this makes sense. It also makes sense to us that the perpetrator(s) are not Soham people. We buy maps and friends and family head off into Suffolk. Nicola and I stay behind, numb, distraught and stressed out. And I have something I must tell her. I confide that I have not passed over all the relevant information to the departing search parties. What I did not say was that, yet again, the mediums were sure the girls are already dead.

We spend time with Oliver. In the background on the television, Manchester United are playing in their European Cup qualifying round, first leg in Budapest. The result does not go to plan with a 1–0 defeat but there is something else which captures our attention. One of the advertising hoardings has a message to help find Holly and Jessica with a telephone number. (The message had been arranged by the National Missing Persons Helpline.) But as I half watched the second half, I failed to notice the appeal at all. What kind of father does that make me? By midnight, we can take no more. For once we both fall soundly asleep within minutes.

Thursday 15 August

No news, no leads, no overnight developments, nothing. We almost don't expect anything more positive now.

Chris and Stewart arrive just before 10 a.m. and want to pursue the uncomfortable and postponed project of the 'who would Holly get into a vehicle with' list. They make it clear that we are doing this list NOW. Chris and Stewart know I believe no one among our family and friends would harm Holly. Even now, 11 days into the search, I'm certain that no one we know could be involved.

They hand me a copy of the list. I am asked if I can highlight people who Holly would have 'really trusted', enough to get into a car with. I think she would have got into a car with almost anyone on that list.

I say nothing.

Chris changes tack. He reads out individual names from the list and asks for a specific reply. Yes or no, would Holly have got in the car with this person?

I have no desire to be rude, but I hate this. I don't want to be 'obstructive' as they see it, though, and Chris has been subtle. The way it is now, I am not putting forward these names myself and I feel I should answer direct questions from the police, even if I am being asked to betray family and friends. Of course, if I imagined for one second someone on the bloody list might be guilty I would say so, but I don't.

As we start, Nicola comes back from her sister's. Nicola does not have to be at her most sensitive to work out what is happening. As she enters the room, the names of Robert and Trudie Wright are read out from the list.

I have mentioned how close Nicola and Trudie are. I often say to people that Nicola is closer to Trudie than she is to me, and I mean it. I never, under any circumstances, make the slightest negative comment about Trudie within earshot of Nicola.

Chris and Stewart are about to find out the depth of the affinity between these two friends. Nicola says it is out of the question that her friend would do anything to harm Holly. You might as well put the Queen in the frame. That is the end of that. I smile and watch the boys floundering. Nicola completely misinterprets my smile and bollocks me. She carries on with 'shred the husband'. She is livid that I would discuss this list in her absence.

I tell Nicola that I only agreed to review the list as the goal-posts have been moved a little. Stewart and Chris explain why they feel this is so important. They stress the 'need to go back to basics' and that 'the answer to this lies in Soham'.

Nicola hates this as much as I do but, finally, we do it together, and respond to the names on the list. As we limp towards the end of the task, we are both relieved. Soon over, or so we think.

But the police have more psychological exercises for us. Now we are asked to highlight the 'top three' about whom we feel the strongest reservations. We can't discuss our choices with each other. I have to pick my three alone and the same goes for Nicola. It is another really tough, unfair call. But we do comply, if reluctantly. Once we finish, Nicola and I do not discuss our selections and it's obvious we are both uncomfortable having done this exercise. Stewart and Chris compare our two lists.

Something makes them feel they've hit on an important find. Chris informs us that 'two out of the three you have both named are the same'. To the police, that does seem to point the finger. We know differently, however.

After Chris and Stewart head back to headquarters, we decide to write the letter to Holly and the abductor(s) as FLO Trudie said it would need to be completed for tomorrow. We sit in my little office and feeling reasonably focused, we write the opening line, 'Our darling Holly'.

A second later, we're both in floods of tears. We can't cope any more. It seems so brutally unfair.

You cry and you wipe away the tears. You tell each other you must not give up, break down, abandon all hope.

When, some considerable time later, the letter is complete, it reads:

'Our darling Holly,
  Please be strong. We miss you so very much. Believe us that the end is in sight and you can come home to your family.
  Holly, you have done nothing wrong, darling, so just try to be brave for now. No one sleeps at home as we wait for your return. Snoozums still waits on your pillow and you will cuddle him again soon, we promise. Every person prays for your safe return.'

The appeal immediately follows:

'If there is any individual aware of the identity of this kidnapper, please step forward and help. Do not allow any misguided loyalty to affect your decision. One phone call can end this misery and change people's lives for the better.
  We know there is goodness in every person's heart, please find yours now and save Holly and Jessica.'

We sign the letter.

Then, we get an unexpected ray of hope.

Holly's godmother, Donna Paxton Tomb is flying back 'home' from America, to be with her childhood best friend, Nicola. Donna's mother, Coral Paxton, has been using the services of a medium after losing a very close friend. The medium's name is Ron Moulding and he has told Coral that he has seen the faces of the two people responsible and seen them very clearly. The first is a dark, short-haired man, and the second is a younger woman with mousy features. Ron can come to our house and give detailed descriptions tomorrow. Ideally, we want to have a police artist on hand who can draw to his description.

I immediately contact Chris Mead to request the services of a police artist. Chris says he will see what he can do, but it is very short notice. This is quite a moment. I feel confident that since I know so many people round here, I have a good chance of recognising the guilty man and woman once their faces are drawn.

Tonight there is a public meeting at the Lodeside Hall, part of the Village College. I want to go but the police worry they cannot manage our presence. So the only people who are not allowed to go are the families of the missing girls.

The police have a new message for the community. DCI Andy Hebb tells the packed hall: 'Look at the behaviour of your friends, relatives, neighbours. Are they doing anything differently?'

If the police are turning the spotlight on Soham, Soham is turning the spotlight on the police. People are frank about how frustrated they feel at the lack of progress and make suggestions. One idea is to have the police search every house in Soham. We know how the police will feel about that, given our attempt to get just 25 houses searched earlier. Never mind that it is common sense. No innocent person in Soham will refuse to have their house searched if it means helping find Holly and Jessica!

Needless to say the meeting is told why such a search would be impossible.

Afterwards, the media need someone to interview. The caretaker, Ian Huntley, proves to be the one person willing to speak. He's already carved a little notoriety for himself as 'the last person to see Holly and Jessica alive'. He repeats what he has said before about talking to the girls and makes much of his regrets.

Midnight is the deadline for the kidnapper(s) to make contact. We don't wait in anticipation. We do not expect contact to be made in any way, shape or form.

At the time we didn't know what was going on at Police Headquarters. The present head of the investigation, David Beck, was about to be joined by Temporary Detective Chief Superintendent Chris Stevenson to bring some direction to the investigation. All the senior officers were reviewing their own lists of likely suspects. They had three names and were about to analyse whether any of them was likely to be guilty. At the top of that list – and first to be analysed – was a certain Ian Huntley.

Friday 16 August

Ron Moulding may change everything. By mid-morning, God willing, I hope to have two faces drawn, which will allow me to identify the people who have taken Holly and Jessica. But when Chris rings he is much more interested in the fact that there is a press conference at 11.30 a.m., which we need to attend. No one has said a word about this before.

Like us, the media seem to feel the enquiry is back to square one, with nothing in the pipeline. David Beck's head is on the block. One criticism seems to be that he has only just visited Soham himself. We are asked if we feel that criticism is justified and when we say we don't, we are asked to assist in defending his position. We agree to offer a short quote.

'We would rather he find the girls and we were happy to be kept informed by the Family Liaison Officer.'

There is no time to think about this further. Ron Moulding, the second medium to enter our lives, turns up at my home. Ron is extremely keen to get to work, but he wants an assurance that an artist is coming.

I am able to confidently assure him that this will not be a problem as 'I have spoken to Chris.'

But when I open the door, I just see Chris, Stewart and Trudie.

'Chris, Ron is already here. Have you organised the artist?'

'We have not been able to arrange one in time, Kevin,' Chris says.

I am absolutely deflated and feel very bitter. If we could get the faces drawn, we might have a real lead. Why isn't this being treated with more urgency? Why can no one else recognise that this could be the first clear break?

How difficult is it to get a police artist? I suspect not very. I have relied on the FLOs and they have not come through for me. I am hurt and disappointed. If the three of them cannot read my body language, they're in the wrong job.

In our small house Ron can't help overhearing the acrimonious exchanges. The man has travelled from Norfolk to try and help. He has already refused any payment and I am feeling embarrassed by my failure to produce an artist. Ron's journey now looks point-less. I join him at the table to see if he can, at least, describe the two faces he has seen.

As he does so, it is apparent to us all that he is describing a man and a woman very similar to the people Dennis described – a woman with a mousy face and a man with short-cropped hair. It is a very chilling moment.

Yet again, I find myself impressed by skills I don't really under-stand. Ron adds that the girls will be found East of Soham. Chris, Stewart and Trudie are all clearly sceptical and make little effort to hide it. The only thing they want is to get us to the press confer-ence. I am not of the same mind, however, and, as they have clearly let me down in the grandest of fashions, I say their press confer-ence is not our top priority right now and they should go without Nicola and me.

It is the biggest stand-off yet between the police and us. I've really upset them. Chris warns, 'There may be negative press specu-lation if only one family does the press conference.'

'Then so be it, Chris.' If I had been thinking more clearly, I could have reminded him that Nicola and I had already done one press conference without the Chapmans, so blowing his argument apart.

Ron continues to talk, saying that he could see a vast open space with what looked like a small house in the distance. Stewart and Chris now hover over Ron. I know it is going to cause the Family Liaison team problems, but I am not shifting my position. You could cut the atmosphere with a knife.

I don't want to look at Chris or his colleagues, so I take the redundant pencil and paper and begin to write the numbers I through 10 in a straight line, from left to right. I repeat the exercise, making sure that the 1 and 10 run exactly parallel. It is my rather pathetic intention to fill the whole page like this.

Ron, who is watching me, breaks the silence. 'Why have you just written "Keeper's Cottage"?'

I turn the paper round and show him I've just written two lines of numbers. He replies that he clearly saw the two words 'Keeper's Cottage' on the page. There is an immediate reaction from Stewart and Chris. Both step forward, suddenly interested.

We are now about 8 minutes away from when we are supposed to go out live on television. Neither Nicola nor I have any idea why this press conference has been called. Stewart and Chris continually get phone calls asking where the hell everyone is. I suspect they have not told their senior officers that Kevin Wells is not cooperating.

I am, after all, the person assessed as being difficult though, of course, I was not told that at the time.

I'm not going to any press conference now, as I want to explore the 'Keeper's Cottage' observation further. I remember window cleaning for a customer with that house name so I'm going to have a look around. That house is in a remote area in the fens, though, unfortunately, not East of Soham. My FLOs interrupt, asking again if Nicola and I will leave to go to the press conference.

No, I tell them.

Chris and Stewart are obviously upset and, on the spot, they decide to tell us something highly sensitive – and we move to where Ron cannot hear. Nicola and I are told, 'There has been a significant development. It is a priority that you attend the press conference now and post that press conference the details of this significant development will be shared with you.'

We are both stunned. Were the police actually going to mention anything to us at all if we weren't refusing to go? Does this explain why no artist is present? Is the development bad news? Do they think we are not to be trusted with information now?

As these questions race through my mind, I slump with my head in my hands. I am close to breaking down very publicly. I cannot accept that the right way to deal with us as a family is to dangle carrots before us. I have worked alongside the police in an unquestioning fashion over the last 12 days and, now, only by accident, only because something has happened that made me turn stubborn, I've discovered they have news that could change my family's life forever. And they weren't going to share it.

We now have six minutes to get to the press conference.

Not telling us there is a new development breaks our agreement on how we would work. I feel completely let down. I also have a sense that the 'significant development' is untrue and is just a ploy to get Nicola and me to the press conference.

It is now five minutes before the conference starts.

Stewart breaks the silence.

'Kevin, we need to go and we need to go now. I am asking you to trust us. Rest assured this is a significant development. Will you place your trust in us? Have we let you down so far?'

It is a personal appeal. It may well be all they have left, but this is very specific and direct. The three of us have built up a special bond. That has already been tested this morning with the non arrival of the artist. Would they dare to risk the working relationship by overstating their position just to get us both to a press conference? Common sense says no. A gut feeling says no.

Stewart does make me change my mind. I apologise to Ron, he promises he will be available to meet again and we are out of the front door.

Matt Tapp, the Cambridgeshire Police media consultant, is waiting for us. This press conference is going to be better organised. He promises that if the Chapmans or we wish to stop, we just have to give a hand signal and it's over. Matt says he will pick individuals to ask a question so we don't have a chaotic deluge of shouting hacks – as happened at previous press conferences.

Is this how gladiators felt as they entered the arena? As we walk down the corridor leading to the main hall, the noise is very loud.

There are more press than ever before. We pause to try and focus before facing the cameras. We've had no chance to prepare and worse than that, Nicola and I know that there is a significant development in the pipeline, which must be kept completely secret. The Chapmans know nothing of this development, which does not sit well with us at all.

I try to block out my earlier anger and frustrations. Many questions reflect the morning papers and ask what we think of the quality of the investigation. We're exhausted, have not been told why we are here, have been let down over the artist and have no leads apart from the significant development they were going to keep from us.

At this moment, I'm tempted to agree the hostile press are right – the police are useless. But I know that to say it would be very destructive.

It takes a monumental effort but I exonerate the police over the 'night of the Newmarket mounds', confirming they were following specific instructions from the family – to keep us informed of every single development at the earliest opportunity. I add that we know that everything is being done in the search for Holly and Jessica. Obviously, there is not a clear lead to work on at the moment, but we don't blame the police. I could not have given a clearer message of support and it certainly has not been scripted. But we want to get home and hear what this 'significant development' is.

It needs one more call by the FLOs to their senior officer to confirm what can be shared with us. Like eager children, Nicola and I await the information. Something is not right though. Stewart and Chris go outside to talk in private. We're on tenterhooks. Then, hesitantly, Chris tells us that, 'Ian Kevin Huntley is now being treated as a significant witness.'

'What does that mean?' I ask.

'He is to be invited to assist the police as potentially the last person to see the girls alive by being *cognitively interviewed*.' This is police language for a structured interview; a police officer will go through 4 August step by step with Huntley.

'Witness means he has seen something. It does not mean he has done anything. We are no further forward at all, Chris.'

Chris and Stewart both know that this does not constitute a 'significant development'. We're perfectly well aware that Ian Huntley has come forward to say he may have been the last person to see the girls alive. The man has been on television countless times saying just that. In fact, Nicola and I had previously expressed our sympathy for him over the constant media intrusion. We learn that Maxine Carr, Huntley's girlfriend, is also being taken in for questioning, and that the police now plan to search their house.

But the fact remains that no, this is not a 'significant development', far from it. Nicola and I have been misled on a grand scale. They got us to the press conference under false pretences.

I am bitterly disappointed on two counts. First, there is no good news in the search for Holly and Jessica. Second, my link with the police has been compromised. I do not have to debate the options or, indeed, ask Stewart and Chris to leave our house. They know what they have done, no doubt following orders, and both simply choose to go. I am unsure if I will see either of them in their capacity as Family Liaison Officers again.

Trudie stays in the house. She did not lard on the 'significant development' stuff and we don't feel betrayed by her as we do by Chris and Stewart. Nicola and Trudie work on statements. I pop into my office to make some calls and find out how friends and family are getting on with their searching. I explain the artist's impressions did not materialise and that Ian Huntley is to be interviewed. After I have made these calls, I give this position some serious thought. I conclude that I sort of know Ian Huntley because of helping lock up the school. I met him on a number of occasions. He never behaved strangely or gave me reason not to trust him. I suspect the police are just following up the fact he said he was the last person to see the girls alive.

Although Huntley and Carr are 'helping police with their enquiries', there is a local rumour of a woman staring at children on the Sunday night the girls went missing. This incident happened near to Saucy Meg's Restaurant, very near to the Soham war memorial, and it worries people. Could this wide-eyed woman somehow be involved? It's a rumour that could contain an element of truth. If there was a woman involved, Holly and Jessica may have been duped or coerced into a car and a nightmare.

I start to think of all the things we said – and didn't say – to Holly. Did we ever mention to her the possibility of a woman helping a man abduct girls when we discussed stranger danger? I know the answer only too well. No we didn't. We were careful, we taught Holly to be careful, but we didn't imagine Soham was a place where children needed a 100-page handbook on how to be safe.

It is now 6 p.m. Stewart and Chris return to my home. They ask if we can speak.

Fine, I say, in spite of the earlier stand-off.

They say they are deeply unhappy with the way things went earlier in the day. They feel they have let our family down and realise that they need to recover the family's trust, and do it quickly. They add that they are, and will always remain, focused on providing the level of service they feel we need. We have made up the ground – and made up.

As we sit to talk, they tell us it will be some time before we get any update from the Huntley and Carr interviews. We hand over our letter to Holly, which the police will give to all the Sunday newspapers. We also hand over a sample of Holly's homework and her cuddly toy, Snoozums, for the photographers. The missing person's hotline also needs a photo of Holly.

Oliver has been in and out of the house all day. He asks if he can stay round his friend Ryan's house to sleep. It seems to be his way of dealing with things at the moment.

All talk in Soham is of Huntley and Carr. There are rumours of vigilante action and feelings are running exceptionally high. The media are good at sniffing that out. Some reporters know that members of my extended family will be in The Ship, our local pub, and seek their viewpoint. Nicola and I don't like to hear others claim to speak on our behalf.

It is late evening before the three FLOs go. All of them look exhausted.

As they leave, I receive a phone call from a very close friend, concerning Huntley. 'Kev, I know where Huntley is being questioned and it is not a police station.' She tells us the name of the hotel and that the room number, if required, is also available.

I am floored by stress and fatigue, but my brain cells are still working. In 30 minutes I can raise at least 30 men to visit the hotel. I think it unlikely there will be more than half a dozen policemen to stop us getting to Huntley. I believe that under threat of violence, he will tell me if he is involved in the disappearance of Holly and Jessica and where the girls are. I'll have enough time before police back-up arrives.

Although Stewart and Chris are 'onside again', I can justify not phoning and not telling them. Earlier in the day, we were kept in the dark. This will balance the books a little.

I also think that if Huntley is found to be involved, and charged and arrested, this will be my only clear opportunity of getting to him. Decision made. I am going to the hotel.

Nicola is in complete shock when I tell her. As the reality of my plan sinks in, she starts to look terrified. She thinks my decision is a bad one. With so many people in the house, we have to whisper in our bedroom. She says going to the hotel is an enormously risky step and, quite frankly, a selfish one. My wife is now in tears and desperately asking me to change my mind. But I'm sure I'm right. I can't get her to agree, but I have to go through with it. I feel I have no choice but to gather my family and friends, because it is no use relying on the police. I will get the truth out of Huntley.

As I leave the bedroom, she sobs, 'Kev, if you get into the car, I will ring the police myself to let them know your plans. I'm sorry, but I can't let you do this.'

That one sentence kills my plan. I need the element of surprise at the hotel. It would be an impossible task if the police could prepare for our arrival.

I'm furious at Nicola, but it doesn't last too long, which is just as well. She's absolutely right. My burning desire, as a father, to help my daughter, is overriding all logical thought. These really are desperate, desperate times. We hug, cry and eventually pull ourselves together to go down and rejoin our friends and family.

Our planned swoop on the hotel is cancelled, but there is another opportunity to be active. We've heard that Ian Huntley may have visited his father's bungalow in Littleport over the last few weeks. There is a rumour that Huntley was seen there in the early hours of Monday morning, after the girls went missing. I have no idea if the police are aware of this, but Rob and I head over to Littleport. We are both angry to be foiled yet again. There are people and vehicles outside the bungalow. We pull over to watch from a distance for a while but no one seems to be leaving the house. We also realise that we have no idea what Ian Huntley's father actually looks like, so we begin our frustrated journey back to Soham.

Despite extensive police searching, there was no evidence found to implicate Huntley's father.

Saturday 17 August

At exactly 7 a.m. the early morning call from the police comes through. It's become routine, and I say, 'No doubt you will be with us in the usual 45 minutes or so.'

'Kevin, we are at your front door,' Chris says.

My heart sinks. Panic begins to rise immediately. I cannot speak for a few seconds. Nicola realises that something is wrong and becomes more and more agitated.

'Nic, they're at the door already.' Nicola starts crying.

We both know this has never happened before – and just how serious it may be. Together we go downstairs, not even bothering to dress fully.

If ever twelve steps take an eternity to descend, it is now. We open the door to find Chris standing in front of Stewart. His eyes are glazed. He looks totally dejected, the bearer of the saddest news possible.

'Can we come in, please?'

In silence all four of us walk to the living room. In a state of fear and bewilderment, Nicola and I listen.

'In the early hours of this morning both Huntley and Carr were arrested on suspicion of murder. This followed the recovery of Manchester United tops and other clothing.'

There is a long silence. Chris telephones headquarters to let them know the news has been shared with the family. We really do not know what to do or say. Yes, this is bad news, but at the same time how does this take us forward? Where are the girls? It may well be the abductor would change the girls' clothes, so what does this really mean? This and other questions fill my head. Sadly, so do the answers.

Nicola and I telephone our respective family members. The initial reactions are heartbreaking. Soon our house is packed. But we don't have much information. On the television, DCI Andy Hebb reads a statement to the media. He uses the phrase 'due to a significant find' to explain why Huntley and Carr are now in custody. All of us know that we have to maintain confidentiality.

On television we also see the home of Huntley's father, in Littleport. His bungalow is being searched, leading us to speculate that he may well be involved. We all ask Chris and Stewart question after question. There are no real answers; the phones are now ringing incessantly. But we have nothing we can say to our friends so we sit down to watch the rolling news programme on television. An ex-cop from the Flying Squad is on, second guessing the position, which does not sit well with us.

Nicola and I need some space and quiet and Chris draws the short straw in taking us for a drive. We head to Littleport, taking the route Huntley would have taken if he visited his father, stopping periodically to search places that look like potential dumping spots for two small bodies. It's heart-rending.

It is time to face the reality. Nicola says out loud what I, and probably Chris, are thinking.

'In our hearts we know the girls are dead. What we want now is to know for sure and to find them.'

We stop searching and continue to Littleport. It is a waste of time, as the media are all over the place and the last thing we want to do is offer a photo opportunity that might harm the investigation. We do a U-turn back to Soham. There's nothing we can do but watch television.

At 1.20 p.m. Chris takes yet another telephone call. This time, however, he stands and leaves the room. As he paces in the garden, I feel my heart beat faster. Chris is listening rather than talking and his body language has changed yet again. As he comes back into the dining room, he asks Nicola and me to sit down. Quietly, Chris tells us, 'Two bodies have been found in Suffolk.'

Nicola and I exchange glances and she begins to cry. I try very hard to suppress my own tears. I can't do it. If it had been a single body, maybe it could be some other unfortunate soul, but there are two. We both instinctively know that one of those bodies is Holly.

We can't go next door and tell people. This is the moment we've feared since Holly went missing. The two FLOs tell our relatives. Once again we find ourselves embroiled in mass family grief.

After a long time, we collect ourselves a bit. It is time to glean some facts. Are the two bodies those of children? Are they both female? Where in Suffolk are they? The only question which is answered is the location, Wangford. Not a single person in the house has ever heard of it. Chris fetches a map and we see that it is right next to Lakenheath, East of Soham. We all know Lakenheath. Some members of the family searched there recently.

The first two questions, however, are the important ones. Bizarrely there is no further information. As the pressure mounts, the tension simply becomes too much for the FLOs. They both take to pacing in the garden while making calls.

Surely someone can tell us if the bodies are those of children? Is information being deliberately withheld from us? Are we back to the 'no trust in the family' position after my brother confided in that journalist? Do the bodies have any clothing on? How long have the bodies been at Wangford? Does one of the bodies have blonde hair?

I repeatedly ask Stewart and Chris and, repeatedly, get no answers. The information loop is not working. At the bottom end of this loop are members of my family, myself included, whose lives are being fucked about because someone, in a senior position, is choosing to withhold information. In desperation Chris even tries contacting Suffolk Police direct. It is to no avail.

Much later, we find out that the police decided to inform the families of the grim discovery because they were frightened the press would find out and publish the news. The police told us at once, and, therefore, they could only give us very limited information.

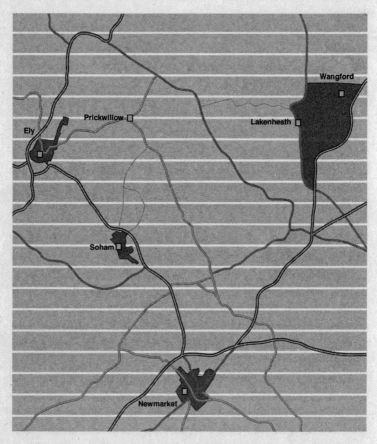

The deposition site at Wangford, to the North-East of Soham.

But no one tells us those details at the time. Not to know if it is Holly is unbearable. Unbearable even though we all believe we are about to get the worst news of our lives, and no one holds out any hope of a reprieve.

It is now 7 p.m. We have been waiting for an update for over five and a half hours. This delay is inexcusable. People are getting ratty and irritable with one another. There are short fuses around – and many of them. A lot of this pent-up frustration is directed at the FLOs. People get angry with them and then apologise. These are strange, terrible times.

The vicar turns up again. He too finds it incredible that no information is forthcoming. Stewart and Chris return from the back garden. For the third time today, their body language warns us it will be awful news.

'We have a significant update for you. Where do you want to be told and who do you want present?'

Tim immediately starts to leave the dining room. I tell him to stay. Over the last two weeks, I have seen many qualities in Tim and I know he will keep any information confidential.

Nicola shepherds Oliver into the dining room; once again we shut the door to the packed living room. Chris and Stewart begin to tell us the heartbreaking news. They explain that 'the two bodies found are now thought to be those of Holly and Jessica. Unfortunately, given the time they appear to have been dead and the rural location where they have been found, both bodies are badly decomposed. It will not be possible to identify them visually. There are also signs that both bodies have been burned. Until a DNA check has been completed there is, technically, a small element of doubt but it is "highly likely" the bodies will be those of Holly and Jessica.'

We sit in stunned silence. Then, Chris speaks with Oliver and explains in simpler language. Oliver says he understands. Then, Chris turns to Nicola and me.

'The candle that has been burning for the last two weeks has just gone out. We are so very sorry.'

Chris, like the rest of us, is affected by the emotion of the moment. I shake his hand and sincerely tell him, 'We have travelled down a very long tunnel and have now come to an end. You have been an absolute star.' I mean it wholeheartedly. Over the last 13 days, he has been truly remarkable.

We now have to tell everyone in the living room and, despite our sadness, Nicola and I manage to do it together. But we can't let our sense of loss make us careless. Chris and Stewart remind everyone of the need for confidentiality. It is also the catalyst for people to leave. There is much hugging and false bravado before people shuffle off to their homes. Their faces – sad, anguished, bloody perplexed by how it could have come to this – will stay with me for the rest of my life.

The vicar is also ready to go. He is in a predicament and explains his position. He has already written the sermon for tomorrow's televised service. The wording of that service indicates that there is no official confirmation that the two bodies are those of Holly and Jessica – and he has now heard differently. The FLOs ask him not to alter his sermon, reiterating the need for complete confidentiality. Tim agrees.

Once Tim has gone, Nicola spends much of her time with Oliver. Goodness only knows what he is thinking. Nicola has little or no success in getting Oliver to open up to her at this moment. We're both terribly worried for our son.

Later, Chris has a little more news from the deposition site at Wangford. A decision has been made that the girls' bodies will remain *in situ* overnight. This should allow enough time for all the experts to visit and complete their tests. The priority now is to secure as much evidence as possible to convict the person or persons responsible for the murders. That makes sense. But what hurts at this moment is the fact that Holly, although dead, is going to be left in a ditch. It seems so demeaning.

Stewart and Chris leave at 10 p.m. Quiet descends on this house. Nicola and I break down. So does Oliver. We start to grieve as a family. Holly will never come home again. There is no escaping that. In the early hours of the morning, completely debilitated by grief, we go to bed. After settling Oliver down, Nicola and I sit in Holly's bedroom. It does nothing to mend the reality but seems to bring us nearer, somehow, to our daughter.

Sunday 18 August

With the intense desire to search for Holly gone, I am experiencing a terrible void. Though I'm tired, I disappear into my office to make some written observations. This also allows me to try and deflect the pain of this dreadful Sunday morning. I write a series of questions:

- *Why has someone killed Holly?*
- *Why has someone killed Jessica?*
- *Under what circumstances can two girls be killed together?*
- *Where were the girls killed?*
- *How were they killed?*
- *Who died first?*
- *When can we bury Holly?*
- *Had there been a sexual attack before death?*
- *Did the surviving girl see her friend killed?*
- *What kind of a person can kill a child, let alone two?*
- *Ian Huntley and Maxine Carr have both been charged, how can a woman be involved in killing two children?*
- *I know Ian Huntley.*
- *Nicola knows Maxine Carr.*
- *They are not local people. I have received messages of concern about the caretaker from a number of local people.*
- *I have met or seen Ian Huntley on at least three occasions during the last fortnight.*
- *Ian Huntley was in his office at 4.30 a.m. on Monday 5 August, a few hours after Holly's disappearance. Was Holly alive at this time?*

- *Did Ian Huntley lie to me and my friends about his reason for being in his office?*
- *Did Ian Huntley lie about the building already being searched by the police?*
- *Are the police actively looking for someone else?*
- *What is happening about questioning?*
- *What police station are Ian Huntley and Maxine Carr being held in?*
- *How long will forensic tests take?*
- *Are there any obvious links between the girls and Ian Huntley?*
- *Has the search of 5 College Close been completed?*
- *Are there any obvious signs of the girls ever being in the house?*
- *What is the up-to-date position in regards to Ian Huntley's father's bungalow being searched?*
- *If Ian Huntley's father was involved then that would bring the number of adults to three. This would accord with Dennis Mackenzie's earlier observations.*

I log Dennis Mackenzie's observations in some detail:

- *Ian Huntley and Maxine Carr do have a northern accent, as he predicted.*
- *Ian Huntley has dark hair, as he predicted.*
- *Maxine Carr has mouse-like features, as he predicted.*
- *Ian Huntley's car is a red Ford Fiesta, as he predicted.*
- *The letter J features, as he predicted. It is part of the registration number of the Ford Fiesta.*
- *The house at 5 College Close is next to a straight piece of water, complete with ducks, as he predicted.*
- *Huntley's address, College Close, has a C and O in it, as he predicted. Two Cs and two Os, in fact.*
- *Beyond the trees to the rear of Huntley's house stand a number of huge metal grain silos, which resemble a 'wind-*

    mill without sails', as he predicted.

- *The girls have been found away from Soham, as he predicted.*
- *The description of a road without pathways matches the track at Wangford, as he predicted.*
- *I walked or biked past Ian Huntley's house, whilst searching, many times, as he predicted.*

There are a few predictions that seem wrong or bizarre – namely, that the girls were wrapped in something, possibly bubble wrap or carpet. I have no information to prove or disprove this at the moment. Does the name Prickwillow mean anything? Again, I am unsure if this is going to be relevant.

    Finally, seeing the number 18 by looking out from within the house at College Close. I am unable to see the relevance of this point. I know the area very well and cannot think of a property that would be numbered '18'. I do know, however, that the school site is number 16 Sand Street, so I need to find out if that site becomes No. 18 at any stage.

ABOUT RON MOULDING'S OBSERVATIONS

- *The descriptions of Huntley and Carr were accurate.*
- *The deposition site at Wangford is East of Soham, as he predicted.*
- *The 'Keeper's Cottage' he 'saw' me write can clearly now be interpreted as 'Caretaker's House'.*

OTHER MEDIUMS' OBSERVATIONS
A number are similar to some of those offered by Dennis and Ron, but some others now stand out:

- *A road, the name of which begins with the letter C, in a state of disrepair. I am confused by this, but later we would be told the deposition site is known locally as 'The Carr'.*
- *Holly and Jessica will be found, almost by accident. This*

has happened, with the local gamekeeper checking out a strange smell coming from the drainage ditch.
- *Can see 3 villages/towns, beginning with the letters M, B, and W. The village beginning with B is the biggest. It is a sobering moment. Mildenhall, Brandon and Wangford are all in the area. Brandon is also the biggest to my knowledge.*
- *The village beginning with W features yet is 'too far'. There is a very bad feeling about this place. The deposition site is on the outskirts of the village of Wangford.*

There are also a number of observations that make no sense to me at the moment:

- *The names 'Muggsy', 'Muttley' or 'Muggly' do not feature.*
- *Dark-haired person standing outside an Italian Restaurant. Although we have an Italian Restaurant in Soham and it is located within Holly's walking boundary, there are no suggestions that Ian Huntley was seen standing outside it.*
- *Man living with grey-haired mother.*

This is the first time I have analysed these predictions from nearly two weeks ago. I am completely stunned by how accurate many of them have turned out to be. I remember telling Nicola that I felt Dennis was a very talented medium. Here now in black and white is startling proof that he is the genuine article. It is a clear, first-hand indication that there is something 'on the other side'. I do not have to debate this with anyone. I've seen it for myself. I am completely unsure as to how this may affect my future thinking on spiritual matters.

Between the mediums, there was enough information for me to have made an informed guess and identified Huntley earlier myself. Quite why I did not have the intelligence to see the overall picture is a question that haunts me. If it turns out that Holly or Jessica were killed after I received this information, I will not be able to forgive myself.

Nicola and I watch the televised Sunday church service. It gets dramatic, as Soham is at the centre of a storm. Claps of thunder punctuate the transmission. One mighty crack puts an end to reception and we never see another minute of the service. So, there is no way of seeing if the vicar keeps to his promise of not altering his sermon, but I trust him completely. Storm clouds, thunder-claps, the cessation of the broadcast, it all seems apt.

One soul is not woken by the thunder – Oliver. That gives Nicola and me time to speak alone. It is extremely difficult to know what to do or say to one another. I hate seeing Nicola looking so forlorn. Not only have we lost our beautiful daughter, Nicola has lost her shopping companion, friend and soul-mate. I feel her loss is even greater than my own. We both know, without any doubt, that we have lost the star of our family.

For the moment, however, we decide on a small plan of action.

The house is going to be inundated again today with family and friends and we plan to share our news. In all likelihood an official police statement is going to be made later in the day, so this is the right thing to do. Friends and family should not hear things first on the television, if we can possibly avoid it.

We decide to try and give everyone the impression that we're being strong and focused. Many family and close friends feel the loss of Holly as much as we do. We do not want to add to their woes by continuously breaking down in front of them.

We also decide not to cry in front of Oliver, if we can help it. Instead, we will spend time with him alone to try and gauge how he is coping, once the house is quiet.

Finally, we agree that if the house becomes too busy or our emotions are in danger of overload, we will simply ask everyone to leave.

As soon as we've fixed on this plan, visitors arrive. We tell each one the truth. For some the truth is too much. A few leave imme-diately while those who stay become involved in counselling others. If it is Ian Huntley and Maxine Carr who did this, then I wish they could see the depth of despair they have created in this house.

It is 2.15 p.m. before the police return. Chris has been to see our family doctor, Dr Partha, to obtain Holly's medical records. They have been taken to Lakenheath police station and then presumably down to the deposition site, which we are now told is called 'The Carr'. Oddly, this is the surname of Maxine who is under arrest. Chris has also been trying to access dental records for Holly, but there are none. Nicola offers one of our blown-up photographs of Holly, which shows the alignment of her teeth, to see if this will speed up the process of identification.

There is no update from the deposition site. Chris, however, has an immediate question. 'Can you prepare a short statement which will be used when the body has been identified as Holly?' It is a sombre request. We eventually agree just one sentence: 'Although still numb after losing our gorgeous daughter, Holly, please accept our heartfelt thanks for everyone's help and support throughout this traumatic fortnight.'

The police also want to discuss Holly's post-mortem. We listen, too tired and stunned to react, as we hear Holly will be taken to Addenbrooke's Hospital later today. We are told that we have a right to be present at the post-mortem, but need to consider the following appalling facts:

- *What is left of Holly is unrecognisable.*
- *There is little or no flesh left at all.*
- *There is not even a hand to hold to say goodbye.*
- *There is severe maggot infestation.*
- *The smell of decay is overpowering.*
- *There are signs of the body being burned.*
- *Do we want this to be our last image and memory of Holly?*

All these details are beyond imagining. We don't know what to do. Eventually after talking it through – and it is the worst night-mare – we decide not to visit the mortuary and see the remains. As a compromise we ask one of our FLOs to be present on our behalf and Trudie agrees to go. Trudie would not only be there to make sure the appropriate level of care is in place for Holly's body, but also to report back with an honest assessment of the situation. For Nicola, this is very important. She wants to see her daughter again, whatever her state, but everything we hear makes it sound unbearable. The decision not to pay our last respects would come back to haunt us.

In the afternoon we hear the police have decided to make an official announcement. Although no formal identification has taken place, all parties agree that it is Holly and Jessica. No one asks us what we think as parents. The imperative is to quell the media frenzy, now almost beyond control. In one way the niceties of police procedure hardly matter but, yet again, we, the parents, are somewhere near the very bottom of the information chain.

In the early evening, at the church gates, Deputy Chief Constable Keith Hoddy begins his statement:

'It is almost exactly two weeks since Holly Wells and Jessica Chapman disappeared from this town sparking a massive enquiry to find them. It is with great sadness that I have to tell you the following news.

It may be some days yet before we are able to positively identify the two bodies found at Common Road, near Lakenheath in Suffolk, yesterday lunchtime. However, we are as certain as we possibly can be tonight that they are those of Holly and Jessica.

Holly and Jessica's families have been told this terrible news. Before I say anything else, can I suggest that we pause for a moment in silence in memory of these two little girls and out of respect for their families and their many hundreds of friends.

Holly and Jessica were reported missing on the evening of Sunday August 4th and since that time a huge effort has been mounted to find them. We, like the families, refused to give up hope that the girls would be found alive and well. Our heartfelt sympathy goes out to Holly's parents and brother and Jessica's parents and sisters at this ghastly time.

An enormous effort involving hundreds of police officers, supported by civilians and scores of experts, worked tirelessly to trace the girls and the sense of sorrow now is felt acutely. Holly and Jessica's families continue to be supported by trained family liaison officers at this, the bleakest of moments. They are being given every possible support and this support will continue in the days, weeks and months to come.

A man and a woman are under arrest for the murder of Holly and Jessica. The man is also under arrest for abduction. They remain in custody this evening and will spend another night at separate police stations in Cambridgeshire. Because legal proceedings are active I am unable to say anything more about this line of the enquiry.

Now is the time for quiet contemplation. It is a time to respect the grief of Holly and Jessica's families and I ask that you respect their need for privacy. They have asked me to read the following few words to you:

Statement from Sharon and Leslie Chapman

"We would like to thank everybody for their kindness and support during this very tense and traumatic time especially family, friends and the Family Liaison Officers. Whilst we appreciate your support and all your assistance in this very trying time we would like as a family for you to respect our privacy and allow us some time alone."

Statement from Nicola and Kevin Wells

"Although still numb after losing our gorgeous daughter, Holly, please accept our heartfelt thanks for everyone's help and support throughout this traumatic fortnight."

The people of Soham have had their lives turned upside down by the presence of the media during the last fortnight. You have all played a very important part in the hunt for Jessica and Holly and for that I thank you.

But perhaps now I may invite you to consider that it may now be an appropriate time for all media representatives to withdraw from this community to allow it to come to terms with its terrible loss.

Thank you.'

It is a strange sensation listening to this information being shared, but Nicola and I have a sense of relief that the truth is now clear.

By late evening, Trudie leaves to travel to the mortuary. Chris remains with us and we all watch the television, in respectful silence, as the bodies are driven away from the deposition site at Wangford.

In keeping with our new agenda, we decide to ask everyone to leave. Then Oliver reminds us that he knew Holly would be found in a ditch somewhere. Both of us had forgotten his words to Ruth mentioning that very fact. We talk things through, as best we can; we feel Holly was not killed in the ditch, but left there. There is nothing that any of us could have done to find her alive. We hope it will settle his mind a little.

When Oliver has left the room, we talk about our concerns for him. He is a few months away from his 13th birthday. We're scared of the impact all this will have on him. But there's nothing we can do except keep an eye on him.

But everything is dwarfed by our sense of loss, unfairness, grief and confusion. What is going to be the outcome of this terrible time in our lives? We have no idea.

Monday 19 August

Nicola and I are up early, waiting for Chris and Trudie. Neither of us has had any sleep.

I don't envy Trudie having to describe the visit to the mortuary to us. She is very matter of fact and tells us she is sure we made the correct decision in not going to see the remains of Holly's body. She knows we both wanted to say 'goodbye' to Holly, but our daughter was not identifiable. Trudie tells us nothing we are not expecting but it's still terrible to hear the reality.

One wry 'consolation' – Holly's body was not burned as badly as first thought. Because there was so little flesh left to burn, the fire appears not to have lasted long. The police believe the damage was caused by a flash fire rather than prolonged burning.

The LOVE necklace we knew Holly was wearing is damaged but still intact. There is also some of Holly's hair which has escaped any obvious signs of singeing. Trudie asks if we'd like some to be saved. Nicola asks for some hair and the necklace.

Our first opportunity 'to see Holly' will be at the Chapel of Rest in Addenbrooke's Hospital. Chris asks if there is a certain perfume Holly used to wear – if so, it can be used in preparation for our visit to the Chapel of Rest. Chris is being delicate. He knows we will have no opportunity of seeing, hearing or touching Holly ever again. A scent that reminds us of her may be some help. But as Holly simply used to borrow whatever was available from her mum's collection, there is no perfume that was specifically hers.

But we can't visit yet and there may even be a delay of a few days. The legal teams representing Ian Huntley and Maxine Carr may want to commission their own post-mortems. So what is left of Holly's body may be ripped to bits three times. Nicola and I are very upset at the thought of this violation. If the Home Office pathologist has done a post-mortem, why can't this be good enough for all the legal teams? Surely there is no need for bloody three.

Chris returns in the late afternoon and we are a little calmer, but he can't give us any satisfactory answers to the questions we raised yesterday. We know we are at the start of the investigation, but it's unacceptable to be given absolutely no information.

Ironically I have information for Chris. My cousin Tina, who lives in Lakenheath has telephoned to say Huntley was seen visiting his grandmother in the village last Wednesday afternoon; according to the 'home help', he was acting very strangely. This puts Huntley in the same area as the deposition site. To us, that seems crucial but Chris's reaction is quite low key. He is shattered. That's obvious when he takes DNA swabs from Nicola, Oliver and me.

The rest of the evening we discuss Huntley's visit to his grand-mother and tell family and friends about it. Everyone has so many questions and I find myself in the maddening position of not being able to answer them. It gives me some insight into how my FLOs must feel when I ask and ask them questions. But insight or no insight, keeping the parents in the dark just feels wrong.

I also realise I'm going to have to think about work. It's crucial for me to be involved in this investigation and help bring those who killed Holly to justice. Some part of me that's not entirely conscious senses that working towards that goal will occupy me. And being occupied will mean I don't dwell on my grief so much. But where does that leave work?

Very late at night, Chris rings to say that there is no more infor-mation from the interview of Ian Huntley. He adds, however, that they're now in the process of assessing Huntley's fitness – or lack of it – for facing formal police interviews. We are utterly confused. Huntley has been on the television and dealing with local people all the time in the last two weeks and he seemed fine. Is his dramatic decline an admission of guilt? Or is it just an attempt to hold things up? We already believe that the police have the right man, so to hear that he seems to have some choice about being interviewed is most disconcerting.

I feel very strongly that the so-called system has betrayed us. Huntley has only just been arrested and the authorities seem to be pandering to him. I don't see much sleep coming tonight either.

Tuesday 20 August

Huntley is supposed to be in court tomorrow. But when Chris rings, his tone is defensive – with good reason.

'In the early hours of this morning, Ian Huntley was deemed unfit for interview. He has been detained under the Mental Health Act 1983 and has been admitted to Rampton psychiatric hospital in Nottinghamshire for a full psychiatric assessment,' Chris tells us.

This assessment is likely to take 28 days, but till Huntley is assessed, he will not appear before Magistrates. It may also take longer if the psychiatrists want more time. There have been cases where it has taken six months, even a year, to assess someone.

We are both fuming at this development. To wait for a month, or even longer, before Ian Huntley can be interviewed, seems completely inappropriate. In theory he might never be interviewed! We are experiencing, first-hand, a system that pays no mind to the victim's rights, or their family's.

Chris tries to placate us. In his opinion, people can't fake psychiatric illness. Huntley will be under 24-hour surveillance, so if he is play-acting he will be found out. We hope and pray he is right.

There is also 'good news'. The investigation is still in full swing and even though Huntley is in Rampton, he will be visited by police officers today and charged with the murders of Holly and Jessica.

I suspect Chris deliberately keeps this piece of news until the end of our conversation. It is a hugely significant development. Given that Maxine Carr has been charged with perverting the course of justice, this must mean that the police believe only Ian Huntley was involved in the murders. We don't understand how that could have happened. As Holly and Jessica did not know Ian

Huntley, they would not have gone into his house or car if Maxine Carr was not around. Had Huntley tricked the girls somehow? How could he kill one without the other fleeing?

In the late afternoon Acting Det. Supt David Beck comes to visit us. We are introduced to his team and to his staff officer whose Christian name is 'Holly', which knocks me back. It seems a little insensitive, but we say nothing, though I feel rather frosty towards Beck as a result. Then he offers his condolences – and they are obviously sincere. Nicola and I thank him for his efforts in the investigation.

Just as the police are going, we're told that the staff officer's name is, in fact, Polly, not Holly. The police would not have brought someone called Holly to our house. I must have mis-heard. It is a strange end to the meeting.

Soon after they have gone, Chris confirms that Ian Huntley has been formally charged with the murder of Holly and Jessica. There is nothing new on Huntley's condition, however. Chris goes on to raise a second subject, which is much more heart stopping. Do we want to visit the deposition site before the media are given access? The police are under enormous pressure from the media. Nicola and I are not sure what to do. We think it would be right to visit the site, and to leave some flowers as a mark of respect, but the very idea frightens us. We decide not to visit. When we say that, Chris points out a few home truths.

Even if you do not go, images of Holly's last resting place will appear in the media. How will you feel about that?

If you change your mind in the near future, you will run the risk of being pursued by a photographer during what should be a private and very emotional moment in your lives.

If you go tomorrow, the site will be cordoned off and the visit will be completely private.

His arguments change our minds. Our next decision is whether or not to take Oliver. We must give him the opportunity to decide for himself. We are slightly surprised to get a categorical 'no', but we accept his decision as final.

Inside our house, there's grief, and grief envelops you. We are so far inside the 'eye of the storm', as to be only partially aware of the outside world. Our friends and family are staggered by the number of condolences, and moved by their sincerity. The churchyard has become the place people send flowers as a mark of respect. Many soft toys are also coming with the messages of condolence and the toys are kept safe inside the church. The vicar has set up a vigil area where people can light a candle for Holly and Jessica. There is also a book of condolence to sign.

People are also leaving tributes at the war memorial and the school gates. The television news shows they are also leaving flowers at the entry to the deposition site in Wangford. It is very touching to have this support and we need every ounce of strength to carry on.

Before the FLOs leave us there are further matters to deal with, though. I log them because I had really no idea that in the middle of a terrible family tragedy we would have all this inundation of detail, matters arising from the bureaucracy of death:

- *Do we want to meet either the Coroner or Home Office Pathologist in person? (No)*
- *Will we accept some flowers from the enquiry team? (Yes)*
- *Will we accept some flowers from Manchester United? (Yes)*
- *Can we contact Manchester United concerning a one-minute silence before their game at Chelsea on Friday? (Yes)*
- *The police have also been in discussion with Royal Mail, as there are huge numbers of items being sent in the post.*
- *Do we want a PO Box opened? (No)*
- *Do we want the postal items delivered or held at the moment? (Delivered)*
- *Will we give some thought to a memorial service for Holly and Jessica, as the degree of public empathy is overwhelming? (Yes)*
- *Will we give some thought to this service being held and televised from St Paul's Cathedral, London?*

We decide that this is really not suitable. Any service must be for our family, friends and community – and that means it must be local. Finally, so grimly:

• *Although no one knows when our daughter's body will be 'released', will we give some thought to Holly's funeral?*

We decide Holly will be buried in Soham, the village she lived and died in. Ironically we are relieved to have all those details to handle, because thinking about never seeing Holly again is just too immense at the moment. The grief, pain and anger are too much, confronting our memories feels too frightening. But we can hardly avoid them.

Our very last photograph of Holly, taken on the day she went missing, has become the image in the media. Holly and Jessica were happy posing in their Manchester United tops. It made a great picture. In good faith, we handed over this photograph to the police to help during the search. Now this photograph is used by all and sundry. It should not really matter, yet somehow it does.

Wednesday 21 August

Another sleepless night, weighed down by the thought of visiting Holly's final resting place in the morning. It is difficult to try and find anything positive about this forced insomnia, so, in the early hours, I decide to start writing a poem for Holly. Hopefully, when we meet the vicar to discuss the memorial service, he will allow me to include my poem amongst the prayers and hymns.

Chris, Stewart and Trudie join us, along with Nicola's parents, on the sombre journey to Wangford. We are supposed to be there for 11 a.m. When we reach the entrance to 'The Carr', I realise this is the very spot my late grandfather used to bring my brother and me to see the aeroplanes at the US Base. Those old, happy memories are overwhelmed by these horrific circumstances.

The track itself is typical of local private roads: part concrete, part rubble, part mud and grass. The muddy areas are very churned up and make walking rather slow. Once we have been signed through both the police cordons, Det. Supt Russell Wait meets our group. Like all the scenes-of-crime officers, he is dressed immaculately in suit and polished shoes, as a mark of respect. Given the quagmire around us, it is a gesture that we appreciate deeply.

We are gently guided to the spot in the ditch where Holly and Jessica's bodies were discovered. Although the area has been cut back a bit, there is evidence that some vegetation burned recently, above the level of the ditch. It is awful. In hushed tones, we are told of the body positions of Holly and Jessica and how Holly had her arm wrapped round Jessica. It somehow seems appropriate, for in life Holly was so caring and kind. There seems, however, very little point in staring at an empty ditch for too long, poignant though it is. We lay two bunches of flowers and stand in silence for a while. For me, it is a defining moment.

The fact is that some bastard, some lowlife, has thrown my daughter in a ditch as though she were a piece of rubbish. I promise myself, whoever this person turns out to be, he will not take anything else away from my family. It is time to dig deep and stand strong for Nicola, for Oliver and for other family members who feel the loss of Holly so acutely. We will not go under.

The place is so far off the beaten track that I think we can assume four things.

First, only someone with local knowledge could possibly know of its existence. Second, whoever put the girls in the ditch must have felt they had 'got away with it'. Third, the girls were not killed at this spot. Fourth, I know Ian Huntley has a close association with this area. I start to be very sure the police have the right man.

We travel back in silence. As we do so, it suddenly dawns on me that the route home is only one turning away from the village of Prickwillow, the village that the medium Dennis Mackenzie, mentioned. If Huntley wanted a quiet, discreet route to Wangford, he could have driven through Prickwillow, away from street lighting, and, crucially, far away from any CCTV cameras. Yet another detail where Dennis Mackenzie's predictions may have been right.

We meet with Tim Alban Jones, the vicar, to discuss the memorial service for Holly and Jessica. He is warm to the Chapmans and us. One of the first questions is the title of the service. It is felt more appropriate to use the words 'Celebration of Life' than 'memorial' and although we're not unanimous, we agree on 'Celebration'.

Tim has a rough outline of how the service will run. Although the suggestions seem very formal, they are not set in stone and he asks both families for their observations. Everyone agrees that Ely Cathedral, which can accommodate 2,000 people, is the right venue. St Andrew's Church in Soham could only take about 400. The new venue throws up an unexpected problem of protocol. Tim explains that the Bishop of Ely would be expected to read the main sermon in 'his own' cathedral. We all immediately state that Tim must be responsible for the main reading. Tim promises to talk to the Bishop; Tim suspects it is more likely than not that the wishes of the families will override protocol.

Both families agree to include a poem in the programme, one for Holly and one for Jessica. It is not clear who will read the poems but I am already writing mine and Les and Sharon Chapman seem confident of having one for their family. I have one more request to make and, unfortunately, it does not seem to go down too well. I ask for a lone piper to play 'Amazing Grace' at some stage during the service. The vicar and Les Chapman seem unhappy about it. It has rather stopped me in my tracks. I am confident of being able to insist on the piper being included if it is just Tim who objects, but not Les. I sit in silence frantically thinking what I can do. Should I explain what a lone piper signifies to me? Should I explain my large Scottish family background and what it would mean to them? Should I simply plead with Les to allow my request? Then, Les breaks the silence; he objects to the piece of music, not to the bagpipes themselves. He simply dislikes 'Amazing Grace'! My small crisis is over. I reassure Les that another appropriate piece will be found. I know I do not have, or even know, a piper, but hopefully the Scottish members of my family will save the day.

As there is going to be a programme printed for the service, I am asked to complete my poem as soon as possible and to confirm what piece of music will be played and by whom.

When we get back the FLOs are there. Unfortunately our police business is far from over for the day. They confirm that plans have been made for us to visit the mortuary at Addenbrooke's Hospital this Sunday. It will be our only opportunity of seeing Holly before the lid is secured on her coffin. We are asked whether we wish Holly to be wrapped or unwrapped for our visit and we decline the latter option very quickly. We are also asked to give some specific thought as to what we wish to take with us on the visit.

Nicola and I have already discussed this trip and what we can hope to achieve from it. We know we are going to be unable to see Holly physically. Learning to accept this has taken much of our emotional energy over the last few days. Having worked out when we are visiting the mortuary, we ask family and friends to leave our home once again. We want to spend time with Oliver in an atmosphere of quiet and calm, as we need to speak to him about visiting his sister this Sunday.

When Oliver is safely tucked up in bed, it is time to speak with Nicola about my silent pledge at the deposition site earlier today. It is a very personal address from me to her. I promise to deal with all issues up until Holly's funeral and tell her I don't want to cry any more tears until then. I am unsure if she really needs this comfort from me, for she is a very strong person, but she seems relieved. Before trying to sleep, we make a list of what we will take on the mortuary visit. It takes much longer than any of us would have guessed. By the end of a very long day we agree to take:

- *A letter to Holly from Mum and Dad.*
- *A letter to Holly from Oliver.*
- *Some family photographs.*
- *Some photographs of Holly and her friends.*
- *Holly's pink box, to put the photographs in.*
- *A Manchester United scarf.*
- *One of Holly's cuddly toys.*

Thursday 22 August

It has been another sleepless night. Nicola was exceptionally teary throughout the early hours of this morning and there seem to be no right words to say to her. This is the first time that we have not cried together, for one of us normally starts the other off immediately. It is desperately sad to see her like this.

Today's agenda is becoming rather obvious. Early this morning, we receive another lorry load of cards, letters and gifts from the general public. The volume is staggeringly high, indeed our post is wheeled to our front door in metal cages, like the ones you see at grocery stores. We have not had the time or strength of character to deal with the post over the last few days and, at a guess, there are about 15,000 items that need opening. Help, we ask all friends and family. Between us, we set about sorting the correspondence into cards and letters, and then break down the piles further into divisions of local, national, and foreign.

Separate boxes are created for small-sized gifts such as candles, CDs, poems, picture frames, soft toys, drawings and paintings. In the living room we also have many beautiful floral tributes, in fact, they're overrunning us. None will go to waste, however, as all postal helpers are unofficially paid in the floral currency of the moment. Nicola and I keep the message cards that come with the floral tributes before allowing any to leave our home. It feels inappropriate to give even the flowers away. But Nicola suffers terribly from hayfever. We can't fill the house with pollen.

Every unofficial postman in our kitchen is, at one point or another, overcome by the wonderfully written letters and poems. The power of the written word when you are feeling emotionally vulnerable is incredible. Here in black and white, thousands of total strangers try to offer comfort to a family they've never met. It is humbling.

Tim Alban Jones confirms that the Celebration of Life service is going to be next Friday and that he needs my finished poem along with the name of the piper and details of his chosen piece of music, plus the composer's details. It is time to ring Scotland and call for help from Uncle Fergus. Over the years Fergus has regaled us with stories of seemingly knowing everyone in Scotland by either living next door to them or meeting them whilst fishing or drinking. It is time to test the big man.

I am delighted to learn from Fergus that some former neighbours, many years ago, (no surprise to me) had a 'wee boy' by the name of Archie who 'could play a bit' and he promises to try and locate him. He rings half an hour later with Archie's number.

The telephone call is quite an emotional one for both parties. At once Archie says it will be a privilege to travel down and pipe for us next Friday. It is a huge weight off my mind and I feel indebted to him. By the end of our conversation 'the wee boy who could play a bit' transpires to be 46-year-old Archie Steele from Seil Island, near Oban. He is a former member of the Scots Guards and has piped at the famous Edinburgh Military Tattoo as well as state banquets at Buckingham Palace. It appears his CV is more than acceptable and good old Uncle Fergus has done it again!

I tell Archie we don't want 'Amazing Grace' and he immediately suggests a slow air called 'Samantha's Lullaby'. He does not know the composer but heard and learned the piece by ear from a CD. He feels the piece to be perfect for the occasion and we agree to both try and locate the composer.

Remaining and rather pending are the daunting tasks of finishing the poem and writing a letter to Holly, both of which will have to wait until the house is quieter. Away from home, the police and Crown Prosecution Service are becoming very concerned about the continuing level of publicity about Ian Huntley and Maxine Carr. A formal note from the Attorney General is sent to all editors to remind them to consider carefully the conduct of their journalists:

'In light of the torrent of publicity that has continued to be published since Carr and Huntley were arrested and charged, the Attorney General feels bound to remind editors that criminal proceedings against Maxine Carr and Ian Huntley are active within the meaning of the Contempt of Court Act 1981; and to remind them of their obligations not to engage in conduct, nor to publish material including comment, that may create a substantial risk of serious prejudice to the course of justice in these prosecutions, whether under the strict liability rule or otherwise.

The Attorney General is currently considering specific examples of this coverage drawn to his attention today by the Crown Prosecution Service.

The police investigation in this matter is still in progress and the Attorney General reminds editors to consider carefully the conduct of journalists to ensure that nothing is done which could impede the investigation or the administration of justice, for example in relation to approaches to people who are or who may be witnesses.'

The last paragraph of this note is becoming pertinent, for witnesses in Humberside who have had links with Huntley are being contacted by the police. Alarmingly, these potential witnesses have already been signed up or offered money for their stories by the press. They quite simply refuse to cooperate. It is not the best of starts for the investigation. We are deeply concerned at the impact this may have on the trial.

Our own 'operation' of opening the never-ending postal mountain continues: 15,000 items are a lot. And there is an unforeseen twist. It has been nearly three weeks since I've joined Scott and the boys at work. Clearly Scott is under no illusions in expecting me to physically return to work, but I also deal with all administrative aspects of the business and herein lies the problem. Somewhere in the remaining forty or fifty boxes of post are cheques from customers which are vital to our cash flow. Many have sent this month's payment with a letter of condolence or tucked inside a sympathy card. It is impossible to differentiate between post we need to open now and post we intend to open at some stage.

The vicar, Tim Alban Jones, is also receiving many hundreds of items, reflecting his high-profile interaction with the media and the central position of St Andrew's Church in Soham. To add to his burden, many people write to him, requesting that he pass on items of correspondence and gifts to both families, which he does on a regular basis. If we are at home during any such visit, Tim is always invited in and updated, confidentially, on our current position. At this moment in time, I am pleased to have someone representing my home town so well in the media and find myself warming to this most capable of individuals. Unfortunately, many others see him rather differently, and I repeatedly hear concerns over Tim's eagerness to represent Soham at the drop of a hat. It is a no win position for Tim and I defend him whenever the subject comes up. Part of my reason is the alternatives do not appear too great. Whilst Tim was on holiday from 11 to 17 August, his place as a spokesperson for the Church was filled by one Rev. Alan Ashton. Along with every person I mentioned him to, I had absolutely no idea who this man was. Although he did a decent enough job, he most certainly was not from Soham, so how could he speak on behalf of the locals when no one in town knew him?

When our guests leave, I am going to finish the poem for Holly and I have some way to go yet. Oliver has long since gone to bed. Nicola and I worry about his continuing quietness.

As I said at the start I am no believer in the supernatural. But, throughout the evening, strange things have started to happen in our house. The television has abruptly begun to switch itself off, and then, after a few seconds, back on again. Three light bulbs, all in different rooms, fail, one after another. Could it be that Holly's spirit is with us this evening? Is Holly trying to signal – electrically – that she's here? Neither of us knows what to make of it and we eventually decide to go to bed, feeling somewhat uplifted at the thought our daughter may have found her way home.

I don't manage to sleep. In the early hours of the morning I creep downstairs to finalise the poem.

Friday 23 August

By 4.30 in the morning I have finally completed the poem for Holly. Although I have written four verses, I decide to omit one because I worry about my ability to read it in front of so many people next week. Tim Alban Jones tells me I should think again about reading in person but I know in my heart that I must do it for Holly.

Soham's Rose
Your right to grow, to mature and to play
So cruelly denied, in a sinister way.
Attentive and caring, a parent's delight
But so young at heart, needing comfort at night.

The garden is quiet, the house is too
But pausing for a moment, we can still sense you.
Your trusting nature and desire to please all
Allow us your family, to remain walking tall.

Our memories, now shared, with the Nation's hearts
Small crumbs of comfort, now it is time to part.
We will never forget you, Heaven's gain, as it knows
Is simply you Holly, our beautiful Soham rose.

It is hardly a literary classic, but I'm pleased with it. Every sentence is about Holly and how we love her. I've never claimed to be a poet and it's as good as it is going to get under duress.

I now find myself willing Nicola to wake up so I can share the poem with her. Silently, I read the poem over and over again to get the right expression. Eventually I hear Nicola go to the bathroom. I creep upstairs to announce, 'The poem is now finished, may I read it to you?'

I feel so emotional when I say the title, I falter. My bottom lip begins to tremble and I can't stop the tide of tears about to surface. Yet again I can't speak. Embarrassed, I break down and sob uncontrollably at the end of our bed. I hand the poem over to Nicola to let her read it for herself. She reads it fast and a few moments later, she's also sobbing. We both miss Holly so much.

Slowly, we calm down. We gently rebuke each other for losing control of our emotions so easily. Half an hour after I first tried, I finally manage to read the poem to Nicola. It is a small step. I'm going to practise, intensely, so that I will be able to do Holly and the poem justice, come the big day.

At 9 a.m. our FLOs show up. There is, unfortunately, no information about the investigation, or the well-being of Ian Huntley and Maxine Carr. As potential witnesses, we are not allowed to know anything, although, apparently, there is no information to share anyway.

The FLOs have a number of tasks for us. The most crucial is today's opening of Holly and Jessica's inquests by David Morris, HM Coroner for South and West Cambridgeshire. It will be adjourned today, too, as seems to be the custom. We are shown a copy of Mr Morris's statement, which is appreciated. We are now in a position to plan for Holly's funeral. We also hear that an interim death certificate will shortly be issued, but because there are a number of unknown details, the wording will be vague. There will be no formal medical cause of death on the certificate and there will be no date or place of death, as no one knows what these might be. So the certificate will just confirm the location where Holly was found dead and the date of her discovery.

Everything else today is trivial by comparison. We hear we are going to be invited to Old Trafford if we feel up to it. It is difficult to know what to do. Nicola and I know this offer is designed to cheer Oliver, but we both feel we are not ready for such an excursion. We have hardly slept over the last three weeks. Going to a match at Old Trafford would place us under enormous pressure. But when we tell Oliver about the invitation, he's so happy and excited that we can't refuse. So we will be going to next week's European fixture against the almost unpronounceable Hungarian champions, Zalaegerszeg.

A national newspaper has offered to name a rose after Holly and Jessica. What do we think? As I have written a poem called 'Soham's Rose', I am uneasy about the coincidence being thought intentional and inappropriate. Even though the offer is well intended, I decline.

The same newspaper has also offered money towards funding of a Child Safety Centre at Alconbury. What is our reaction to that? Obviously, we don't object to any project promoting safety for children. In fact, it doesn't need our approval but we're asked because we have become useful, symbolic. Our names can now be used to raise money and we do not know where this is going to end. It worries us.

Organising the Celebration of Life service is proving tense. The vicar, Tim Alban Jones, drops by and has news of the ticket allocation details. We have to say that the allocation is woefully wrong and causing trouble. Without any reference to my family it has been decided to allow us 300 tickets, but we need double that figure. I am completely and utterly hacked off. One of the points of the service, as I see it, is to allow members of the Soham community an opportunity of attending in person to pay their respects. This is where the bulk of the tickets must go, as those of us who live in Soham have experienced first-hand the shock and intrusion.

Instead, what I see is a totally political allocation. Of the 1,580 tickets, 980 are destined for uniformed organisations, town council, press, police, army and schools. It needs changing.

To his eternal credit, Tim shoots off to sort out a compromise. I am unsure if he will be able to achieve it, simply because he is too nice. I really hope I am wrong, but I also leave the FLOs in no doubt about what we need in terms of tickets.

And then, there is the mail, the mail, this mountain of unopened mail. As we sort it, we notice some odd facts.

Many hundreds of people express their sympathy in the form

of poems. Some have written their own, whilst others send books. The poems sometimes feature wonderful calligraphy, often framed for good measure. The poignant 'Footsteps' poem repeatedly appears in small gifts and cards. We've probably received that poem from the general public more than 600 times.

Religion doesn't matter. We have condolences from Protestants, Catholics, Methodists, Jehovah's Witnesses, Muslims and even the Chief Rabbi. Some suggest passages of the Bible or Qur'an which may offer spiritual comfort. As well as many copies of the Bible and Qur'an, we receive books about coping with child loss, bereavement, hope and the psychic connection.

Many items have nothing to do with us here in Soham. Our tragedy has unleashed hundreds of letters from people wishing to share their experiences, most of them tragic. We've become a trigger. Usually, they begin with references to Holly and Jessica, but then heart-rending tales of murder, illness, accidents and loss follow. And they offer advice. Time heals – a little. We will have to learn to mourn Holly for the rest of our lives, but it will get less intense. Some of the letters are incredibly moving and well-written.

But not all our correspondence falls into this well-written, well-meaning and uplifting category. I am about to discover hate mail. The first example is about ten pages long and seems to focus entirely on the subject of paedophilia. I am accused, not only of being the murderer of my own daughter and her friend, but also of killing Milly Dowler and Sarah Payne. For good measure, I am said to be actively involved in child-trafficking rings, and promised that vengeance is coming. It is extremely distressing and frightening to receive letters like this.

Over the next few weeks similar letters would accuse me, among other things, of being the leader of international paedophile rings. Some were even more disgusting, and a few from religious crackpots. One unsigned letter shrieked that Nicola and I 'got what we deserved for allowing Holly out to play on the Sabbath'. It seems completely unbelievable that someone could be so cruel.

We were astonished by the nature of the mail – and no one warned us. We had similar experiences with the calls we received. Once the bodies of Holly and Jessica were discovered, many calls came in offering profound sympathies. Often they started with condolences, and then turned into tales of tragic events the caller had suffered. People sobbed and broke down on the phone, leaving Nicola or me to try and comfort them! Worse, some of these callers became almost addicted to talking to us.

Two ladies, both clearly distressed and perhaps in need of professional help, begin to plague us with their calls. In the end, reluctantly, we are left with no option but to ask the police to intervene. The Chapmans change their number and go ex-directory. We can't do this. My business has been established for five years and the same telephone number appears on all my advertising, headed notepaper and customer records. Changing telephone numbers will have to wait, but we do go ex-directory.

It would have been nice if the police had flagged these potential problems early in the investigation.

We experience the kindness of strangers and, sometimes, their cruelty. But our friends are supremely kind. Three special people have travelled back to England to offer moral support, Holly's godmother, and Nicola's childhood friend, Donna Paxton Tomb, from America, my cousin Julie Mitchell with her 15-year-old daughter, my goddaughter, Sarah, have flown in from New Zealand. I have that same childhood link with Julie that Nicola shares with Donna. We are amazed to learn that the search for Holly and Jessica was carried both on TV and in the national papers in New Zealand.

On the news tonight is the minute's silence at the match between Chelsea and Manchester United. We watch the images of the players bowing their heads, all wearing black armbands. It is a moving moment. Then, as if it could have been scripted, David Beckham, Holly's hero, scores with a sweet left-foot strike. After the game, he dedicates the goal to Holly and Jessica.

Saturday 24 August

We still have to write a goodbye letter to Holly. As the visit to the morgue is tomorrow, we must complete this most difficult of tasks. Nicola has decided that the cuddly toy she would like to leave inside Holly's casket is 'Snoozums'. I am against handing Snoozums over, for this is the single toy she loved most. I can smell her on it and I want to keep it.

Nicola says Holly would never go to bed without Snoozums, so it is right that Holly should have Snoozums with her in her final resting place. It's an emotional argument but in the end, I admit that Nicola is right.

To our surprise, we get another letter to Holly – from one of our babysitters, Donna Fiebig. After reading the letter together, we both break down and succumb to a torrent of tears. Donna's memories, thoughts and observations about Holly are absolutely spot on and we know Holly saw Donna as her trendy, beautiful, older 'sister'. It doesn't make it easier to write our own farewell letter. We put that off until tonight.

At least the tickets for next week's service at Ely Cathedral are sorting themselves out. Tim has managed to increase our allocation to an acceptable 550, which I can live with. The tickets themselves are colour coded and Nicola immediately ensures that three lilac ones are reserved for our FLOs to join us in the seats at the front.

Soham has now become a tourist destination as people come to visit the graveyard to view the floral tributes. There are four times as many bouquets as a few days ago. Nicola and I decide to walk up to the church, by ourselves, later today. It is not a decision we make lightly. The press could ambush us without our FLO support to rely on. If hundreds of people are already visiting in and around the church, we probably won't get much privacy.

Premiership matches will have a one-minute silence and one will take place at Headingley, at the test match between England and India. I worry as I know people drink a lot before the start of the afternoon's play. I've seen that in person and done it in person. My reservations are misplaced, however. The crowd and players stand in silent tribute and we, in our house, suddenly stand too and remember Holly and Jessica.

Nicola and I decide to venture out together for the first time since Holly's disappearance. We're nervous. As we turn into Sand Street, there are cars queuing over the bridge next to The Ship pub. We know this is going to be difficult, but we also know from friends and family that some of the messages of condolence are heart-rending. There are tributes from Holly's friends, family, Brownies and Majorettes. We hope we can find them amongst the 15,000 floral arrangements. We are also keen to see a rather special tribute from the local radio station Q103 – 1,000 red roses in the shape of a heart, which seems an incredible gesture. Above all we want to go because it is exactly a week since Holly's body was discovered and to see that others care and grieve makes us a feel little less desolate.

We walk the length of Sand Street without meeting a single person but when we get to the High Street, it becomes clear that people are actually trying to avoid us; they look away or suddenly dash into the closest shop. So many people cross the street, that if it were a boat it would capsize. We did not expect our neighbours to give us the cold shoulder.

The churchyard is full, there's a throng of people with their heads down, reading the thousands of messages. Every blade of grass has been covered with tributes. Resting on the wall of the Lady Chapel is the magnificent Q103 1,000-rose heart – our friends and family are right, it does look spectacular. As we walk through the sea of flowers, slowly but surely, we find messages from Holly's friends and activity club members. As I read these messages to myself, I hear the words spoken in a child's voice, not mine. I also find a tribute sent by a group of prisoners.

Gradually people in the churchyard get used to us being there. Timidly, a few come and give us a consoling pat on the back or a reassuring hug. We both know it is well intended but it leads to a kind of a stampede and soon we are completely engulfed. People tell us how sorry they are, offer support and tell us they too want to see justice done. No one knows how to respond naturally to our painfully unnatural situation.

At home, the mountain of mail is still there. Once more all visitors are roped into our makeshift sorting office, which occasionally doubles as a diner. As we sort the mail, I realise we have a small logistical problem. The three lilac tickets for the Celebration of Life service, which Nicola reserved for the FLOs, have gone. It does not take long to work out that I have accidentally allocated these tickets to friends. I apologise immediately to the FLOs who accept inferior seats with very good grace. But Nicola is furious with me and says so publicly.

Late in the evening, our visitors go and we can no longer distract ourselves from the task of writing the farewell letter to Holly. The first two words – 'Dearest Holly' – trigger a cascade of tears and we can't stop them, though we try. Oliver is coping much better than his parents! He completes his goodbye letter to Holly in a very matter of fact way before heading up to bed. He doesn't tell us what he wrote. Although intrigued, Nicola and I agree not to open it. Our son has the right to his privacy.

Alone now, Nicola and I can try to write once more. Once we finish, some four hours later, we put the letter with the rest of the items we're taking to the morgue. In the letter we offer our deepest apologies for failing Holly as parents. Unsure what has happened to our beloved daughter, we ask whether we could have guided her better, warned her of the dangers she might face. We ask humbly for her forgiveness.

Sunday 25 August

This morning's newspapers are worrying. The broadsheets discuss the question of whether Huntley and Carr can receive a fair trial after some papers have written so much about their background and history. We all feel angry and bitter that there is the slightest risk of Huntley and Carr escaping justice.

There were many public tributes to Holly and Jessica yesterday, all of them touching. There were silences at most football matches, at Newmarket and Worcester race course. Golfers offered their respects at Gleneagles. The *Sunday Telegraph* carries a front-page photograph of the Soham Town Rangers team, arms linked for a silent tribute. Supermarkets and town centres organised their own ceremonies to coincide with the 3 p.m. kick-off time of today's football matches. We feel the whole country is with us, and it is some comfort, though surreal.

Through the front page of the *News of the World*, their readers now know that the police have Holly and Jessica's clothing and trainers. The release of this information from a police source marks a significant moment. Both the Chapman family and ourselves have kept this confidential over the last week. Both families have proven themselves trustworthy. I hope the police will let us back into the information loop.

We have an ordeal today, the visit to the Chapel of Rest. On the journey to Cambridge, Chris and Trudie tell us that the police have a password system to gain access, as they fear a rogue press reporter might get in otherwise.

When we arrive at Addenbrooke's, Chris disappears for what seems like an eternity to check the route and morgue are clear. We get out of the car and walk to the Chapel of Rest in silence.

We are ushered into the smallest of rooms and prepare ourselves. Through the door lies Holly's casket.

There is a viewing window in the chapel door. Looking through the glass helps us compose ourselves. Together all five of us go in and gather round Holly before Chris and Trudie quietly withdraw to the little room. Now is the moment to stand as a family of four for the very last time.

You rejoice when a child is born. You never imagine you will have to be here – with her casket. Never, never, never.

We put the things for Holly over the quilt-like garment that neatly conceals the crinkly plastic cover loosely defining Holly's body shape. We hope that the thought and care taken in the writing of the letters and the selection of different items and photographs somehow gets through to the daughter and sister we'll all miss forever. All of us whisper our final messages of love and farewell to Holly.

Then it's over. We step back into that small room where Chris and Trudie are waiting.

We drive home.

One of the strangest features of this period in retrospect, is the fact that there is so much to do, and it doesn't matter that you are in no mood for much of it.

At home, we tackle the outstanding postal mountain. Our kitchen is not actually part of the Royal Mail, I remind myself. Many people also continue to send letters to us via the vicar, Tim Alban Jones.

It seems strange that people are writing to Tim to pass letters to us, but as he is so much in the media, perhaps the public perceive him to be at the heart of things. In Soham there is a growing feeling of disquiet over his eagerness to comment. Nicola and I have never sought counselling from Tim or asked him to speak on our behalf, but people seem to think that he is doing both. It bugs me, but I see no point in starting a conflict. In most ways he has been a positive presence and we are going to have a lot of contact with him in the run up to both the Celebration of Life service and Holly and Jessica's funerals.

In the mail mountain, I get a letter from Kevin Proctor, the managing director of the White Dove Company. Kevin is offering to release doves at the Ely Cathedral Service next Friday, which would have been a wonderful moment. Unfortunately, this offer has come a fraction too late as the printing for the order of service is already underway, but his offer does get me thinking. The Village College is still closed and local people are worried whether the school will actually be handed back in time to start the new academic year. The community is even more worried about what frame of mind the kids will be in.

It seems to me that if Kevin would be prepared to release his doves at the start of term, it might prove to be a good experience for teachers and pupils alike. I make a note to speak with Kevin and get all parties together for discussion.

We go to the churchyard one last time to take in the scale of the floral tributes. This time, learning from our previous experience, I drive to the car park. Even though it is twilight, the churchyard is still milling with people and many come forward to meet us. As politely as possible, we withdraw as quickly as we arrived.

Monday 26 August

Today, Chris and Stewart are taking my brother-in-law, Graham, to the deposition site at Wangford. Graham is distressed as he wonders whether he should have found Holly and Jessica, when he was searching there. The police believe that if Graham sees how remote the deposition site is, he will realise that the most willing searcher in the world would not have located the girls.

This morning we finally open the last batch of unopened mail. It's a moment of light relief – and there haven't been many of them. We have tried our best to sort mail into different categories in the last three weeks. That gives us the chance to review our boxes. It is quite staggering to see how many items have come from outside the United Kingdom – Australia, New Zealand, America, Zimbabwe, France, Spain, Belgium, Germany and many more countries. Of course, most of the mail comes from the 'home' countries and we keep about two hundred letters which we will reply to eventually.

One box contains cards and letters from high-profile people and organisations. Many were delivered by the police by hand and that made getting them quite intense. We always will be grateful for the kind words in those letters and cards.

The letter from Mary McAleese, the President of Ireland, is interesting. We have had thousands of letters from all parts of Ireland. The Irish 'mail' outnumbers its nearest 'rival' by 2 to 1. It is extraordinary to receive so much support from across the water.

Today's *Daily Mail* carries a headline of, 'Please don't pass us by say parents'. I'm rather surprised. I had told the vicar about

139

being cold-shouldered on our walk through the High Street, but I am slightly miffed that this has been turned into copy which claims we 'made the appeal to their local vicar'. The piece also refers to the Chapman family, which is a surprise since they are not dealing with Tim. I'm beginning to wonder if some of my family and friends who have been critical of the vicar are perhaps a bit right. Is Tim less man of God and more man of the media? Has Tim gone public because he cares for us and worries about us or has he done it to stay in the public eye? I am beginning to waver in my support for him.

But whether the vicar says too much is not very important compared with another media issue. The police have issued a press release which affects us all close to Holly and Jessica.

Regina vs Ian Huntley and Maxine Carr

This is a message for all media outlets covering the police investigation in Cambridgeshire surrounding Holly Wells and Jessica Chapman.

On 20 August 2002, Cambridgeshire Police issued the first of a series of advisory notes to all media outlets about the provisions of the Contempt of Court Act 1981.

On 23 August the Attorney General issued advice to editors reminding them of the provisions of the Contempt of Court Act and of their obligations to the criminal trial process.

Regrettably, further information published in the media since that note has continued to approach the boundary of what is likely to be regarded as acceptable by the trial courts.

Such continued further publication is viewed by both the investigation and prosecution teams as serious since it flagrantly ignores the advice given to editors by the police and the Attorney General.

Cambridgeshire Constabulary and Cambridgeshire Crown Prosecution Service strongly urge the media to exercise restraint and caution in reporting details of the case thereby ensuring that the public interest in guaranteeing both defendants have a fair trial is not frustrated by the publication of material prejudicial to the defendants or to any of the issues in the case.

No matter how many times I read this notice, it makes me feel sick. For Huntley and Carr not to stand trial is unimaginable and we are feeling exceptionally vulnerable just now. We must get justice for Holly.

Before leaving, Chris and Stewart agree to accompany Nicola and me up to the churchyard to have one last 'uninterrupted' look at the tributes. The two FLOs discreetly guide members of the public away to allow us some privacy, and it is much appreciated. The next time we see the churchyard, the flowers will all be gone.

Tuesday 27 August

Oliver is so excited this morning. It will be the first Manchester United game he sees live. We leave for Old Trafford at 1 o'clock and we are given an insight into police procedure. The rules demand that when going on a glamorous trip to Britain's greatest football club, you have to be escorted not by one, not by two, but by all three of our FLOs. It's very risky, Old Trafford.

Joking aside, Nicola and I are very uneasy at going out socially in the present circumstances. Everyone close to us knows that we're going because of Oliver, but we wonder how people will perceive this outing. We're leaving ourselves open to criticism. We're going to be sitting in the Director's Box – and we would not be there if our daughter hadn't died. I am not sure if either one of us is strong enough to face snide comments.

On the way up, we get a telephone call from the Family Liaison coordinator, Gary Goose. The Home Office have been in touch and Chris asks, 'Can he have the thoughts of Kevin and Nicola in relation to the Home Secretary, David Blunkett, attending the Celebration of Life service?' The service is meant to allow family, friends, community and individuals directly linked to the investigation the chance to gather together and show their respects. We don't consider the Home Secretary to be part of that group. After a short discussion, Nicola and I say we don't think it right.

I don't suppose the senior officer who gives that answer back to the Home Secretary is congratulated. It was a clear 'no', but we get another call ten minutes later. 'Have the Wells family given any more thought to the Home Secretary's request, as he is keen to be present to extend his respects?' Obviously, as we were totally clear, we have not given the position any more thought. We say a curt and factual 'no' and hope this is the end of the matter.

A few miles later, the phone goes again. This is becoming irksome. We repeat, once and for all, that 'our position will not change, please do not ask again'.

When the phone rings again, we all howl. Impossible surely. I don't believe it! Though the call is from the same source, it's something different and we're not asked to review, revise or reconsider our decision about Mr Blunkett turning up – to everyone's relief.

The traffic is bad and we get to Manchester late. We just have time to check into the hotel, change our clothes and head for Old Trafford to meet our chaperone for the evening, Keith McIntosh.

We're very late for dinner. Everyone else has finished so while we eat, our table is entertained by Magic Matt, whose tricks and funny one-liners completely enchant Oliver. It is so good to see him smile and laugh again.

We are shown to our seats in the Director's Box with a few minutes to spare. It is not really a box at all, but a large seating area in a prime position opposite the halfway line. Sir Bobby Charlton and the President, Martin Edwards, are a few rows down. The players who have not made the team tonight sit to our right. These really are the best seats in the house.

Tonight's game is a very important one for United, as they need to overhaul a first-leg deficit of 1–0 to continue in the Champions' League. By half-time we are three goals up thanks to van Nistelrooy, Beckham and Scholes. Beckham's free kick would have made Holly cheer and scream with adulation for her favourite player.

The second half brings two more goals. At the end of the match we return to our corporate table. I see the former goalkeeper Alex Stepney and I decide to ask our chaperone Keith to ask for the great man's autograph. I build myself up to request this small favour, but it simply does not happen. It's not that I'm nervous and it's not that Keith is unapproachable, no, it doesn't happen because Keith stuns the table by announcing Sir Alex Ferguson is waiting to meet us.

We walk through to the manager's lounge. After nervous introductions, Sir Alex places us all at ease. He offers his condolences
and then presents Oliver with a football signed by the players.
Oliver is thrilled and we all examine the ball. Then we're asked
to stay to have a drink and something more to eat. Sir Alex makes
it clear he intends to spend some time with us all. We're amazed
as it's a busy match night.

The manager's lounge is clearly a castle. Back-room staff knock
at the door and pop in to speak with 'the Boss'. One visitor is
Tony Coton, the goalkeeping coach. This huge guy has also
brought a gift for Oliver, a set of gloves from United's keeper,
Fabien Barthez. Oliver is just so happy. I instantly forgive Tony
Coton for having played so well for Manchester City.

You obviously do not stroll into Sir Alex's lounge without
knocking even if you are the biggest of the stars. Another noncha-
lant knock. Sir Alex says, 'Come in, David.' Can it be? No surely
not? It is, it's David Beckham. I get up to introduce my family to
him – and introduce the three FLOs. We're gob-smacked people
are being so kind. Some 10 minutes later, David Beckham
announces to our son that he thinks he can improve on the gifts
Oliver has already received, and he disappears. A few minutes
later David Beckham is back with his match boots, both signed.
Oliver is even more thrilled and he was already as thrilled as a
12-year-old can be. Chris Mead captures it all on camera.

After the best part of one hour Sir Alex has to go. Circumstances
apart, it has been a privilege to meet everyone and enormously
beneficial and therapeutic. I hope that all these famous people did
not feel too uncomfortable in our presence; it must be so difficult
to know what to say to us at the moment. What is certain is that
the difficult task of moving forwards as a family has taken its first
tentative steps here tonight. We are, and will always be, eternally
grateful.

On our way out Keith shows us round the dressing rooms, much
to the delight of Nicola and Trudie, who both insist on sitting at
David Beckham's changing place, feeling this is appropriate as

they are now his close friends! We are also allowed a walk down the players' tunnel and out onto the hallowed turf and I imagine myself to be my childhood hero, Martin Buchan, leading the team out. In the dark and silence of the night, with the 66,000 crowd long gone, this is an image of Old Trafford I will never experience again. It is a very emotional moment.

We return to the hotel in a bit of a dream-like state, and decide to buy a drink for our three FLOs for their support on this fantastic day. We find the quietest part of the bar and it does not seem to matter too much that we are being stared at by other guests, for we really are on cloud nine. It suddenly dawns on me that David Beckham's boots, if they are the same pair as he wore last Friday against Chelsea, have each scored a goal and they now belong to Oliver. Even a fight in the toilets between two guests and the arrival of police officers can't dampen our spirits.

I wouldn't have missed tonight for the world.

I would have missed it happily, if it meant Holly were still alive.

Wednesday 28 August

At breakfast we glance at this morning's papers and, though we were not aware of any pictures being taken during the game, our images appear throughout, some on the front pages and some inside. I do not think Nicola or I will ever be comfortable at being in the spotlight.

Diana Law meets us when we go back to Old Trafford. I want to tell her that I used to celebrate my own goal-scoring feats with a single raised arm and pointed finger just as her father used to do. But I suspect she has heard it all before and refrain from doing so.

We are taken round the ground for the standard tour, which is great, before heading off to meet young Matthew Sheldon, our very well informed guide for the museum. I could have stayed in that museum for the entire day but it wasn't to be. Under pressure from Nicola ('*you've got all the books at home anyway*'), Oliver ('*I need to get home to show everyone my gifts, Dad*') and Stewart (*a Liverpool supporter, feigning polite interest*), the decision to head home is taken by the majority!

The evening belongs to Oliver. He bursts with pride every time he shows off his Beckham boots and signed football. Bizarrely, everyone, without exception, insists on not only trying the boots on, but also on sniffing them to see if Beckham's feet smell! Becks has an ally in Nicola, as she reassures anyone who'll listen that this national icon is not only much better looking in real life, but also that it is simply inconceivable that he could have smelly feet. Heroes do not pong.

Thursday 29 August

This morning, as now usual, Chris and Trudie, cannot update us on Huntley, Carr or the enquiry. And as usual, we are frustrated. The position that, as we are witnesses we cannot have our evidence tainted by knowing any developments, is beginning to wear thin. Every time I met Huntley other people were around and they could give any evidence needed. Nicola's evidence only concerns past details about Holly and the Sunday barbecue.

So why can't a little common sense be used? Why can't the legal teams work together to allow my family access to crucial developments? This exclusion can only upset us in the months ahead and we don't deserve to be placed in this position. Chris promises to take my concerns forward to see what can be done.

Maxine Carr is due in court today – or not – as the case may be. We are told that she will be answering questions via a prison video link. It is hardly a priority but why should she be protected from crowd noise or crowd scenes? Surely she should be made aware of the public anger against her. We believe she must break her silence, tell the police what she knows and put some distance between herself and Huntley. So will today's 'appearance' bring a change of position from her?

The date for Holly's funeral is being kept secret but Nicola and I have already spoken with Reg Brown, the local funeral director, to arrange a simple service. It was a difficult decision to make but, in the end, we decided on a single hearse to collect Nicola, Oliver and myself for the short journey to St Andrew's. Close members of the family who feel they want to be part of the funeral cortège are not totally happy, but the loss of our daughter has been so public, that we ask them to accept our need to be by ourselves with Holly.

Chris, Stewart and Trudie want to confirm some arrangements for next week:

- *Can the Family Liaison Officers attend the funeral? (Yes)*
- *Can the Chapman family attend Holly's funeral? (Yes)*
- *Do we wish to attend Jessica's funeral? (Yes)*
- *Would we like a motor cycle escort to the cemetery? (No)*

We do not want the media at either funeral. The police say they can give no guarantees. Holly's funeral will be one day after Jessica's. We worry that local people will discuss the fact Jessica's funeral has taken place and so alert the media to our daughter's.

We learn from Chris and Trudie that the investigation has taken a small negative turn. The police want to view footage involving Ian Huntley which all the main television networks possess, particularly footage which has not already been broadcast. The police want to see if Huntley's behaviour or words offer any clues. We are appalled to learn that only one television company provides the material. The others insist on receiving a court order to comply with the 'request'. I just do not understand the mentality.

It also becomes obvious that forensic testing is not going to yield results very quickly. Probably nothing will be forthcoming for at least six weeks, and many tests will take much longer than that. There is no great point in becoming upset at this news, as we cannot change this position, but it's something else that makes us feel frustrated and anxious. If things are taking this long to sort out, when is the court case actually going to start?

We are asked two questions which need an immediate answer or explanation.

'Are you aware of a box of chocolates and a card from Holly to Maxine Carr?'

'Yes. Holly was most insistent on getting something for Miss Carr at the end of term.'

'Did Holly ever mention to you something about being Maxine Carr's bridesmaid?'

'No, never, why do you ask?'

'Sorry, we cannot say.'

And so the cat-and-mouse game continues.

My Scottish relatives have arrived this morning – with the piper Archie Steele. They are all staying at Mike and Ann Jarman's house, just off College Close, the address of Huntley's house. It is cordoned off by the police and they control access. The police officer looks very surprised when Nicola and I ask for permission to go through, and we share a wry moment.

Seeing everyone for the first time is emotional and tearful and we all hug one another. Archie says we should hear 'Samantha's Lullaby' at least once before the service, as it could be upsetting if the first time we hear it is in the cathedral. Nicola and I are both sobbing by the end; there is something very haunting and very appropriate about this piece for it is not just a slow air, but a lament. I have this gut feeling that this piece was composed following the death of Samantha, whoever she may have been. We feel that our part of the service, the poem and the bagpipe solo, is as good as it can be. Sad, ironic, we have a small feeling of pride in this fact. Our daughter will be remembered in style.

Friday 30 August

I have not slept, hardly the ideal preparation for this afternoon's reading, but there is no time to dwell on this as we have to be at Ely for 11 a.m. for a practice run.

As we drive to Ely, there is the most stunning view of the cathedral, almost floating in the distance. In the sunshine, the roof reflects a beautiful silver colour. It's easy to see why the cathedral is referred to as the 'Ship of the Fens'.

The cathedral is such a commanding building that I feel almost embarrassed to mention to my FLOs that this is my first ever visit. The sheer magnificence is overwhelming. Sunlight floods the stained-glass windows, the painted Octagon, the exquisite wood and brass effects. Inside the cathedral it is very busy – TV journalists setting up, technicians completing lighting and sound checks. Eventually, it is my turn to stand at the microphone and have a practice read, but I cannot. Already feeling overawed, I offer my apologies as I feel I am only going to be able to read the poem just the once in this setting. Instead I read two lines of a hymn before deciding that will suffice.

At 4 p.m. Nicola, Oliver, Trudie, Chris and I join the Chapman family and their liaison officers for tea with the Bishop. Everyone is friendly but I am knotted with nerves and I really don't want to deal with sandwiches, chit-chat and Earl Grey. I leave Nicola and Oliver to their own devices to pace outside with Chris. If I could drop out of reading the poem at this moment in time, I would do so.

The FLO coordinator, Gary Goose, is talking with Mrs Adams, the mother of Victoria Beckham, who wants to arrange some private floral tributes on behalf of her daughter and son-in-law.

Gary is helpful which is more than the funeral director, Reg Brown, was when Mrs Adams first called. Mother of celebrity or not, she was fobbed off because Reg Brown kept to the police's request for absolute secrecy and discretion.

We go in by the side entrance of the cathedral. It was supposed to be private but one crew is there. I feel I'm walking a longest of short walks into the camera lens and that does nothing to settle my nerves.

The cathedral is hushed. We are escorted to our front-row seats, where (and still feeling guilty about this) our FLOs leave us to find their less good seats. There is a little nervous chit-chat, Nicola tries to reassure me I will recite the poem well. I hope she is right for at this very moment, Canon John Inge starts his welcome. Immediately after his address, the choir in their resplendent red cassocks glide past my left arm singing 'All Things Bright and Beautiful'. It does feel awesome, holy, as if angels are watching down on us.

Bishop Anthony is next up and leads us into a reflective period of silence and a prayer. Then Brian Stevens, one of the Family Liaison Officers for the Chapman family walks to the lectern. I know my own moment is imminent. To my surprise, I lose my nerves; I know what I have to do. 'This poem is for Holly and I must not let her down' is my only thought.

As Brian Stevens begins reading a poem called 'Lord of Comfort' there is an eerie echo. The sound demons are at work and we can also hear the Italian commentator on the service ad-libbing his translation. With just a slight pause Brian elects to carry on and reads the poem with great clarity and expression. I hope that their moment is not spoilt for the Chapmans by this technical interference.

I now have a dilemma. Do I dutifully go up and try my best to master this Italian interference problem, or do I ask for the glitch to be fixed first? As the verger is in front of me waiting to accompany me to the lectern, there is no time to debate the position further. I lean forwards and say, 'Sorry, I am not going up until the technical problem has been sorted.'

'Quite right,' he whispers and disappears down the side of the cathedral. For what seems like an eternity, I sit and wait for him to come back. Will I ever get to read the poem at all? The verger glides back and gives the smallest nod, which I take to mean everything has been sorted and it is time to make the short walk to the lectern.

I walk forward. Sitting to my right-hand side are many of my cricket club colleagues. Amongst them is John Stannard, who forms part of my contingency plan. If my voice fails or if I become overcome with emotion, I have decided to simply return to my seat rather than embarrass myself. John has every reason to be nervous; he has agreed to step forward to read the poem if that happens.

Fortunately for both of us, I manage to read the poem unaided. The Italian gremlins don't make themselves heard or felt. Nicola and Oliver both greet me with a well-done message. I feel so relieved.

Next Archie Steele will play 'Samantha's Lullaby'. As he walks forwards his shoes make a very distinctive clicking sound on the cathedral floor. He comes to a halt just in front of our seats, and the clicking stops and that is an informal introduction to his playing. The smallest pause as he prepares himself, and then the unmistakeable haunting sounds of the bagpipes begin. He plays perfectly. By the end of the piece I have lost my composure completely. I just about stop myself sobbing.

I notice both Nicola and Oliver have shed a few tears too. Thank goodness we have no cameras in front of us.

Then, after some words from Holly and Jessica's headmaster and the hymn 'Give Me Joy in My Heart', Tim Alban Jones takes to the pulpit.

Tim speaks of Holly as 'the perfect daughter with her love of dancing and football and the way she enjoyed helping other children with her winning smile.' It is particularly relevant that Tim includes helping other children, for at St Andrew's School, Holly was one of the older children entrusted with looking after a younger playground 'buddy'. Holly's 'buddy' was a six-year-old girl called Eleanor, the daughter of Tim Alban Jones.

Tim goes on, 'Jessica and Holly were two trusting and loving girls and the way they lived is surely the right pattern for us. The very worst thing that could happen as a result of what took place in Soham is that a whole generation of children should grow up without being able to trust anyone.'

I'm struck by how sensitive both his words and his delivery are. Tim goes on to say, 'Holly and Jessica have become a part of the lives of a great number of people in the past few weeks – a far greater number than ever were lucky enough to know them during the course of their lives. Let us hope that as we continue to remember them and give thanks for them, we will also continue to try to model our lives on what St Paul calls "the more excellent way" – the way of love. For in that lies healing and salvation and, ultimately, hope for the future of us all.'

I feel genuinely uplifted by Tim's address, it captures the moment. There is now a little more time to reflect, for in front of us the choir are singing the anthem 'Lord you are the light of life to me' and they do so beautifully.

Then the Methodist Minister of Soham, the Rev. Malcolm Hope leads prayers and gives a well-meaning, but long, address. It is a strange moment really, for this was the only part of the service we did not know about in advance. Tim told us that the prayers would be short at this point and I now find myself feeling slightly peeved towards the over-long Malcolm Hope. I am also slightly confused why the Methodist Church has been chosen to do the prayers when, round the corner, the Baptist Church, with the biggest congregation of all the Soham churches, has not been asked to feature.

Finally, the Bishop returns for the Blessing:

'May the love of God and the Peace of the Lord Jesus Christ
Bless and console you
And all who have known and loved Holly and Jessica.

May God give you his comfort and his peace
His light and his joy.
And the blessing of God Almighty,
The Father, the Son and the Holy Spirit
Be with you and those you love, both here and in eternity.
Amen.'

This most emotional service ends with the *Nunc Dimittis*, sung by the Cathedral Choir, as they walk through the nave. I am about to dissolve in tears again. So we leave the cathedral in this slightly volatile state. We walk outside into the glare of the sunshine and the waiting press and television crew, where our visible frailty becomes a matter of public record.

We don't see a car as we drive back to Soham. We join our FLOs and collect a Chinese takeaway for everyone and watch a re-run of the service in private. This time, Chris and Trudie have the best seats in the house. Nicola and I are crying by the end, not just because it is enormously emotional, but because we feel privileged to have been given the opportunity of celebrating the life of Holly in public. We are very much aware that other bereaved parents have not been, and will not be, so fortunate.

While we have been gone, 250 volunteers have been clearing away the floral tributes from the churchyard. Neither we nor the Chapmans were consulted, but many of the flowers are beginning to decay. And there is a strong feeling that Soham has had enough of 'grief tourists' who visit the churchyard. One man even arrived with a deck chair, and settled down to eat his fish and chips in amongst the floral tributes.

This afternoon has also seen another small yet significant piece of police activity. The school site was formally handed back to the Village College. Margaret Bryden, Howard Gilbert and the rest of the staff can now plan for the forthcoming term.

In the evening many close friends and family join us to share in the emotion of this most extraordinary day. Archie Steele takes his place in the corner of the garden and pipes 'Amazing Grace'. This wonderful piece of music seems intrinsically linked to today's events and everyone gathers together outside to hear Archie perform. It seems strangely fitting.

Saturday 31 August

Over the last few weeks our doctor, Dr Partha, has sometimes dropped by. He wanted to check the emotional and physical well-being of Nicola, Oliver and myself, without giving us an opportunity of 'preparing to welcome him'.

Oliver shows Dr Partha the signed football and the coveted David Beckham boots. A little later, I see that Dr Partha is playing football in the back garden with my son. As I watch Dr Partha confirm he is a better cricketer than footballer, I suddenly notice Oliver is wearing David Beckham's boots! As a matter of urgency the game is interrupted and the boots retrieved in the nick of time before any damage is done.

Our FLOs have this weekend off. All three deserve a break. It gives us time to catch up on local news and the ever present rumour mill. One such rumour suggests Ian Huntley may have attacked Holly and Jessica, because Jessica's mother, Sharon was offered the school job ahead of Maxine Carr. Certainly for a while, Nicola and I were both under the impression that this job rumour was true, but it is not. Maxine Carr was a general classroom assistant, on a voluntary basis since the spring of this year and was upgraded to paid temporary staff until the end of the summer term. At this time Sharon Chapman was a learning support assistant working with special needs children.

There is also another story. Only this time the content is quite soul-destroying. The Scottish newspaper, *The Herald*, have sacked one of their journalists, John MacLeod, following his column last Monday. MacLeod wrote, 'Had the parents of Holly Wells and Jessica Chapman kept the Lord's Day, their daughters would still be alive. They would have spent the day at rest or in the private and public worship of God, and not been wandering the countryside, prey for whatever evil finally befell them.' It seems inconceivable that this ill-judged, irrational view can be published in a national newspaper. Is MacLeod saying my daughter's death would have been acceptable between Monday to Saturday?

Members of the church, health centre and schools have been meeting to discuss what arrangements are needed when school starts again. There will be a number of help lines and access to counsellors available. Although I am unsure if these services will actually be used, it seems appropriate to have them in place; even if they help just one person that must count as a success.

I also meet with my business partner, Scott. Our cash flow has not been unduly affected by the loss of work experienced so far, as payment for our work completed in June and July has been coming in. But our cash flow is going to take a serious dip in the next two months. We agree I will go back to work part time in the next couple of weeks and that, meanwhile, I will do some of the paperwork so Scott can concentrate on the practical side of the job. I am pleased to be able to lighten his load a little as he has proven an invaluable friend over the last month, and also because Scott and his wife are expecting their first child.

My personal cash flow has been boosted by a visit from Paul Hedger on behalf of the Isleham High Street Baptist Church. He brought a cheque with a wonderful letter confirming that, 'We, as a congregation, were anxious to convey our love and care in a practical way.' It is deeply moving and appreciated, not least because of our historic links with Isleham. Nicola was born in Bowers Lane and, over the years, I have been lucky enough to captain both football and cricket teams for this wonderful village.

We are still getting so much mail. One letter today comes from Sara and Mike Payne, from Surrey, who had to battle tragedy and the media after the murder of their beautiful young daughter Sarah. Sara and Mike's public crusade must be known to every parent in the country with their efforts to introduce 'Sarah's Law'. Their kind words are very much appreciated.

All day and well into the evening, people drop by, talk about yesterday's Celebration of Life service and tell us of their own emotional moments in the cathedral. We are so lucky to be surrounded by so many genuine, caring people. It is such a shame that it has taken something this heinous for Nicola and me to see the true strength of our family and friends.

Sunday 1 September

Today would have been Jessica Chapman's 11th birthday. Our sorrow for Les, Sharon, Becky and Alison Chapman is made worse by the fact that we were the last adults in charge of their precious daughter and sister. Our duty of care not only extended to Holly but to Jessica and, at this moment in time, no one needs to remind us of this fact – it is weighing very heavily indeed.

For the Chapman family, their relatives and friends this is no doubt the most testing of times and it is their feelings of loss, confusion and grief that really matter. We hope and pray for them all, for in addition to the poignancy of today, their minds will also be focusing ahead to tomorrow. At 11 a.m. in St Andrew's Church, it will be Jessica's funeral.

Monday 2 September

Acknowledging the Chapman family's desire for privacy, I only confirm that Nicola and I attended the funeral of Jessica Chapman.

When we get home with our two FLOs, I ask Chris, 'How does a man like Huntley get a job working with children? What checks are put in place?' He says nothing much in reply but we will discover there are some major police concerns about Ian Huntley and his past.

By late afternoon our FLOs depart to allow us and our many visitors a chance to reflect about Holly's funeral tomorrow. Last Friday's Celebration of Life service led to a deluge of post. These letters have been, and continue to be, a source of comfort to Nicola and me. One such letter is from a lady who has also lost her daughter. Initially it is the address which grabs my attention as it is from the Isle of Seil, where Archie Steele the piper lives. Having never even heard of the Isle of Seil before, it is quite bizarre that this remote area of Scotland should figure twice in such a short time. The moving letter hits home:

'You will have many, many letters from strangers, so may I be one more, please, to send heartfelt condolences and prayers. I hope you feel a little comfort that so many feel for and with you, during dark, dark days. I wish I could say it gets better: but today sees the 5th anniversary of the death of my beloved daughter, Diana. I can say, it gets gentler and easier, but she lives in my heart, with great affection and I miss her every day. That doesn't change, or ever will, but our other children need us, and brighten our life, and I hope from now, life will be kind and gentle for you and yours, and that most of all – you have peace to gather your lives, far away from those who pry and the media.

I shall be with the crowd, who prays for you all and the souls of Holly and Jessica. May they rest in peace.'

The letter is from The Hon. Mrs Frances Shand Kydd and her 'beloved daughter', of course, was Princess Diana.

Tuesday 3 September

We don't sleep at all as we count the clock down to Holly's funeral this morning. The last four weeks have been so traumatic I am relieved the funeral is today. As a parent, this is an odious thought to have.

Our planning for the service, we hope, has been meticulous. The order of service has been printed in Holly's favourite colour, lilac, by my old cricketing colleague, Ian Hobbs. On the front is a photograph of a cheeky-looking, smiling Holly, which is just the way we want to remember her. This photograph is special, for it was taken in the back garden of Donna Paxton Tomb, Holly's godmother. Donna has agreed to read a poem for Holly during today's service and no one envies her the task ahead. We hope that selecting this photograph somehow shows our love and support before her big moment.

Nicola and I have chosen as the first hymn 'Morning Has Broken'. After Tim Alban Jones completes his address, we are going to play 'Angels' by Robbie Williams, the song which Holly and I used to sing together on the karaoke. It is going to be hard. Especially as the lyrics are so relevant to today's proceedings. Prayers will follow 'Angels' before the final hymn of 'All Things Bright and Beautiful' (for that was Holly) will lead into the commendation.

We have asked for no visitors this morning. Nicola and I want to spend time talking things through with Oliver. We tell him not to be too distressed when his mum and dad begin crying and that, if he feels like it, he can cry at any time. Oliver is very quiet but stresses he does not want to hold hands as we walk behind the coffin. Well that is fine if it is what he wants.

I'm glad to be surrounded by Soham people. Neville Green arrives with the hearse and is the one person, apart from the owner Reg Brown, who everyone associates with C. E. Fuller and Co., the undertakers. He is a quiet, gentle man who has offered sympathy and understanding to hundreds of Soham families for countless years. We end up hugging in our grief.

We drive to the church in silence and as Holly's coffin is taken out of the hearse, all three of us stand together ready to begin this uniquely sad walk.

As all three of us sit down in a front pew, the enormity of seeing Holly's coffin, just in front of us, is too much to bear and we start to cry. Unable to sing any words of the hymn, our composure fortunately returns before Donna walks to the front to read her poem. She recites the poem perfectly. Tim Alban Jones delivers the address sensitively which leads on to the playing of 'Angels'. As the song starts, I tell myself to keep composed, but, within seconds, I have completely broken down as memories of sitting at the end of the stage with Holly come flooding back. The more I try and stop myself crying, the worse it gets. It is Nicola who manages to compose herself to comfort our young son.

We leave the church upset and we can't see properly because our eyes are full of tears. The only person I can remember seeing in the congregation is Jessica's father, Les, which is most bizarre. The police have closed the road. We walk back to the church gates in uncanny silence. It's so quiet that a tumble weed blowing across the road would not have been untoward.

Some of our relatives don't find getting to the cemetery easy. Their taxis are caught up in the well-meaning roadblocks, but the FLOs improvise and everybody eventually finds themselves gathered together for the last part of proceedings.

Quietly, with just a tiny nod of recognition, Tim begins. Fortunately this time, Nicola and I do not dissolve into tears as the coffin is gently lowered into its final resting place. We did not want to place some soil over the coffin, so it is the quietest of verbal farewells, 'Goodbye, dearest Holly.'

This moment is the painful conclusion to the last four weeks of our lives. It has been a time when people's character and inner strength have been tested beyond imagination. It somehow seems appropriate to thank and hug every person present for their unstinting and loyal support. As all three of us walk back towards the hearse, laid out on the grass verge are all of the floral tributes. Next to our own white and lilac HOLLY, there is a red 7 from David and Victoria Beckham. Holly would have liked that.

In the Dark

4 September–31 December 2002

Wednesday 4 September

Nicola has decided to return to work today. She wants to stay busy. Fortunately, no clients come to the Suffolk subsidiary office of Lorimer Longhurst and Lees Solicitors, so she will only need to deal with the familiar face of her boss Paul Harrington. There has been no pressure at all from her employers.

This allows me to spend time with Oliver. He is going to return to school himself, sometime next week. Although he is not keen to talk about Holly, he will discuss school and the problems of meeting everyone for the first time since Holly was murdered. We agree that probably his friends will not ask specific details. If normal conversation fails, then he can fall back on the Manchester United trip. He seems to grasp the importance of getting back into a routine with a degree of maturity beyond his twelve years.

For all our family the fact that Holly's smiling face appears frequently in the newspapers and on television does not make it easier. Emily, Holly's three-year-old cousin, also misses her terribly and asks where she is. We all hope her heart-rending questions can somehow be addressed sensitively and without creating too much anxiety for her. (What do you say to a three-year-old girl who thinks that borrowing a set of ladders is the sensible way of getting Holly back from the sky?)

I have also been thinking about Tim Alban Jones. He handled the Celebration of Life service and both Jessica and Holly's funerals very sensitively. My reservations about him now seem ridiculously misplaced and I feel I should have given him the benefit of the doubt. Without discussing this with Nicola, I decide to begin going to church. It may well be for the wrong reasons in that I feel a debt of gratitude to Tim and a public show of support may well stop any local criticism of him from developing further. But I have also witnessed the rather alarming accuracy of the mediums. I now know first-hand that there is something else out there, so to speak. I need to review my reticence towards religion.

By coincidence Gillian Bristow chooses this moment to share some very personal observations with me. Gillian is now retired and is an astrologer, a Reiki Master and a Louise Hay Teacher. I have known her all my adult life and have always found her to be remarkably informed, observant and intuitive. We both know that, last Christmas, Gillian predicted a major incident in my life this summer. 'Be careful, Kevin,' she said, 'you are going to have a traumatic event in your life, you will come through it and you will be a better person for it, but it is going to be a long journey.' We both took that to mean I would be involved in an accident. How wrong we were!

We have a long silent hug before Gillian explains why she has come. She wants to share with me a couple of observations. 'It is important for you to know that neither Holly nor Jessica was sexually molested although I cannot discount there may have been intentions of a sexual nature towards one or both, but, Kevin, something happened. All I can see is anger, just so much anger. I am really sorry to have to tell you that your daughter and her friend happened to be in the wrong place at the wrong time.'

Gillian apologises profusely in case she has caused any upset, but what she says is the first chink of good news in the last four weeks. I am sick of reading about Ian Huntley and his past sexual liaisons with young blonde girls who looked like Holly. Gillian brings me real hope. If she feels there was no sexual contact with Holly, that is good enough for me. After she leaves, I return to my office and break down in relief. Maybe, just maybe, my daughter was spared the harrowing indignity of being raped before she died.

This evening Nicola and I discuss Holly. It is the first time that we have reminisced at length about our daughter. Memories, incidents, milestones, observations and the unfulfilled potential of Holly make it heart-rending, but as we talk, our grieving process truly begins. This is not a 'community disaster'. It is a personal disaster which has left two families trying to cope with the loss of their youngest daughters. We feel confused, scared, unsure of the future. Will we still be together as a family when the police investigation ends? We genuinely do not know. What we do know is we love and miss Holly so much that it hurts and we will fight for justice on her behalf, no matter what it takes.

5–30 September

The easiest to say – and the hardest to do – is to establish a pattern to move forwards as a family. Our priority is to offer a secure, loving, trusting and truthful environment for Oliver. We agree to always tell him the truth about Holly and the police investigation; we will also encourage him to ask any questions he wants. If possible Nicola and I will grieve together in the evening once Oliver has gone to bed and try and reintroduce a little bit of humour and fun back into his life. But that does not mean not talking about Holly.

We ask friends and family to treat us normally and share thoughts of unity to make sure together that the murderer of Holly does not wreck our lives more.

Two things dominate my thoughts – the burning need to get justice for Holly and the very real possibility of no trial occurring. I start to make a specific plan. Over the last few weeks I have seen the strength of the written word many thousands of times over. I have also seen how writing a farewell letter to Holly was a way, not of coping with or deflecting, but of expressing extreme emotional distress. By way of regaining a small degree of control over my life, I decide to record my daily observations on matters of a personal nature and on issues relating to the investigation:

'To a much loved and very special little girl who we never had the privilege of meeting.

May you rest in peace.

From Stewart, Chris and Trudie.'

Our three FLOs wrote these words on their floral tribute at Holly's funeral. There would be no more important people than these three during the year ahead as they became trusted members of our family and social group. They would be tested to the extreme, so would their knowledge and professionalism. We would come to rely on their confidentiality, sensitivity, reassurance and kindness. We know this saga will not end quickly. Confusion, anger, guilt and even denial accompany the strongest of all our emotions – sadness.

On 9 September 2002, the new term for Holly's old school, St Andrew's, starts. We destroyed the class photo of 2002 because Maxine Carr was in it. Like the Chapman family, we attend the morning assembly which will be followed by the release of two doves by Kevin Proctor. We hope that our being there is not too startling or distressing for the children. Four hundred and thirty children stare fixedly at us as we take our seats. The head of the school, Geoff Fisher, tells the children not to be afraid to talk about the events of August and says this new term can represent a new beginning. He is heard in total silence. I feel desperately sad for Geoff. He has so much respect from the community but who would want to be in his shoes today? Holly's year group sits to our left. Nicola and I know most of them as they have appeared on many of Holly's school year photographs.

The short assembly ends and the children are asked to stand outside for the release of the doves. It's pouring with rain but the children don't complain a bit as they look upwards. High in the sky, Kevin's two doves complete two circles of the school grounds before disappearing towards the grey horizon.

I feel it is now appropriate to do one newspaper interview to say thank you to the police, community and the vicar for everyone's efforts. I give the interview to the local *Cambridge*

Holly aged 7.

Holly aged 18 months.

Holly aged 6.

Holly aged 2
years 6 months.

Family holiday in Gran Canaria.

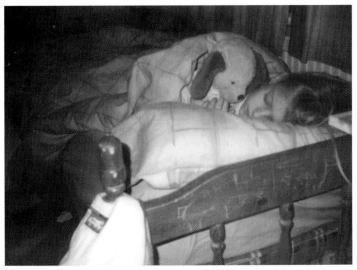
Holly aged 9. In bed with Snoozums during a sleepover at Jessica's house.

Holly aged 10 (October 2001). Nicola and Holly are bridesmaids at Robert and Trudie Wright's wedding.

Holly aged 10 with Oliver aged 12.

2001. Holly, Oliver and Ryan Fitchett. The first Christmas at
Red House Gardens.

Holly aged 10. Her last
school photograph.

Family photograph at Rob and Trudie's wedding on
20 October 2001.

Family photograph with Donna Paxton Tomb on her
wedding day. Holly was bridesmaid for her godmother
Donna on 15 August 1998.

Holly as a bridesmaid at Mark and Sarah Saunders'
wedding in August 1997.

Christmas 2000. Holly aged 9 and Oliver aged 11.

Kevin and Holly being silly at the penultimate family barbecue on Sunday, 28 July 2002.

Holly and Jessica's last ever photograph. Holly was aged, as she used to say, 10 and three-quarters.

Evening News and my friend James Fuller. He is well prepared and that makes it easier than anticipated. Only a couple of months ago, James thrilled Holly by taking her for a ride through the countryside in his sports car, and here he is now writing about her death.

We also go to the Village College for another release of doves. Again, we hope that this symbolic release will help start the new term on a positive note. Arrangements are slightly different this time, however, as the 1,335 pupils are out on the school field following a fire drill. They fall in line as we approach; they are all silent, which is amazing with over 1,000 children. The weather is better than last Monday, Kevin Proctor again steps forward with the basket of doves. He opens it and they fly high into the sky and, then, suddenly change direction. Everyone watches in disbelief as they fly straight towards the caretaker's house and complete two circles above it. It couldn't have been scripted more poignantly.

Nicola and I visit various parts of the school to bless them in the company of Tim Alban Jones, but we know we can't stay long. The police want us home because there has been a significant development and it is too serious to share over the telephone. We spend so much time now trying to second guess what is happening. Our conclusions are:

- *Something has happened to Ian Huntley.*
- *Something has happened to Maxine Carr.*
- *Maxine Carr has announced her intention to 'change sides'.*
- *New evidence has been found to implicate a third person (based on the medium's observations).*
- *Ian Huntley has made a confession.*

We are miles out. The police tell us one of the Family Liaison Officers for the Chapman family, DC Brian Stevens has been arrested this morning on child pornography charges. It almost beggars belief. We are, of course, relieved that nothing has happened that will directly affect the trial, but the implications are ghastly. First, there will be another period of intense media coverage, just when we want the very opposite. For the Chapmans it's far more personal, of course. Brian Stevens read the poem for their family at the Celebration of Life service and this wonderful service has just been tainted. If Stevens is guilty, Nicola and I will have to accept that Holly has not only been murdered by a potential paedophile, but also that her funeral was attended by one.

I have already said how worried we are that the psychiatrists would allow Huntley to escape being tried. We are relieved when we learn he will be placed back into the prison system rather than the hospital system, as he has been finally assessed fit to stand trial. We did not know then that a former girlfriend had given a statement that Huntley had once told her that, when he murdered a girl, he would play the mental card – to get away with it.

But we still have problems with the police and their 'best' – don't make me laugh – practice of not telling us real information we desperately need. Still, one of the few things they do reveal is that Maxine Carr was definitely not in Soham that Sunday. Local rumours and we thought 'credible' witnesses had led us to believe the opposite. We had been asking, 'How could she be involved with hurting two girls who she helped to teach?' Confirming she was not in Soham that terrible night makes us hate her a little less and hate Huntley even more. He must have tricked the girls into the house, as his story of Maxine Carr being upstairs in the bath cannot have been true. Surely, if Maxine Carr has an ounce of decency in her, she will step forward and say what she knows?

Nicola has been asked to give a statement detailing not only what food we had at last August's barbecue but the manufacturers of each and every product used. The police are so keen that Chris escorts Nicola down to the local shop to buy the same desserts again. The police need a chemical analysis of the ingredients so that they can be compared with the contents of Holly and Jessica's stomachs. This is macabre but, since we know when Holly and Jessica ate at the barbecue, and since the rate of digestion can be calculated, this analysis will reveal more about the time of their death. It will also show if Holly or Jessica ate anything else, or had been given drugs or alcohol. We console ourselves by thinking of the point of all this. If the contents of the stomachs only contain the barbecue and the food has hardly been digested, then both girls died soon after finishing their meal. It eliminates the traumatic thought that either girl could have been held captive for a long time and been subjected to sexual incidents.

Our lives have changed so dramatically that we have to hope for the 'good news' that the children died quickly.

Some better news comes from Harkness New Roses. After hearing my poem at Ely Cathedral they have offered to dedicate a new rose as a lasting memorial, to be called 'The Soham Rose'. We all need a lift and this helps. The Soham Rose is commissioned and, very generously, a percentage of sales are offered to the Holly and Jessica Memorial Fund. The rose is going to be the palest of pink, which looks absolutely superb against the dark green leaves.

Behind the scenes two independent advisors are being selected to represent the community on the investigation which is named Operation Fincham. We have said we think this arrangement is unnecessary and have been ignored. The Chapmans and ourselves are already out of the police information loop. If two community members are appointed to monitor and participate in the decision-making process with the police, two people in our community will know more about the investigation than the parents of the victims. How can this be right?

We get an unexpected call from Archie Steele, the piper. Archie had been asked to pipe at a wedding in the Scottish village of Kilchrennan. On the outskirts, he called at a house to confirm directions for the church. The lady owner asked him if he was the piper who played during the Ely Cathedral Service and invited him in for a cup of tea.

'Do you know who wrote "Samantha's Lullaby"?' she said. Archie, of course, had been trying to find out. Before she could divulge the name of the composer, Arthur Gillies strolled past the window. A few seconds later, Archie was talking with the mysterious composer himself.

Trying to get back to any normality at home is hard. On Saturday 28 September, Oliver asks if he could be allowed to swap and move into Holly's bedroom. It is twice the size of his own and he could do with the extra space. Our own emotions surge somewhat as we come to terms with maybe 'losing' Holly's bedroom in its present form. But if Oliver has no fears or concerns about moving into his sister's bedroom, as parents, we should follow his example. (Privately both Nicola and I are pleased at Oliver's request and think of it as a positive sign of how he is coping.)

There is no time like the present, so all three of us walk into Holly's bedroom to begin to store and clear her personal effects. Nicola concentrates on sorting out Holly's clothing for charity, and gasps very loud as she holds up a pair of Holly's trousers. Nicola explains that these are the trousers she told the police Holly was wearing when she left the house on 4 August. We must contact our FLO Stewart to tell him this was wrong. He reassures us this will not affect the case in a negative way and that a new statement can be completed during his next visit.

All afternoon we examine different toys, games, books and knick-knacks Holly played with. They evoke many happy memories. We get upset, of course, as we remember and talk about big and small moments of Holly's all too brief life. As we pull ourselves together, Nicola notices an envelope attached to Holly's clipboard. Inside is a letter Holly has written to a record company, informing them that she is enclosing a demo tape. The tape features soon-to-be superstars Holly Wells and her friend Natalie Parr singing a few karaoke-based tracks. It's very clear from the letter that this is not the first time Holly has gone to such trouble! How we miss this fiercely independent, clear-thinking young lady from our lives.

Over the last few Sundays I have been attending church and I have slowly begun to gain a little understanding of the strength of faith. But this has caused a few problems, as some friends and family question the purpose of my 'directional change'. My wife Nicola is my sternest critic. Every Sunday morning, she asks the same question, 'If you get in contact with your new-found God, will you ask him why he allowed your 10-year-old daughter to be murdered?' I promise Nicola that this will indeed be the first question I ask. Like her, I know that no answer will ever be satisfactory.

Through the Bishop of Ely, I have been offered a private confirmation service in Prior Crauden's Chapel in the grounds of the cathedral. I appreciate that and the time is fixed for an afternoon service on 3 October. The only problem is that this is one day before what would have been Holly's eleventh birthday. I have misjudged totally for the run up to Holly's birthday proves too much emotionally to cope with. Out of the window goes our bravado, best-laid plans and future guidelines as the most important date since our daughter's murder creeps ever nearer. On the morning of the 3rd, Nicola is so distressed that I have to cancel or attend the confirmation service alone. Although I feel embarrassed about this, I cannot leave Nicola alone in her despair.

All morning we try to comfort and reassure one another and we eventually decide to attend the confirmation service. Dr Bridget Nicholls, the Bishop's Chaplain, welcomes us. She has gone to a great deal of trouble producing a printed batch of order of services as she expected a large group. Rather meekly, I say there will just be the two of us coming. I'm about to add we do not really have any religious friends to ask to attend. Before I say that, Bridget says, 'A private service, how lovely,' and so, no embarrassed explanations needed.

The service is very uplifting for me and I thank everyone involved. When we get home, Nicola drops her composed 'public face'. To see her in such emotional distress is desperately soul-destroying.

4 *October* 2002

For the last two months there has been a void in our lives and our home. Today would have been Holly's eleventh birthday. It would also have been Holly's last year at St Andrew's School, a year she was immensely looking forward to. Each year the final year group at St Andrew's have an opportunity of going away with the school for a week-long trip to the Isle of Wight. One of Holly's last pieces of school work explained her expectations of year 6:

> 'I am looking forward to the Isle of Wight because I think it will be fun and I will get away from my brother for a whole week! I would also like to be one of the oldest in the school and I would really like to be librarian, however, I am a bit worried about the SATs and what the teachers will think of me.
>
> I think that I will be expected to be sensible and hardworking and also to get good grades in my SATs. I will be expected to have well written work and be proud of it, also to have good behaviour in and out of class.
>
> I think my targets should be similar to my ones last year: to redraft carefully and to use complex sentences where appropriate.
>
> I think I am good at art and literacy because they are my favourite subjects and they're fun.'

God bless you, Holly.

Thinking about how excited Holly would have been today makes me unable to sleep this evening and I go downstairs to write some letters. Two of these are to families who have suffered the same kind of shock and loss as us, and been in the glare of the media. For Bob, Sally and Gemma Dowler, the search for justice for their beautiful daughter and sister Milly is still ongoing. I harbour a sense of guilt because, at least, we have a suspect in custody. And I am touched by the kind words of John and Sheila Tate who, after 24 years, still hope for an opportunity of burying their young daughter, Genette. Her body has never been found.

There are no right words for me to send but I thank them for their letter which explains the long, long journey they have taken together. It gives me a flicker of hope that Nicola and I can come through our own crisis together.

Our daughter has been murdered and we go on holiday. It sounds appalling, but we booked our annual holiday to Gran Canaria and decided not to cancel as Oliver desperately wants to go. We don't want to go, we are nervous of leaving the police protected environment we have got used to, and we want to be on hand if anything happens. But the trauma specialist's advice was to have something positive for Oliver to focus on. So we will go and our nephew Thomas, who is the same age as Oliver, will come too.

Nicola needs to amend her passport, as both Holly and Oliver are listed on it. Our relief at receiving the 'replacement' passport back in time for our departure is shattered when we check inside. There are no new details printed. Instead, a single black biro line has been drawn through Holly's name. It seems harshly insensitive.

A few days before our departure, I meet with Meridian Broadcasting Limited. They have asked me to consider writing and presenting this year's Christmas message for Channel 4. Every year they ask a member of the public who has come through adversity and, this year, they feel I am right. It is a very humbling offer and I agree in principle. It may also help raise a few pounds by way of a donation from Meridian to the Holly and Jessica Fund. It is also something positive to concentrate on.

I ask if Chris and Stewart could accompany me to the meeting and they are worried. They want the Crown Prosecution Service (the CPS) to approve before I can accept any offer. Chris and Stewart worry that if I give the Christmas message, Huntley and Carr's defence will be able to argue that their clients cannot get a fair trial. Given the huge amount of publicity this case has already attracted, including the sordid past of both Huntley and Carr, how can my message, which will explain how we are coping as a family and trying to plan some future, be relevant to the fair trial issue?

Within 24 hours, the CPS advise the police not to allow me to proceed with the broadcast. It's more than advice. There is the veiled threat of applying for an injunction to prevent the broadcast. This kind of interference in my life is becoming tedious. The CPS also reveal that my interview with James Fuller and the *Cambridge Evening News* will be disclosed to the defence teams and that they may use it to claim Huntley and Carr cannot get a fair trial. What a sad fucking world it is. The CPS add that I may be a 'live' witness and this may somehow taint my evidence, which again seems rubbish. I know no one who believes the defence team will want to cross-examine the father of a murdered daughter in the witness box, so why can't they accept my statements so we can know more of what is going on with the case? I wonder if the police and the prosecution have any idea of the hurt and anger we feel as a result of being excluded. Is anyone pushing on our behalf to help rectify this position? Unfortunately I suspect not.

Nicola is in tears as we pack for our holiday. This will be the first time in ten years that we go on holiday without Holly. Nicola decides to pack a heart made of plastic beads which Holly had made for her earlier in the summer. Unfortunately the heart is broken in half and there is only one half to take. I try and cheer Nicola up by confirming that this is okay as we too are broken-hearted. Nicola packs the half heart and we think no more of it.

In the queue at Stansted Airport, people go quiet as more and more of them turn to stare at us and, then, look away. We queue in total silence. Our fellow passengers seem quite anxious, perhaps fearing they may actually have to sit next to one of us on the aeroplane! Murder embarrasses. No one knows what to say. Better if we were invisible. By the time we reach the front of the queue, we too find ourselves staring downwards to avoid any uncomfortable eye contact.

At the hotel we unpack our things together and Nicola finds the half heart and places it on top of the chest of drawers. As I pick up the empty suitcases to place them inside one another, the missing second half drops out from the lining. We look at each other for a few seconds before breaking down once more, for we both take it to be a little sign that Holly is with us, after all.

When we go to the swimming pool, Nicola insists I walk round the entire complex searching for a sun bed. I must not miss an unoccupied bed so I peer around and notice that everyone is either sitting up or standing still, watching my every move. It is an exceptionally uncomfortable feeling. Eventually I find a sun bed. You'd think that people would have the good manners not to pay us any attention, but no. Guests next to us slowly but surely gather their things, in silence, and walk away. We now have plenty of sun beds to choose from and it makes us wonder what it is like to be German on holiday!

In the evening, people point fingers, stare with their mouths open, or look twice at us as we visit the occasional shop or bar. But in one way it is worse than at home. Here people sometimes recognise Nicola and me, say a friendly opening 'hello' or 'fancy seeing you here' – and then they have a no-memory moment as they try to work out just who we are. Sometimes the penny drops, after a few lines of conversation, but sometimes it does not, so I have to make a small speech explaining why they 'know' us. Said speech would be on these lines:

'I know you think you know us and you are probably going to feel terrible about this, but you only recognise us because regrettably we have all been in the news recently as it was our daughter Holly who was murdered in Soham.' Many people break down and cry on the spot, and so, quite bizarrely, we have to try to comfort total strangers in the Canary Islands!

Then we visit the Trafford bar to watch England's match against Macedonia. The bar is packed with England supporters and, as I make my way to order some drinks, I become more and more aware of the growing silence behind me. When I place my order and put my money down, the only sound is the sound of the commentary on TV. The young English lady serving picks up my

Goodbye, Dearest Holly

money, places it gently back into my hand and whispers, 'You don't have to pay for your drinks here.' It is all too much and I return to my seat with tears welling up.

It is 11 long days before we have a real conversation with any one, but for the last couple of nights, we socialise with the Gemmell family from Oban in Scotland, near the Isle of Seil. As I share the details of Archie the piper, and how he found out who wrote 'Samantha's Lullaby', Dorothy Gemmell comes up with the answer of Arthur Gillies. Not only does she know the man, but her teenage son John who plays the pipes has been judged by Arthur in competition. It is indeed a very small world.

Throughout I have been in contact with Chris Mead, asking for any updates or developments. I have been allowed a police-issue mobile telephone for the duration of the holiday, which is appreciated. Over two weeks I hear certain details about Huntley and Carr but I am not privileged to hear the specifics. Result – I feel even more frustrated and excluded, especially as we are away.

Huntley and Carr were meant to be interviewed during the first week of our holiday. But Huntley and his legal team successfully block this. This is bloody frustrating and seems to me to have all the hallmarks of a guilty man running scared. Common sense dictates that an innocent person would talk freely with the police. Huntley has already been charged and, in the eyes of the law, this means there is enough evidence in place to justify that. Therefore the defendant does not have to 'voluntarily' be interviewed after being charged. (Technically, defendants can still be interviewed to clear up ambiguities, which the police try to do. But, Huntley blanks the interview and continues to feign mental illness.) Our prosecution team must convince a jury 'beyond reasonable doubt' that Huntley murdered Holly and Jessica. The onus is wholly on the prosecution and Huntley has a right to remain silent. I have never had any reason to think about this before in my life, but it seems almost unbelievable and grossly unfair that this is how the legal system works. To make matters worse, Chris also explains that each and every part of the case against Huntley and Carr

must be disclosed to their legal teams. This 'gesture' is not recip-
rocated. The defence teams do not have to inform the prosecution what their line of defence will be and they can use a 'hijack
defence' at the last moment in court. So every set of forensic
results, as well as each statement against Huntley and Carr, is
handed over to the defence who, in turn, hand this information
over to their clients. As they wait in custody with nothing better
to do, they can read, re-read and then put together an explanation that fits around the evidence, as presented. I find this terri-
fying.

The loss of Holly is catastrophic, but the thought of losing her
without gaining justice would be life- and soul-destroying.

The police once again offer Maxine Carr the chance to clear
up any ambiguities. It looks like she will accept, but then her
legal team declines to proceed. The road ahead is going to be a
long one. There may be a little chink of light on the horizon,
however, as the prosecution papers to be served against Carr will
be ready for November. This may well act as a catalyst for her
legal team to suggest a different strategy, but only time will tell.
If Carr does decide to 'change sides', then this may well ease the
negative public perception against her and get her a shorter
sentence. The police feel she is under enormous pressure and
showing signs of beginning to crack. Carr has also admitted
charges relating to DSS fraud. She claims she was forced to do
it by Huntley, which shows she is prepared to lie for him. The
police and CPS now have a difficult tactical decision to make.
Do they prosecute Carr for fraud before the main trial or wait
until afterwards?

As we are on holiday, Nicola's mother is at our house doing a
little bit of cleaning for us in our absence, when she answers a
telephone call. It is yet another call from a certain Mr Westgate.
I have been receiving calls from him since August 2002 and what
starts as a fairly lucid attack on 'the system' quickly degenerates
into erratic and illogical comments which I find distressing. But
this time it is not me who is accepting the call, but Diane and we

feel powerless to ease her concerns, stuck as we are many hundreds of miles away. Sensibly, Diane rings the police.

Chris is right about Maxine Carr feeling the pressure as she collapses and is taken to hospital. I do not know what the specific reason is for her collapse but I do know that the police have some damning statements against her character, following her antics in a night club. Ian Huntley was hardly the ideal partner either and their relationship was not going too well in August 2002. While Carr was away, he had been trying to arrange a date with a woman in Soham for the Sunday evening. If Huntley believed Maxine Carr was going away to have a 'good time' and he didn't get the opportunity of doing the same, would this 'failure' affect his mind-set in such a way that he could kill two girls? Logic says not, but as we are not dealing with a straightforward individual, it cannot wholly be ruled out. Once again we will have to be patient and wait for the full facts to emerge.

The police have interviewed 28 of Huntley's former girlfriends and they appear pleased with their findings, though they do not explain why to us.

In Gran Canaria, we also learn that there is to be an arrest in Soham of an individual who is linked to the same porn charges as Brian Stevens. The police intend to keep this low key and away from the attention of the press. Yet again it is worry about the unfair trial argument, which will be used by both defence teams.

Some better news eventually comes from Chris. The police are very pleased with the way the case is developing and they now have some forensic results which will take the case forwards. We are delighted. We also receive the grim news of the analysis of Holly's stomach contents; what she ate at the barbecue was not digested and her stomach did not contain alcohol or drugs. Holly died virtually straight after eating her tea. It is, of course, any detail relating directly to Holly which causes us the most distress and Chris senses that. He uses an analogy which we will often come back to over the next 15 months; it is that of a pack of cards. 'At the moment both legal teams have some cards each.

Over time as the case comes together, we will slowly but surely add to the strength of our hand and at some stage they will have to show theirs. Hopefully, we will play the last card.'

We get some sad news when we return to Soham, as Mark, the brother of our former babysitter Donna Fiebig, has been killed in a car crash. It is another stark reminder about how random life is. Mark is buried next to Holly and Jessica in the Fordham Road cemetery.

November 2002

There is more police work to do. We are shown photographs of Holly's knickers in order to give a statement confirming them to be hers. We are also shown a photograph of the bin in which the clothing was found inside the Hangar building on the school site as well as being asked to provide hair samples. It is hardly the best way to start the month, but worse is to come. We are so frustrated at being denied information and having to second guess developments that the head of the investigation, Temporary Det. Supt Chris Stevenson calls to see us in person. He acknowledges our frustrations and pledges to try and improve our position. The timing is good for he is about to start a three-day meeting with the Crown Prosecution Service. We wait on tenterhooks for Mr Stevenson to tell us what has been decided. But we hear nothing and so we get even more frustrated, and I am sorry to say the brunt of our anger is directed at the FLOs.

Eight interminably long days later we are eventually told the outcome of the meeting. Mr Stevenson, the CPS and Counsel for the Crown have decided not to pass on any further information with immediate effect. No information at all. We are completely distraught. With the trial at least one year away, this is going to make our life impossible. Maybe at some stage of my life I will be able to accept that the need to protect the integrity of the investigation is greater than the needs of a victim's family, but now I cannot. I also see Mr Stevenson in a new and unflattering light.

He has not upheld his personal pledge to us and he has not had the decency to let us know of the U-turn in person. The fact that this decision has been made and withheld from my family for over a week is almost unforgivable. Despite the rhetoric and the best efforts of our FLOs, my family and I remain at the bottom rung of the senior management's priorities. We don't fucking matter. This hurts very much indeed. I also wonder if senior management, feeling that our FLOs are close to us, have started to withhold information from them too.

Over the last few days I have tried desperately to find a way to move forwards and eventually realise the idea of writing a book can address these issues. It will give me an opportunity to tell people about Holly, about her unfulfilled potential, her talents, her character and why we feel her loss so deeply. It will let people see the debilitating effect losing a child can have on a family. It will give me the chance to put a victim's views across and let me explain what it is like to be involved in a police investigation. Hopefully it will also allow me to 'reclaim' Holly. Each and every one of these reasons is individually important but, added to my desire to be proactive, my writing project feels like my personal salvation and catharsis.

I have previously written invoices and business plans. I know nothing about what to do next in terms of finding someone to guide me in writing a book. Clearly I also need advice from the police as to how this project can be managed and what, if any, restrictions will be put in place. I will not do it if it poses any risk to the trial ahead, personal salvation or not. The police ask their media representative, Matt Tapp, who is also the managing partner of Talking Heads, based in Cambridge, to come and speak with me later in the month.

On 15 November, the common sense of writing becomes clear to me. In Norwich Crown Court it is decided that the trial is going to take place at the Old Bailey, London. For us this is a disappointing decision. We are going to have to brace ourselves for a long journey to the capital each and every day we wish to attend. The main reason for moving out of East Anglia is to enable a 'fair trial' for Huntley and Carr. This phrase 'fair trial' is beginning to wear remarkably thin.

In the late afternoon I am window cleaning in Upware. Chris, who is with Gaye Meadows, the FLO for the Chapman family, finds me and asks me to come down the ladder and join him in the car.

'Kevin, did Holly ever suffer from nosebleeds?' Chris asks.

'I don't think so recently, but I cannot be certain. Why?'

'It is to clarify a point that has arisen in the enquiry.'

'What point is that then, Chris?'

'*Sorry*, you know I cannot tell you.'

My mind races with the implications. Have the police found some of Holly's blood in Huntley's house or car? Have they found some of Holly's blood on her own clothing? Have they found some of Holly's blood on Huntley's clothing? Is this a clue to the manner of Holly's death?

As I get more agitated and try to hold back my tears, I implore Chris to explain. Chris asks me to telephone Nicola and ask her the same question. Nicola's answer is more detailed than mine. Holly did occasionally suffer from nosebleeds, usually during hot weather, although not regularly. Holly had not had a nosebleed on 4 August before she left the meal table. Chris makes an on the spot decision to try and quell my distress. Satisfied that both parents have answered the question without knowing the reason for it, Chris believes it is his duty not to leave us in a position where what we imagine is, in fact, worse than the reality. He has a duty of care to us, he explains. I am simply told that the police have a witness statement from 'somebody' who has said that Huntley had told them that one of the girls suffered a nosebleed. There seems little point in asking details of whom, where, or at what time, this witness had seen Holly but it does not stop the mind racing.

For me the emotional effects of thinking about Holly and her nosebleed and whether she had been struck so hard by Huntley to cause this, are far-reaching. Over the last few months, as a coping mechanism, I have told myself that Holly did not suffer in her death; now the reality seems different. I am forced to confront Holly's last moments. (In the weeks and months ahead my fears over how much Holly suffered would manifest themselves in the form of countless vivid nightmares. Some of the images would be so clear and repetitive that I would record them with the police, in case, somehow, they became relevant.)

Grieving is taking its toll. Nicola cannot sleep and she feels drained as well as looking terribly drawn. She is trying so hard but it is obvious her spirit has yet to return. Even shopping is terribly difficult as members of the public make it uncomfortable for her. We agree she needs to leave this pressured environment and decide that after Christmas she will go and stay with Donna in America, to get two weeks of peace and anonymity. I also can't sleep but the reason is slightly different, for I do not want to go to sleep, as every other night I am awoken by nightmares of Holly's death.

On 26 November, Matt Tapp comes to see me to discuss my book project. My memories of him are positive from the last press conference he organised and our FLOs feel he will be able to give good advice. Matt Tapp breaks it down into pre-trial and post-trial options, with the latter being the most important. He says the options are:

- *Book: serialisation in newspaper.*
- *FLO training courses nationwide.*
- *Police Press Officer training courses.*
- *Legislative change – a champion.*

The top option is the only one I need to seek Matt's further advice on, but the bottom option is also thought-provoking. Chris believes this case may lead to a change in legislation. Matt Tapp has access to senior officers and when he agrees with Chris that I could get involved in campaigning for the law to change, it is a sign that all is not well. It is difficult to see how things can get any worse, and all this just adds to the frustration of being excluded.

By the end of the first meeting we have a basic plan of action. Matt agrees to identify some literary agents who may be interested in such a project. All I want at this moment is an opportunity to write, but I fully appreciate the need for confidential professional advice. The police have provided me with that. I am most grateful.

December 2002

I never thought I would need a literary agent just as I never thought I would meet royalty. Both are happening now because Holly died. We have been invited to have tea with Prince Charles at Sandringham, Norfolk. The invitation was extended to us through the Bishop of Ely and the gesture is yet another sign of the enormous empathy for both families. The vicar, Tim Alban Jones, has also been invited and offers to drive us to Sandringham. In the morning of 4 December I do paperwork and write the books up for the business.

I open the bank statements, and am completely shocked to find that there is virtually no money in the account, which should not be the case. It seems my weekly cash and cheque deposit envelopes, normally banked through the hole in the wall letter box at Lloyds TSB in Soham, every Sunday, have not been credited. Other deposits as far back as October and November, have also not been credited. Three thousand pounds are missing, mostly in cash. I am so angry at this development. I have an excellent relationship with my bank and have been using the weekly deposit envelope for many years, but will they believe that I have banked this amount, mostly in cash over the last month or so? The short answer turns out to be no. The bank will do nothing without some kind of fraud being proved, my account will have to remain short of funds. I have to tell my business partner, Scott, who is as affected with his first baby due by the end of December – and new babies cost.

The start to what should be a memorable day could not have been any worse.

We get to Sandringham some 45 minutes early. It is dark and freezing cold and the thought of just waiting in the cars is not a pleasant one, so we decide to enter the grounds, hoping that this would not cause offence. Once through security, we drive up to the main house which is surrounded by vast open grounds. It is a shame it is too dark to appreciate the view.

No one answers when we ring at the front door which makes us more nervous. For ten minutes in biting cold winds, we try to gain entrance to the home of our future King.

Eventually one of Prince Charles's butlers bids us all welcome and we are shown into the library/office area, while he disappears to arrange some cups of tea. The butler comes back soon with tea and a selection of biscuits. As I pick mine up, I say to the butler:

'Are those biscuits from Charles's own Duchy range?'

'Yes they are, sir, only we would normally say His Royal Highness.'

Point taken!

We are left to our own devices, awaiting the arrival of Prince Charles's Lady in Waiting who is to give a quick lesson on social etiquette, not one of my strongest subjects. Now that the butler has spoken we can relax about it just a little and look at our surroundings. The wonderful floor-to-ceiling wooden shelving is packed with ancient-looking, impressively bound books, which appear far too important to touch. But one small book catches my eye as its title includes the words 'Social Intercourse'. As the vicar and I glance through the book, Oliver sidles up and seeing the word 'Intercourse' on the spine of the book, asks in all innocence, 'Are there any pictures, Dad?' It takes a minute or two to again compose ourselves but fortunately we manage to do so before the Lady in Waiting arrives to speak to us!

'Right, Oliver, do you understand that when Prince Charles arrives for introductions, you offer a small bow of your head followed by a handshake and initially say "Your Royal Highness" before using "Sir" thereafter.'

'Yes, Dad, but can we go last please?'

'I am sure we can.'

Nerves and tea seem to have affected everyone and we are all glad to be offered the opportunity of using the toilets. In palaces, it seems the loos are quite a distance. We walk through the corridors of history lined with ancient armour, war memorabilia and fantastic paintings. Many former monarchs stare down from the walls. It is almost a shame actually to reach the toilets. Inside the toilet area are cartoons and caricatures by famous newspaper artists, originals, of course. As I wait for Nicola to come out, Mrs Camilla Parker Bowles appears. It is the quaintest of handshakes and hellos before agreeing that we will leave the formal introductions for when we have tea.

Once back in the safety of our library sanctum, I regale everyone with the fact I have just met Mrs Parker Bowles in the corridors outside the toilets and wonder out loud if this is what is meant by the 'Royal We'!

Prince Charles's Lady in Waiting comes back. It is time to meet the man himself. The Chapman family and Tim Alban Jones are first through the door and there is just time to go through the order of proceedings once more with Oliver, who has become much quieter. I can hardly tell him not to be nervous as I am in the same state, so I simply guide my young son forward for his big moment. Oliver manages his verbal introduction, bow of head and handshake in one stunning movement which allows a certain father to witness a comic moment. Oliver catches his mum up as quickly as possible, relieved that his worries are now behind him. After my own formal introduction to both Prince Charles and Mrs Parker Bowles, we are all chaperoned into the stunning room to sit down to an old-fashioned high tea. Prince Charles directs where he would like everyone to sit. Nicola and Sharon Chapman find themselves sitting either side of Prince Charles. Opposite, Les Chapman and Tim Alban Jones sit next to Mrs Parker Bowles. I sit next to Mrs Parker Bowles, too, with Oliver to my right. Opposite us sit the two other guests, Rebecca and Alison Chapman.

Prince Charles defuses the potential awkward silence, saying he is delighted we could all make it and that he was really quite unsure if we would accept the invitation. As he talks to Nicola and Sharon, the rest of the table begins to relax. My conversation with Mrs Parker Bowles proves to be quite delightful and I find myself talking to a lady who is not only aware of the details of our troubles, but is a mother who is sensitive. The food is delicate with the tiniest sandwiches and, rather unexpectedly, crumpets with marmite, which take a little bit of getting used to! There is also a range of Duchy short bread and various chocolate biscuits. Mrs Parker Bowles asks my opinion of the dark chocolate as it's a new range. The orange-flavoured plain chocolate biscuits are very good and I say so out loud.

Prince Charles talks with everyone individually around the table and, as he goes clockwise, Oliver is first up.

'So, Oliver, do you like school?'

'No.'

As there is no 'Sir' added by Oliver, Nicola and I try to make eye contact with him to remind him of the earlier lesson, but to no avail.

'You must like some subjects, though, Oliver?'

'Sport's okay.'

Oliver, my etiquette-conscious son, now puts his elbows on the table and supports his chin with the palms of his hands, sulking as he has to talk about the subject which least interests him, i.e. school.

'Do you support a football team?'

'Manchester United.' Oliver can finally relax as Prince Charles moves towards me.

'Mr Wells, how does this window-cleaning work, where does one go?'

'Well it is very hard work, Sir, and at this time of year it is a harsh environment working outdoors. My business is now predominantly based in Cambridge, which is a beautiful city to be working in.'

'I went to University there.'

'Yes, I know, Sir.'

'Do you clean for any of the colleges?'

'The longer-established cleaning companies tend to have the college contracts so it is very difficult to get a foot in the door, so to speak, Sir.'

'Would you like me to have a word?' He says it with humour, which captures the atmosphere of the afternoon perfectly.

'If you have the time, Sir, thank you!'

And that brings to an end my talk with the future King of England. Then Tim, Les, Rebecca and Alison receive the royal attention.

'Are you actually from Soham, Mr Wells?' Mrs Parker Bowles asks. The question is simple enough yet inadvertently it leads me into a terrible *faux pas*. I could have said yes, for indeed I have spent 36½ years out of 39 in my home town. I could have said, yes, other than being born in Ely at the Royal Air Force Hospital, just six miles down the road, but I don't. I give the full spec. 'Yes, I spent all of my young life in Soham and most of my adult life too. I was born just six miles away at the old RAF Hospital in Ely, which is now called The Princess of Wales Hospital.' Oops! I realise that in this place you should not mention Diana. I wait to be lifted from my chair by two footmen (ex SAS probably) who, somehow, have already been summoned. But Mrs Parker Bowles is not phased, I am not thrown out on my bum, and the moment of embarrassment passes. My heart rate goes back to normal.

'I am sure you people have much better things to do with your time.' That sentence from Prince Charles indicates teatime is over. As we prepare to leave, Mrs Parker Bowles asks if I would like to take home the spare chocolate-orange biscuits which I praised.

'No, I am fine, thank you for offering,' I say. But Prince Charles has heard and, at once, summons his butler to get a box of the biscuits. The butler returns carrying a box of same and we are ready to leave again when Mrs Parker Bowles spots that the biscuits are, in fact, ginger and not the orange ones. Do not bring princes the wrong biscuits. Within seconds the hapless butler is sent once more for a second box of biscuits and it is a wonderful light-hearted moment on which to end. Before Prince Charles says goodbye he shows us some of the paintings. This most uplifting of afternoons ends with a handshake and verbal thank you – in my case, while balancing two boxes of biscuits at the same time. I am struck by how kind Prince Charles and Mrs Parker Bowles were.

Oliver created the first laugh of the afternoon and, as we join Tim Alban Jones in his car, Oliver has the last laugh too. 'Who was that man we had tea with Dad and where was the Prince?' he asks. It could only come from Oliver! He'd been expecting to meet Prince William or Prince Harry apparently!

When we get back to Soham we change quickly as Nicola and I are guests for dinner at the vicarage with Tim and his wife, Cathy. We are joined by James and Alison Palmer who would be the first couple to hear the details of our day at Sandringham. I'm so absorbed in regaling them both that I butter my bread roll and begin to nibble. Nicola stares at me. I should not have started wolfing the bread roll. As Tim joins us to say grace before the meal, he adds, 'For what we are about to receive (and for what some of us have already started) may the Lord make us truly grateful!'

The next morning Chris agrees to report a theft at the bank and I am issued with a crime number. He has seen my paying-in books relating to the missing money and how upset and angry I am, and he believes I am telling the truth. Without prompting from me Chris speaks with Simon the manager. Chris asks if the bank had thought about any potential negative publicity if this story gets out. Quickly the bank changes its tune. Within a week of first realising the money was missing, a full unequivocal refund is given. (Many other customers would come forward to complain about missing money so the bank had to reassess its position still further. In the end a courier admitted a number of charges, and got a 9-month prison sentence for theft.)

For Nicola and me everything seems to be taking so long to happen. Each time we have a meeting with any of our FLOs, they ask questions and take statements and items from us. Before the end of the year, Nicola and I answer questions on areas such as: Have you ever been inside Ian Huntley's car? Do you have carpet anywhere in your house which matches this colour? Do you know where and when you bought Oliver and Holly's Manchester United shirts? Do you have any other Manchester United shirts in the house? Kevin, have you ever worn your Manchester United shirt while working at the Village College?

All Manchester United shirts belonging to family members were seized by the police, including a red England shirt for good measure. Different lines of questioning allow us to speculate. Nicola and I second-guess that fibres from Holly and Jessica's Manchester United shirts must have been recovered either from Huntley's house or car, probably the car. Our card hand, thank goodness, seems to be strengthening.

In mid-December the media report that Maxine Carr and Ian Huntley have 'split up'. Although the police do not confirm the story, it could make a great deal of sense. Whether or not Maxine Carr has been advised by her legal team to 'split', or whether she has started to realise her partner is responsible for two murders, remains to be seen. It is my gut feeling that there is something behind this story and that bodes well. Perhaps before the end of this most miserable of years, Maxine Carr may just do the decent thing and come to the aid of two desperate families.

The cameras return to film the annual Soham Village College Christmas carol service, which is held in Ely Cathedral. The Assistant Principal, Stephen Kenna has written a song entitled 'Two Little Angels' and both the Chapmans and ourselves are asked if we are going to attend. We decide we will not be going because neither Holly nor Jessica went to the Village College and so it seems slightly inappropriate. Mr Kenna has said there is a need apparently for a 'community-wide commemoration' but we stick to our position. Nobody tells us, however, that the service has been expanded to include Soham's primary schools and that it will include a reading from Holly and Jessica's friend, Natalie Parr. We would have attended to support Natalie, if we had known.

The East Coast Truckers Charity, the Northampton County Tavern Pub, Cambridgeshire Fire and Rescue Service, and Cambridgeshire Police have all made financial contributions to both families and to the Holly and Jessica Fund in the run-up to Christmas. There have also been smaller amounts from individuals collecting from work or down the local. All of these donations are accompanied by wonderfully uplifting letters which remind us that there is so much goodness in people's hearts. A couple of typical examples: Linda Wood-Mitchell sent a donation from her colleagues in an office at Leeds City Council and John Bull from East Ham sent a donation from a 'few Cockneys'. I hope that by mentioning a few, I will not offend others who donated. Money is also being sent directly to the trustees of the Holly and Jessica Fund. I don't know who to thank but rely on the trustees to do that on our behalf.

The largest donation turns out to be from the Cambridgeshire Police after four officers completed a football ground tour, collecting memorabilia for auction. Inspector Steve Selves, PC Paul Roberts, PC Ifor Maddox and PC Phil Enderby raised over £10,000 and we hoped to thank them in person at a 'sportsman's dinner'. But this idea is cancelled because the police fret – yet again – that any publicity will be used by the defence teams of Huntley and Carr to argue the trial cannot be fair. It is a scary thought, especially given that the media tend to report anything to do with Soham at the moment.

It's astonishing but we have to think about not just the state of

Huntley's relationship with Carr, but also about Huntley's parents' marriage. His parents have split up, it seems. If this is true, this may be bad news as the police believe that if Ian Huntley is going to open up to anyone it will be to his mother. She now seems to be heading to Ireland, so any chance of an unexpected break-through appears to have gone. Meanwhile, Maxine Carr seems to have recovered from her collapse, caused apparently by an eating disorder. Carr has also been downgraded from a Category A prisoner to Category B, so she is no longer segregated. I hope she will now meet individuals who will tell her how it really is and prick her so far missing conscience. Once again we read the news in the papers before the police tell us.

As the end of December draws nearer, we have to face our first Christmas without Holly. It is bleak and inescapable. Even Oliver seems withdrawn and slightly confused as to how he should behave, though we say that it is quite acceptable to be happy and excited, just like any other year. It seems an ideal opportunity to have a more intimate talk with him to see what we can do to make his life better, more normal. Although it is clear Oliver is anxious over something, we cannot get to the bottom of it, so once again Nicola and I agree to keep a close eye on our young son. Oliver gets upset when he sees Holly's picture on the television and in the newspapers. He also doesn't like it when the local newspaper billboards blazon headlines about Holly and Jessica week after week. I understand only too well but can only offer the hope that things will quieten down in the future. Together we speak about Christmas and write our cards in the quiet of my office. I ask Oliver to make an extra special effort to look after his mum over the next few weeks. In return, I promise him that we will both be doing the same for him. As he leaves my office, Oliver completely catches me off guard by asking, 'Who is going to look after you then, Dad?'

Our last dealings with the police before Christmas involve releasing a press statement because their press office is being inundated with calls about what both families will be doing. Although

I consider this to be a little intrusive, if completing a request relieves the pressure on the police, then it is worth doing. We say:

'Thank you for your enquiries relating to our Christmas plans. There are no itineraries in place, other than spending time with family and close friends during this poignant and reflective time. Your continued support in allowing that privacy to be maintained would be very much appreciated.'

All the media respected our request.

Monday 23 December

Nicola and I try to put on a brave face despite our acute sadness. After finishing work early, we go down to the Nursery at East Fen Common to get a wreath for Holly's grave. One of the owners, Helen, simply pushes back our wreath across the counter indicating that no payment is required. This kind gesture is enough to take us both over the edge and we sit in the car park crying together once more. Goodness knows when we are going to feel a little stronger. Nicola has chosen tonight to visit young Natalie Parr and her parents. Natalie is always in our thoughts and Nicola has some gifts to take with her. One is a copy of the cassette with Holly and Natalie singing together and a certificate drawn by Holly saying that Natalie is her best friend.

After Oliver is safely tucked into bed, Nicola breaks down with a very serious emotional issue, that of denial. I try my hardest to comfort and reassure her but cannot influence the direction of her thoughts. Nicola talks about our decision not to see the photographs of Holly's body. She moves to the possibility that the bodies may be those of two other children, before I remind her that the DNA tests were positive. From somewhere deep within her soul, Nicola announces that even though the probability is millions to one against a wrong DNA result, we still have a chance of seeing Holly alive again. We talk about this all evening before eventually Nicola accepts the inevitability of our true position again. She gets there partly by admitting her wish to see the photographs of Holly and Jessica in the New Year to try and put her mind at rest.

We do not realise it, but this will be the last day that Nicola and I have a shared emotional breakdown. For whatever reason, our individual grieving, so in tune for the last five months, is about to change.

For Oliver, extended family and close friends, Nicola and I try to be brave over Christmas. It is hard. We also discuss what we believe happened during August and how the case appears to be developing. We agree the following points:

- *Holly and Jessica left Red House Gardens together and were sighted together throughout their walk.*
- *Although Nicola and I were unable to give a statement to the police confirming Holly asked to go for a walk, we feel it is likely she did ask permission.*
- *The sightings confirm that Holly stayed within her agreed walking boundaries at all times.*
- *Holly was only allowed to walk without adult company if she was with a friend.*
- *Holly did not have her mobile telephone with her, but knew that Jessica had hers.*
- *Holly and Jessica's dreadful fate seems to have occurred by them being in the wrong place at the wrong time.*
- *As parents, we know Holly adhered to all guidelines in place.*
- *Holly and Jessica were two very bright communicative young girls, both a few weeks away from their eleventh birthday. Both were full of confidence and common sense.*
- *Both girls came from a stable family background, surrounded by love in an environment of trust and security.*
- *Holly and Jessica both enjoyed school immensely and had a healthy respect for their teachers.*
- *Holly and Jessica were tricked into the house at College Close by Huntley.*
- *Huntley used Maxine Carr's role of classroom teaching*

assistant to entice the girls into the house by telling the girls
she would like to see them.

- Holly and Jessica would have absolutely no reason to see
anything sinister in this invitation.
- The girls were taught about 'stranger danger' but no one
said you should be suspicious of people known to you in
case they may have a hidden agenda.
- Huntley's account of Maxine Carr being in the bath is
rubbish. It is almost certain, however, that he said this to
the girls to get one of them upstairs.
- Whichever girl went upstairs first, it would not take her long
to realise that something was not right and raise the alarm
by screaming or shouting.
- Either Holly or Jessica would run to the aid of their respective friend immediately.
- Therefore we are looking at the possibility of both girls
somehow being murdered upstairs in Huntley's house.
- The police have said that 'someone' said Holly had a nose-
bleed. We believe this person to be Huntley. We believe this
is an excuse to explain any blood found in his house.
- If Holly had a nosebleed she would have gone into the Sports
Centre or her grandmother's house, just a short walk away,
not Huntley's.
- Huntley's intentions were purely sexual.
- Huntley's reported past shows a fondness for young girls.
- Huntley's reported past shows him to be some kind of
control freak.
- How did Huntley get a job working as a caretaker?
- Huntley's relationship with Maxine Carr was over.
- Huntley had tried to 'make a move' on a local woman.
- Huntley appears to come from a very unstable family back-
ground.
- Huntley can remain calm and convincing while lying on
camera.
- Huntley's Fiesta car looks likely to be the vehicle used to

> *take Jessica and Holly to Wangford.*
> - *Huntley knows Wangford well. Dumping the bodies there shows him to be thinking clearly and not to be 'mental', as he is trying to claim.*
> - *The police are not looking for anyone else in connection with the murders.*
> - *Maxine Carr was not in Soham on Sunday 4 August.*
> - *Maxine Carr appears to have made the extraordinary decision to lie to the police on behalf of Huntley.*
> - *Why would she lie when we are talking about the double murder of two children, both of whom she knew?*
> - *Maxine Carr has already admitted lying on behalf of Ian Huntley before in relation to the DSS fraud.*
> - *Carr must come forward and protect herself by helping the police enquiry and telling what she knows, sooner rather than later.*
> - *Carr has ended her relationship with Huntley, according to the newspapers.*
> - *Huntley and Carr's legal teams are working together and sharing information. Both are painfully slow in addressing any issues or requests raised by the prosecution team.*
> - *The case seems to be getting stronger against Huntley as forensic tests are completed.*
> - *As parents we are excluded from any further specific developments being shared with us for now.*
> - *Will the defence teams accept our statements as fact in order to allow this position to be reviewed?*
> - *Will our representatives continue to raise this issue for us?*

On the way home from church on the last Sunday of the year, I find myself talking with Roger Lane. He and his wife, Anne, have reached generations of children in Soham with their tireless youth work. Roger's sharp mind and wit have helped so many of us, including me, over the last 30 years. Roger now has a different type of battle on his hands with the early onset of dementia and it seems so wrong that this generous man should have to suffer this indignity and get no reward for his Herculean efforts. Our conversation is interrupted by a telephone call from Nicola who says that the *Mail on Sunday* are carrying a report that Tim Alban Jones is to be recognised in the New Year's Honours List. I am struck dumb in disbelief and return immediately to read the report in full. It says Tim has declined to comment and that the honour is thought to be an MBE.

I am angry and upset not hearing about this in person from Tim. Over the last few months we have seen quite a lot of one another. During that time a friendship has developed based on respect and trust and we have shared confidences. It now appears that my openness with Tim has been rather one-sided – and this hurts. He would have known about his nomination for many weeks, possibly months. But he chose to deliberately withhold this information. The irony is acute as I have told Tim how deeply distressed and agitated I am at being excluded from information by the police. The man of God has been doing the very same. (I am told the etiquette is those honoured are supposed not to tell all and sundry, but still . . .)

I am in two minds about this honour. I have seen this highly intelligent, caring man deal with the world's media impeccably. There have been times I wish he had offered the words 'no comment', but usually Tim has said the right thing at the right time. He and his family have also been under enormous pressure since their return from holiday mid-August. But I do feel the incorrect perception of Tim 'comforting' the families was key to the award being offered. As this does not represent the truth, then the MBE can only really be accepted for dealing with the media and speaking on behalf of the community. The timing also seems appalling. I just do not understand how individuals feel it appropriate to nominate, approve and accept this award before we have a verdict. Once more we brace ourselves for the return of the national press.

As the year ends we don't know what happens next but my

personal project of writing a book may well come a step closer. On 30 December, Matt Tapp and Chris Mead accompany me to London to meet the first of two potential literary agents. I am quite apprehensive about this meeting. Matt stresses the importance of making a good first impression. Chris is far less enthusiastic about the trip. In his opinion I am not going to be able to sign a contract or receive any financial advance to take time off work to write the book. That comes as a complete surprise to me. Instead I am told that, as I am still a witness who may be called to give evidence, a cash advance would cause a problem at the trial. Comparisons could be drawn with potential witnesses who have already received cash from newspapers for their stories of meeting Huntley. It would also look bad, Chris suggests. Even my book project – the right to say what I feel after all – is not going to be straightforward.

It pours as we reach London and we are country cousins. We misread the map and spend more time walking in the rain. Then, I arrive on the doorstep of the first literary agent, utterly bedraggled. Rain teems down my head and face as I remember Matt's words 'we must make a good first impression'. By the end of our meeting we are all slightly wiser about the working ways of the literary world and have benefited enormously from meeting this most eloquent professional. It was kind of her to agree to see us outside of normal Christmas working hours. As I look ahead to my next meeting with a potential agent in the New Year, I feel I will have a hard choice to make.

It is a tense New Year's Eve in our home. In addition to bidding good riddance to 2002, we all know that 2003 is going to be a make or break year for my family. If it proves to have the unexpected twists and turns of the last months of 2002, it is going to be the rockiest of rides.

Waiting for the Trial

January–October 2003

Tim Alban Jones has been in the news after the announcement of his MBE. I am slightly troubled that I cannot bring myself to feel pleased for the man, and put it down to our New Years having had such drastically different beginnings. Tim has said that he 'is pleased to accept the MBE on behalf of the community of Soham', which seems rather inappropriate. Many local people are far from happy about this. If, and when, Tim finds the time to speak with either family, perhaps we can discuss it in full.

On 5 January, Nicola flies to America with Kevin and Donna Paxton Tomb. It is a strange feeling watching Nicola leave; her last teary look back as she is driven away from our home is heart-rending. I hope that the next fortnight can somehow revitalise her. If anyone can work a miracle on Nicola, it's Donna.

Then I return to the book. Matt Tapp, Chris Mead and I meet at the Moat House Hotel, Bar Hill, half an hour before our meeting with Sonia Land is due to start. I am immensely grateful to Matt for turning up, for he seems the consummate professional.

Sonia is three-quarters Chinese, very warm, and her approach strikes a chord with me. She grasps that I want the police involved in this project to protect the integrity of the investigation and she does not seem phased by this at all. She stresses my book needs to be a personal story, and that it must be written and published with no pressure or time restrictions. I tell Sonia I will talk about many issues that have never been in the public domain. Somehow, the two of us seem to bond and I have no doubt that she is the right person to become my literary agent.

After Sonia and Matt go, I talk with Chris. Book or no book, the successful prosecution of Ian Huntley is the be all and end all, so I am happy to do whatever the authorities ask. I also realise that Chris must protect himself. If he is to be involved in any future meetings about the book, he must abide by the Criminal Proceedings and Investigation Act. We agree he will seek advice from his senior investigating officer and the CPS as to how involved he can be.

Try cleaning windows on the streets of Cambridge when the public knows you – and knows you and your family have been through a tragedy. Well-meaning pedestrians plague you and, instead of pulling my weight, I feel I'm a burden to Scott and our staff. I will soon have to think of the future. Scott is my business partner, but he is also my friend and that friendship must not be abused. I also know it is unlikely I can write a book on top of doing a full day's work up ladders. As the book is a way of dealing with so many current issues in my life, I make a difficult decision. I will stop working full-time to concentrate on my tribute to Holly.

But how are we going to eat? If I hear from Chris one more time that I cannot receive any financial advance for fear of my evidence becoming tainted, I will scream out loud. I decide to speak with my business bank manager, Rob Laws, to get his advice.

With Nicola away, I find myself very lonely and desperately sad. Once Oliver goes upstairs to bed, I simply cannot stop myself breaking down. I have so much bloody anger festering at the moment; I haven't the wisdom, insight, maturity or whatever, to channel it any other way. I keep thinking about Holly no longer gracing my life. I'm drinking too much – whisky into the early hours of each and every morning. My memories of Holly only make me feel more troubled. Goodness knows how much longer I can continue like this.

On Monday 13 January, my father is taken to hospital following a suspected heart attack. The day after, he looks desperately sick and we are solemnly told that the next 24 hours will be crucial.

I don't want him to die, and I don't want him to die without telling him what is most on my mind. As I am about to leave his bedside, I whisper urgently to him:

'Dad, if I don't see you again, I want you to promise to take care of Holly when you see her next. Please tell her that we all miss her so much and that we hope she is doing okay. I don't know if you can hear me, Dad, but if you do have one ounce of strength left in your body, please find it to stay with us. You must not leave before we have gained justice for Holly.'

I decide not to tell Nicola Dad is so ill. I don't want to spoil her time in America.

The next day, I'm glad I did not panic. Dad has stabilised. Although he is still not conscious, the 'critical next 24 hours' moment has passed, and there is a slight chance we may be able to welcome him back to Soham. As I work in Cambridge, it is easy for me to pop in during the day to check on his progress. I hadn't expected my visits to him, however, to plunge me back into the raw emotional distress of losing Holly. Five months have passed but I can still just dissolve into tears. One morning, I have to pull my van out of the Cambridge traffic, because I cannot see to drive. I'm crying too much.

Even when I have 20/20 vision, I drive like a clodhopper. I crash my car into the side of my in-laws' house, reversing up their drive. I've completed this manoeuvre countless times over the last 20 years. This ridiculous crash, more than any other incident, shows that my mind is totally elsewhere.

On Wednesday 15 January, the CPS sets out the charges both defendants face. Neither the Chapmans nor we have any advance notification – we are well and truly out of any information loop. There is also a new development, an additional charge against Maxine Carr. It is said that she, 'whilst knowing that Huntley had murdered the girls, or committed some other criminal offence, lied about his whereabouts, intending to impede his apprehension or prosecution'.

We are not told what led to this new charge. But I have a very strong feeling that, even if she was not in Soham on the night of 4 August 2002, Carr was involved afterwards, right up to her neck. It is sickening that this classroom assistant, so quick to come forward and talk to the media about Holly and Jessica in her caring voice, now appears to have been anything but a friend to her former pupils. I'm also puzzled when the police ask Rob and Trudie to give further statements. Our friends seem very confused as to why, and I agree to ask what this is about.

It becomes clear the police are still investigating. Later that day I am told something has been found in the boiler house at the Village College and the building has been cordoned off. When Chris produces the familiar refrain that he cannot tell me what has been found, again, yes again, I feel we are being excluded. My friends are to be questioned again, and we were told nothing about the new charges against Carr. Now this. Enough is enough. Chris says these developments are 'not substantial or significant'. Well, then surely they can be shared with us, if nothing else, to stop our minds running wild with worry.

By the end of the day, Chris returns with some answers and I'm grateful, for I know that he would have had to process his request back through senior management. I wonder if the senior investigating officers have any grasp of the pressure and dynamics that exist between the FLOs and my family.

I listen intently as Chris tells me that it was thought a single strand of blonde hair had been discovered, entwined in a piece of string, in the boiler house. Closer examination revealed, however, that the 'hair' is nothing more than a piece of old sacking. The reply as to why Rob and Trudie are being re-questioned is reassuring, at least. In all investigations, certain factors which did not seem to matter when the original statements were taken may become relevant later. That is why the police need to ask and keep asking and taking more statements. Chris also explains the timings and events of 4 August 2002 were critical. To make the point, he talks to me about the Manchester United shirts Holly and Jessica were wearing. 'For example if you, Kevin, could give me a statement confirming exactly what time the girls changed into the red tops, we could virtually rule out any reported sightings which happened before that time, as we would know that it could not be Holly or Jessica.' I accept what Chris says, as he does when I say for the 100th time maybe, that surely, informing both sets of parents before any issues emerge must be the best way to work together. I'm getting sick of saying it, and Chris must be sick of hearing it.

I meet with my bank manager, Rob Laws, to apply for a 2-year business loan to cover the time I expect to set aside to write my book. In many respects the loan application is flawed and we have a little bit of a chuckle together as we assess the facts:

- *I have no experience of writing a book.*
- *I have no contract in place which will guarantee funds in the future.*
- *I will not try to become involved in any negotiations until after the trial is over.*
- *The trial is likely to start at some stage later this year, although no date has been set. No one knows how long the trial will last.*
- *I will not be getting my regular weekly income if this application is successful.*
- *Monthly repayments will have to be met entirely from the borrowed capital.*
- *If things do not work out well, I will have to repay the loan by selling my half of the business.*

I offer Rob my hastily written synopsis plus a great deal of pleading, and he decides to grant my loan application. The man is a scholar, gentleman and banker. He has dealt with the most important objection the police and CPS have. I will finance my writing project myself, so the defence cannot claim my evidence is tainted. I will not be signing any contract or getting one penny for my writing. It's risky doing business this way, but I honestly believe the end justifies the means, and I thank Rob.

Oliver and I have missed Nicola terribly but she looks refreshed after her American break. Quite a lot has happened in her absence, I tell her. The Village College have announced the job of caretaker will not be filled again and the government has sanctioned a £3.5 million grant to help fund the investigation, which seems an awful lot of money. The church have rung a quarter peal to congratulate Tim Alban Jones on his MBE, the first time in 50 years a group of bell ringers entirely from Soham have done this.

But one of the other things we have to deal with is as bleak as it gets – Holly's death certificate. We have both had letters from the Coroner's Office indicating that the formal registration of the girls' deaths can now take place. The Coroner adds that we can wait until the end of the Crown Court trial, during which, hopefully, the date and place of death will have been established for certain. We decide to wait for the death certificate.

On Friday 24 January, at Norwich Crown Court, the trial judge, Mr Justice Moses, presides over a 'Listed for Mention' hearing. He sets dates for the most important event of our lives. The Plea and Direction hearing will be heard at the Old Bailey on 14, 15 or 16 April, with the main trial set for October. Judge Moses intends to swear a jury in on 6 October. Although this is only two days after Holly's birthday, we welcome the news. If the trial starts then, it may well be finished before Christmas. It is the first sign that the system is working – and that we are getting closer to justice. The reality of facing the person accused of our daughter's murder in about 11 weeks' time is a daunting one, but we will be there. After all, if Huntley pleads guilty now, we may never get to face the bastard again.

This timetable for the hearings galvanises the police into action. By the end of January we have discussed who can attend the Old Bailey and the vexed issue of how many seats we will be allocated. We get 10 seats for the Plea and Direction hearing. The police suggest that we travel down to London before the hearing to familiarise ourselves with the Old Bailey in peace and quiet, away from the glare of the media.

The Crown Prosecution Service are mollified because I will not sign a contract for a book but they raise a number of points, which they insist should not in any way be construed as a threat to or interference with my rights. They all sound formidably legalistic. In the writing of my book:

- *The police can assist with dates and times of any facts, which in any way relate to me.*
- *The police cannot provide details about other witnesses or what they have said.*
- *The police cannot give details of any forensic results.*
- *I must not attempt to discuss details with anyone who is a witness.*
- *The prosecution are under a duty to inform the defence of the fact I intend to write a book.*
- *If I am required to give evidence in court, the defence team may ask questions about the book and about any related financial interest.*
- *Once informed about the book, the defence might seek disclosure of any notes/manuscripts to find anything – and not just in my evidence – which might contradict any proposition in the case against the defendants.*
- *If the defence seeks such a 'third party disclosure application', the prosecution could not seek to resist it and might have to support it, as it is their duty to ensure a fair trial takes place.*
- *Any publication of any material before the end of the trial may be in breach of the Contempt of Court Act, 1981.*

It is hard for me to understand how the defence could have the right to access my notes and observations. In being open and honest about my intentions, I have created a minefield. If I didn't need the help of the police to confirm various details and incidents, I would almost certainly lie and tell everyone I have decided to cancel my writing project. I am sick with worry at the prospect that my book, a tribute to Holly, may inadvertently, thanks to the legalities, technicalities, the law is an ass-ities, help the defence.

I wonder – am I doing the right thing in writing this?

I'm stunned by the irony of it all. Tell us, the families, what is going on with the case? Impossible, old boy, a breach of Magna Carta, a breach, no less, of the rights of man, not to mention the rights of perverts, liars and murderers. Yet if I want to say what I feel, I could be nicked!

Second irony: being excluded from all the evidence means I can actually begin to write my book, because I don't know anything that could affect the trial. It has taken a long time for a positive to come from all the negatives of being out of the information loop. But today's the day. I can write because the powers that be have kept me in almost total ignorance.

I need to write because we face so much uncertainty. I meet the CPS, and Marion Bastin and John Goodier point out that the defence have already made it clear that they may not be ready by 6 October. That is a huge disappointment. If the defence asks to change the trial date, this will probably be granted, in the interest of fairness. It all seems a bit one-sided. I like Bastin and Goodier and they make one last point. The defence teams have been told to serve their statements by 28 February. Marion explains these statements should tell the prosecution the main lines of defence and so give us an idea of the likely length of the trial. In four weeks' time we should have an indication of what Huntley and Carr have to say.

By the end of January, a third member of the legal team, Chris Bramwell, is at work, dealing with as yet unused material. We now hear the prosecution case will probably rest on just 10 per cent of the statements taken. No one explains if this is a normal, or abnormal, percentage. We also learn that the CPS has dedi-cated officers to the investigation, full-time, instead of operating from a pool system. That sounds encouraging, especially as CPS officers are now working from Cambridgeshire Police HQ. Our 'attack force' looks to be moving in the right direction.

But before that, there is another Plea and Direction hearing scheduled, this time for Brian Stevens, the officer charged on child pornography offences. Nearly every report of that comes with the now famous picture of Holly and Jessica in their Manchester United shirts.

It is Nicola's birthday on the 27th and, like all first anniversaries after Holly's death, it proves extraordinarily difficult. On the Sunday before, we try to be proactive and put together a photographic collage of Holly. We use 100 photos maybe. It becomes a 3-hour ordeal because we are slowed down by heavy feelings – sadness, loss, and bitterness. But we do manage to decide what items we are going to keep in the 'Holly Tribute Cabinet', which takes pride of place in our dining room. The last objects added are Holly's majorette kit, including a wonderful braided cushion in the troupe's purple colour. The cabinet includes the photograph of Oliver with David Beckham, the signed Manchester United football and the last photo of Holly and Jessica in the team's colours.

February 2003

At the start of February 2003, we learn Maxine Carr may have ended her relationship with Huntley, but that does not mean she has changed sides, or is ready to tell the truth. Instead it is now believed she did it on legal advice. It is a legal ploy in a legal game.

Try keeping your life half-normal after your daughter is killed and when you are discovering there are more tactics in court cases than in a game of chess. We are desperate to find ways of being normal again, but it's hard. Each evening Nicola and I discuss the issues that distress us. We are told of a statistic, which the god of numbers could have spared us. Over 98 per cent of couples who lose a child through murder split up. I have no way of verifying this figure but, at least, neither of us blames the other for the tragedy. Maybe we will join the 2 per cent who stay together.

How do you parent your surviving child through such a trauma? The worry caused by my father's sudden illness took our attention off our concerns for Oliver. Nothing is seriously wrong in any obvious way, but since Christmas, our young son is unusually quiet. Something is troubling him, and we can't get him to open up. Neither Nicola nor I want to say it out loud, but he no longer talks about Holly. We're not sure how to broach this issue or what it means.

On 6 February 2003, Nicola and I have another meeting with our FLOs. We're amazed to discover they want to know if we will contribute to a television documentary with the police. I am shocked that the police are considering working with the media before the trial; it seems insensitive, inappropriate and totally baffling. Stewart and Chris agree to tell their senior officers we don't want to participate, but we gather that the documentary makers will try to encourage other members of our family to take part. Nicola and I speak with everyone and ask them to boycott this project. We are reassured that both FLOs say that they will not participate and will not speak for us as a family when we don't want them to.

We then hit another hitch. I mention to Chris and Stewart that I have accepted an invitation from Matt Tapp to go to Highbury and see Arsenal play. Matt and I hit it off, discovering we both love football. Chris and Stewart's body language changes dramatically. I ask why. I am stunned to hear the list of their objections. Matt and I could be recognised and filmed or photographed. This will inevitably lead to some form of publicity. Questions may be asked as to why we are there together and who paid for our tickets. The all-seeing, right-to-know-everything defence may demand records of our conversation. 'Did Thierry Henry make a good pass or was he off-colour?' Very relevant to the guilt of Huntley and Carr. It could be suggested that Tapp is coaching me as a witness. Any – or all – of the above could harm the successful prosecution of Huntley or Carr.

I only wanted to go and watch a game of football.

On 12 February 2003, I go to London with Stewart and Chris to meet my literary agent, Sonia Land. Sonia accepts the issues raised by the CPS and it is agreed that no contract can be signed until after the trial.

We go to King's Cross to get the train back to Soham but there is a bomb scare. So we go to have a drink together. The drink becomes quite intense. Tim Alban Jones has been canvassing opinions for a church memorial service later in the year to 'address the needs of the community'. Would such a service attract extra media attention, we wonder, would it play into the hands of the defence? I can see their QC saying God is against Huntley and Carr so there can't be a fair trial. Chris and Stewart bitch – if police officers can bitch. Will the service attend to the greater glory of Tim, rather than to the needs of the community? It sounds a harsh assessment, but one which I cannot totally discount.

As we talk, I realise just how focused many of Chris and Stewart's colleagues were – and still are – on seeking justice for Holly and Jessica. But there are many people out there who couldn't care less. Coming back from work, Nicola shows me the details of a competition publicised on the internet. The prize – once the police and forensic experts have finished with them – Holly and Jessica's Manchester United shirts. 'One lucky winner' will get them. The site appears to be satirical, but no one in my house finds it funny.

It has now been over six months since Holly was taken from us and we are grieving as bitterly as in the days after they found the bodies. We may not be so crippled by the intensity of shock and immediate loss but we feel anxiety, sadness and confusion. Both Nicola and I can still be overwhelmed at any moment. During a Friday evening meal with Rob, Trudie, Justin and Rachel, Nicola completely breaks down and begins to pour her heart out. She still misses Holly deeply. Tomorrow is Saturday, the day mother and daughter gossiped, shopped, wittered away together – as men see it. Trudie realises at once what Nicola is missing and promises to join her every weekend to help her and to stop her feeling lonely. You cannot put a price on friendship like that.

On 25 February 2003, Stewart and Chris tell us that we should not expect the defence to provide their statements by the end of the month. There is still a lot of forensic testing going on. So far there are about 2,500 forensic slides, and many more are expected. We are also told for the first time that none of Holly or Jessica's hair has been found in the carpet taken from Huntley's house. The police believe that Huntley's house and car were thoroughly cleaned before he was arrested. It seems so obvious that he and Carr were working together to cover up, but what if they were successful in cleaning the site? Telling a jury that someone should be found guilty because their house is too clean is not going to cut much ice. We need hard evidence. For now, Huntley and Carr may be one step ahead. The cards we hold may not be as strong as we thought.

It shows how slow forensics are that Huntley's vacuum cleaner has not yet been checked for hairs or fibres. As the caretaker, he could have used any one of the school vacuum cleaners. The prosecution, it turns out, may well have to search the contents of the 47 vacuum cleaners Huntley controlled!

Then, there is yet more delay because Huntley's QC, Mr Coward, breaks his leg skiing. The defence ask for a four-week postponement and we worry this may affect the trial date. We are assured this may not necessarily be the case, but once you are in this quagmire, you start thinking like a lawyer. I can't help wondering why a barrister can't function if he breaks his leg. I see that he couldn't turn up in court, but a broken leg does not stop him studying evidence, talking to experts, briefing and being briefed. Asking for a four-week delay seems a move to get more time before letting the prosecution see the defence statement.

The rules are that the prosecution must disclose evidence as soon as possible, but the defence's smartest strategy often is to disclose its evidence as late as possible. So Huntley can look at all the details of the prosecution evidence and then offer an explanation of how the girls died which contradicts that. It's naïve to hope the defence statement will turn up soon. Nicola and I have hoped the trial will be the arena where we find out the truth of what happened to Holly and Jessica – but that hope may be simplistic and misplaced.

On Friday 28 February, Stewart rings with news of the documentary. The police seem to have heeded the wishes of both families and after a 'show of hands' vote from the enquiry team itself, they have decided not to go ahead. It is a huge relief to hear this. Over the last few weeks I have religiously followed the advice of the CPS, as I might be a witness in the case. I have been careful not to put myself in any position that could be perceived as 'gaining a benefit' or 'profiting' from these darkest of events. The senior officers who seem so keen to appear in a documentary are also potential witnesses. They might not be paid for contributing, but it could still advance their careers, and that difference would not matter to the defence. Starting to make a documentary before the trial would also mean the production team learned the facts about the case against Huntley and Carr before the victims' parents. Not only does this seem morally wrong, but information could be leaked. I do not understand why the police are willing to take such a risk and I wonder whether the senior investigating officers have lost sight of what this enquiry is about. When your whole life is bent on the conviction of your daughter's murderer, you don't welcome the thought that the professionals may have other agendas.

March 2003

On Tuesday 4 March, Nicola and I visit St Andrew's School to view the stained-glass memorial window dedicated to Holly and Jessica. We approved the design along with the Chapman family. There is water to represent Jessica's swimming ability and musical notes depict Holly's talent. Two doves recall the impact the release of the birds had at the start of the autumn term. The window is above the entrance to the main hall and, at certain times of the day, it basks in direct sunlight, which is when it can be seen at its gleaming and translucent best. It looks wonderful.

The day after, 5 March, I am relieved to hear from Stewart, finally and formally, that the decision has been made to ditch the TV programme. The biggest glad sigh one could imagine is sighed in our house.

I now want to deal with a very personal subject. In the last seven months, our lives have been touched many times by matters of a spiritual nature. Nicola and I have found these experiences uplifting, for the most part, and we hope they mean that Holly is doing well. 'It' almost always happens in our home. When Holly 'returns', we both feel her presence very strongly. Of course, we have an unrealistic desire to touch and see her again, but we accept that this sixth sense 'feeling' is as close as we will ever get. I want to detail these experiences because they are so uncanny.

Since August 2002 we have had to replace 15 light bulbs, all exploding when we felt Holly was with us. Our main TV set has turned itself on and off with frightening regularity and the kitchen set is doing the same thing, although not as often. The Robbie Williams track, 'Angels', often starts to play when one of us feels very low. One example: when I managed to compose myself after visiting my father in hospital, I switched my van radio on. What did I hear at once? 'Angels'.

There have been other incidents that are difficult to explain rationally: the stereo system in our bedroom occasionally springs to life for no reason and it feels almost as if Holly is trying to communicate through it. The first two times this happened, Nicola was asleep, but not on the third. These incidents occur in the early hours of the morning and they are perhaps the most disconcerting of all.

Holly does not make herself felt only to us. Often, when we experience her presence, other members of the family can sense it, too. Nicola's sister and her partner, Graham, both say they saw Holly's image standing at our spare-bedroom window. Nicola's parents, who live just around the corner, have answered their door-bell a number of times to find there is no one there. What makes this so strange is that their doorbell has been broken for a very long time. And the chimes don't play the tune they are set on. I promise you that before this tragedy, I did not belong to the Soham supernatural club.

One incident sums up our experiences. On Sunday 9 March, in the early evening, Nicola and I can both feel Holly's presence. When Nicola goes to bed I stay downstairs to read *Jonathan Livingston Seagull* by Richard Bach. The book itself is less than a hundred pages long and proves to be remarkably uplifting. It tells how Jonathan Livingston Seagull, who is a bird, as the title suggests, experiences different levels of life's learning curve. The book offers a fresh perspective on how death may be perceived. It captures exactly how I feel this evening and Holly remains with me throughout. After finishing the book, I am able to allow myself a sense that Holly is experiencing a different world, and I pray out loud it's one in which she will be happy. I go to bed with an inner sense of harmony for my young daughter for the first time since her death.

The following morning at 6.15 a.m., I load my van to go window cleaning in Cambridge. As I do so, I notice a solitary seagull sitting on the roof of the house opposite. Bad weather can sometimes bring gulls inland to Soham. We are about sixty miles from the coast. But it's a fine day and I can't help thinking of what I read last night. It takes four journeys to load the van and I fetch and carry under the seagull's beady eye. The bird sits silently, watching my every move. I feel it is a lovely coincidence. As I get into my van, the seagull stays quite still.

Then, through my windscreen, I see a single seagull feather on the outside of the glass. I am completely taken aback and unbuckle my seat belt to retrieve it. As I pick up the feather, I glance at the roof opposite and see the bird take flight. I'm so moved that while watching the seagull disappear high in the sky, I say, quietly, 'Have a nice life, Holly.' I pick the feather up, go back inside and place it in the tribute cabinet.

On my way to Cambridge I think and think about this 'spiritual experience', and I remember the extraordinary accuracy of the predictions of Dennis Mackenzie, the medium. It may just be possible, if we can sense Holly so clearly, that he can make contact with her on our behalf. We may be able to find out some information as to what happened to Holly and Jessica before the trial starts. With some anxiety, I decide to invite the 'big man' back into our lives.

But that will have to wait till after our private visit to the Old Bailey. On Wednesday 12 March, there are, thank God, no media. The historic Court Number One is not in use and we are allowed to spend some time getting used to the surroundings. Chris and Trudie, Gary Goose, Nicola and I are given a tour of the building. We see the cells where Huntley and Carr will be held. The pair will be kept as far apart as possible to stop them conferring. We are also allowed to walk from the cells to the stairs which bring you to the dock itself. Huntley and Carr will walk that route. It is very eerie to do so ahead of them.

I am struck by the sense of history at the Old Bailey, even though much of it has been rebuilt. The resplendent marble hallways lead you into an area full of statues and fine paintings. It's opulent, both impressive and oppressive. We talk in hushed tones before walking into the court itself. It is oak-lined and belongs to another time, another world. I can't help feeling that 50 years ago the system wouldn't have been contorting itself quite so much to protect the defendants.

Court Number One is surprisingly small. We take time to stand and sit where witnesses, legal teams and the accused will be in four weeks' time. A glass screen protects those in the dock but they are not boxed in totally. Any fit person could climb over and hit a defendant by coming at them from above. I could land one punch on Huntley. The thought is an unexpected bonus. I won't do it, of course, I'm not a confrontational person . . . but still . . .

During the journey back to Soham, Nicola speaks with Chris

about seeing a psychologist to discuss Oliver. We have been under immense pressure as a family these last few months and we're questioning our recent decisions as parents. We feel we owe it to Oliver to seek some professional guidance for him.

At the end of the week, we finally get the defence statement from Maxine Carr's team. It reveals little and we are bitterly disappointed. Actually, we are not allowed to see the official wording of her document, which increases our ever-present frustration. It is a short and sharp reminder that legal tactics are at work and it seems to me the phrase 'fair trial' can only be interpreted one way. The police stress that as the judge has already granted an extension to Carr's defence team, he will not be pleased to get so little so late. Fine, but where does that take us?

A more positive piece of news; Huntley has been placed on 24-hour suicide watch. We are not told why, of course, but it seems likely that he has learned of more damning evidence against him. If that caused him such anxiety that he's now a suicide risk, frankly I'm glad to hear it.

Back in Soham, the local newspaper gives its front page to the case. We learn that the online books of condolences have now been closed, after logging over 200,000 messages from around the world. When the sites were first opened, messages were being received at the rate of one every two seconds, an extraordinary statistic.

The paper has two other stories. The number of CCTV cameras in Soham is to be extended to cover the Village College and the caretaker's bungalow. At the moment there is a permanent police vehicle outside Huntley's former home. Given that there is not a single thing left in the house, it seems excessive. I feel sure that the police officers on duty will welcome the arrival of surveillance cameras. They must be bored stiff.

A few days before our meeting with Dennis Mackenzie, Nicola meets another medium by the name of Honor. Nicola is impressed by some of her observations, particularly as the lady did not recognise her before speaking. Immediately after Nicola sat down, the medium saw a spiritual guide looking out for her. His name was Joe and he was a boxer. Apparently he had 'one punch left in him' and he was going to use it to protect Nicola. Nicola has no idea who this boxer might be. Honor also speaks of two young girls playing together. One of the girls is blonde with beautiful blue eyes and is coming forwards. Honor can't get the name of the girl but says that she is carrying a cat by the name of Bits. (We used to have a cat called Bitsy, which Holly adored.) This is enough for Nicola to believe Honor has made contact with Holly. Both the girls seem happy and well. At the end of the reading, Honor highlights a significant date, much later in the year. Will she prove to be right? Only time will tell.

When Nicola tells the family what she heard from Honor, we have a spine-chilling moment, the kind that makes you believe there are more things on Heaven and Earth than . . . well, than 'rational' people are supposed to believe. Nicola's mother, Diane, bursts into tears. When she calms down, she tells Nicola the boxer is her Uncle Joe. He was known as Gentleman Joe and fathered eight daughters, so perhaps it is fitting he is looking out for one more lady now.

As so often in the past few months, we hear from some very odd strangers. During one of my sessions with the FLOs, Mr Westgate, our regular nuisance caller, rings up. Unfortunately for him, I'm so familiar with his voice that I simply pass the phone over to Chris. He listens intently to the man's ramblings and carefully jots down details of the conversation during the 16-minute call. It is a small victory to listen in as Mr Westgate talks himself ever closer to becoming a guest of Her Majesty's Prison Service.

And then, there is the night when Dennis Mackenzie comes back into our home. Nicola and I are anxious and have discussed how we will deal with any information he shares with us.

'Why haven't you asked to see me before now?' Dennis says at the front door.

'Well . . .'

'Kevin, I have made contact with Holly many times over the last few months.' It is the gentlest of opening exchanges, yet knocks me back just a little. The Christian name 'Holly' is hardly ever used by visitors any more and now, here in my living room, is someone who is going to talk about my daughter and who appears to have already been in touch with her. Our anxiety increases as Dennis insists Oliver must be in bed before he will give any details.

Nicola and I have both prepared ourselves for tonight. We have not drunk any alcohol. We do not wish to impart any new information to Dennis and have decided, therefore, not to discuss any issues about the trial that have not already been made public. Dennis picks up our tension and reserve. He stresses he is here to help and asks us to relax.

Dennis first talks about other aspects of his work, including healing, regression and hypnosis. He asks Nicola if she will let him hypnotise her; she agrees and is soon 'under'. Then, the temperature in the house becomes unbearably hot. Despite the freezing cold weather outside, Nicola and I have to remove our jumpers and turn off the central heating. Dennis explains that this happens many times when he visits people, due to the high level of energy he creates. He can harness some of this energy and asks me to stand up in the centre of the room. As Nicola watches, I am knocked backwards as he somehow sends a ball of energy through me. I am completely stunned. I ask Nicola to confirm that Dennis did not push or pull me. No, he did not, she says. I have to accept that I am in the presence of a most extraordinary man. I now need a break because my body is overheating. I go outside, and for 20 minutes, I stand topless in my garden in a temperature of minus three degrees. Then I am ready for the real, hopefully not too agonising, business of the evening.

Dennis uses a spiritual guide to contact 'the other side'. He has two at his disposal, one of whom, a Red Indian called White Cloud, is also used by other mediums. Tonight his guide is a very business-like German lady called Jagna who seems to hail from the 1950s. Dennis proceeds and I write down what he says:

'Holly really misses her shopping trips with her mum, particularly to her favourite shop, *Next*. She says she is doing fine and having a wonderful time. Can you say hello to Olls for her – and she is stressing you must say Olls and not Oliver. Holly feels that Oliver "saw her" 8 days after she went missing.'

It is a most extraordinary opening. *Next* was Holly's favourite shop and she always went there with Nicola when shopping. The reference to Olls is absolutely spot on as it was Holly's nickname for Oliver. No one else has ever called him 'Olls'; if Dennis were going to guess at a nickname, the obvious one would be 'Olly'. As we have never disclosed this nickname to anyone, it floors us. We both feel sure, however, that Oliver would have mentioned it to us if he had seen Holly, but agree to ask him in the morning. (Oliver says he did not.) Dennis adds, 'Holly says she did not feel any pain and that you must not be concerned about the state of her body when it was discovered. Nicola, Holly would like you to wear that necklace of hers, which she was wearing when she was murdered. She knows it's a rubbish necklace but would really, really like you to wear it when you can. Holly says it is okay to move house.' On Sunday 4 August, Holly was wearing a plastic 'love' necklace, which was a free gift from a magazine. The police have recovered it and will return it after the trial, although we do not know what state the necklace is in.

Dennis has also hit on a live issue in regards to the possibility of moving. After much debate, Nicola and I decided to make some internal changes to the house, rather than move.

But then we come to the awful issue of what happened in Huntley's house. Dennis tells us, 'Holly says that she died second and that both she and Jessica were strangled. You will not find any blood in the house although there was a cut to Holly's top lip during strangulation.' We know from the police that the most likely cause of death was strangulation or suffocation and that tests on the bodies excluded death by stabbing or bludgeoning. The police have confirmed there was no blood in the caretaker's house. That seems extraordinary, given that two girls appear to have been murdered there. And I have long believed that Holly died second, as my own nightmares and images have conveyed the same message.

'Both Holly and Jessica were dead before 8 o'clock and there was another male involved in the moving of the bodies. Both bodies were first placed in a store room at the school and were very nearly discovered. Maxine Carr was not in Soham on August 4th,' Dennis adds. Although we know that the girls almost certainly died before 8 o'clock and that Maxine Carr was not in Soham, we do not tell him what else we know. At the moment we have no way of knowing if the girls were placed in a store room or if another man helped dump their bodies so unceremoniously, but both of these claims are extremely thought-provoking.

Dennis adds one other thing, though we have no way of checking whether it's true. Holly says she has stood next to our bed many times, telling us not to be too sad, but to try and remember the good times.

Finally, Dennis passes on our love and best wishes to Holly as we repeat out loud that we are missing her so very much.

This is not the end of the session as Dennis continues to speak through his contact spirit, Jagna. Dennis mentions two key dates that will fall later in the year. Bizarrely, the first one is the same day Honor mentioned to Nicola. Dennis feels this is a day to either receive some good news or money. The second date, Dennis feels is related specifically to the case and will be defining somehow. We can but wait.

Before Dennis goes, I want to talk about the incident last August, when we stopped in front of the low wall opposite The Ship, a spot he felt was somehow significant. I tell him that it was the very place I had first met Nicola. Dennis contacts Jagna one last time and says this is not what matters about the location. Rather, it is linked to a telephone, which I assume is Jessica's missing mobile. I decide I will search that stretch of the river to see if it has been discarded, as soon as possible.

I'm struck again by how much Dennis seems to 'see', to 'know intuitively' – I suppose those are something like the right words.

The next day I tell Chris Mead I mean to search the river towards the end of March. He is not happy and asks me to hold back until he has talked with the senior investigating officer. I agree to wait, but I purchase a pair of Wellington boots anyway.

And then, another landmark, another one of those days to get through for the first time without Holly. It's Mother's Day. Holly would have been making gifts and a card for her mum. We decide not to stay at home and head for Old Hunstanton, on the East coast, where we walk and talk for many hours. We talk about our fears about being in the media's headlights again, and about becoming entwined in the legal process.

There is one last twist before the end of the month. Yet again, the defence statement due from Huntley's legal team on 31 March has not materialised. Instead we have a new date, this time 11 April 2003. No one explains why there's been another delay. Better news is that forensic results continue to come through and we are told there has been a breakthrough in relation to the deposition site. As ever we get no specific details. This hits me hard, because I hadn't thought the deposition site would throw up further clues. Given Dennis Mackenzie's 'claims', I wonder if any forensic evidence has been found which implicates a second man.

I also get the final 'no' from the police about searching the river for Jessica's mobile phone. It wouldn't add much to the prosecution case, they say. I had intended to slip with no fuss into the water at dawn, but the police fear more media coverage, which could help the defence claim that Huntley and Carr will not get a fair trial. After the trial I would learn that this was not the main reason they didn't want me searching. If the phone had been found in the river, so near to Huntley's home, the defence could have argued that Jessica's mobile had never been in 5 College Close.

April 2003

It's always a question of waiting. By 9 April 2003 the subject of seating at the Old Bailey is becoming a problem. The Corporation of London can reserve two front-row seats for its guests due to some ancient rights and we hear that this is likely to be the case for our trial. This is not good news. Many family and friends want to attend and we may not get enough seats. We face the possibility of not being able to sit in front of Huntley and Carr, while Lord This and Tycoon That can pop in for a gawp at their heart's content. It is even unclear if we will be allowed to sit facing the accused at next week's Plea and Direction hearing. It is incomprehensible that we and the Chapmans can be thought so unimportant.

The much awaited defence statement still has not materialised by Friday 11 April. We are told one reason is that Huntley's legal team are simply 'playing the game'. Typical, we think, but all the delays suggest they are in trouble. We are also told that if a defence statement is not completed, there may well be a hidden benefit for our side as it means the defence do not automatically get 'second disclosure' details. Any ordinary person who wants to understand a trial had better buy a dictionary. The police must reveal all material to the defence, especially material which could undermine the prosecution case or help the accused. But if no defence statement is submitted, the prosecution won't know the nature of the defence. You think this is smart defence tactics? Only up to a point. If the prosecution don't know the details of the defence, then they don't have to disclose anything additional after their first statement. That is how you get the phrase 'secondary disclosure'. The defence will want to know any extra details, so our side expects them to deliver their statement at the eleventh hour, and perhaps even hand it to the judge on the day of the hearing. The cat-and-mouse game continues.

I'd read, of course, that faith consoles. But I'd just read it. My grief does make me turn to God – to rant at, to explain, to console. I am going to church two to three times a month now. Nicola can no longer claim I am only attending out of friendship to Tim Alban Jones, as she knows how hurt I was by his actions earlier in the year. She no longer waves me off to church with cutting remarks and I'm glad. I need to go in peace so I can reflect in the right frame of mind.

I have come to a sort of peace with Tim. Since the turn of the year, I have been a guest at his house, and he and his wife have been guests of ours. I have spoken to him of the MBE issues and we have agreed to disagree. I accept his word that he would never do anything to deliberately upset Nicola or me, and he accepts that he has already hurt us. We will both be called on to deal with the media in the months ahead, so it is best to work together. As part of this bargain Tim tells me, before it becomes a matter of public record, that he will be receiving his MBE on Thursday 12 June. For my part, I wish him well.

With one day to spare, the prosecution finally receives the defence statement. The police are baffled, flustered and angry, as the four-sentence statement offers a minimum of information. The long delayed 'meaningful document' reads:

1.   The Defendant did not kill Jessica Chapman or Holly Wells.
2.   The Defendant did see and speak with the deceased on 4 August 2002 at his house and last saw them at about 6.15–6.30 p.m. outside his home, 5 College Close, Soham.
3.   The Defendant did not deposit or have any part in the deposition of the bodies of the deceased at the site where they were found.
4.   The Defendant did not deposit or have any part in the deposition of clothing and possessions of the deceased in the Hangar at Soham Village College.

This is hardly worth the paper it's written on. We still don't really know what Huntley's defence will be. That means the two sides cannot agree on any evidence, which would reduce disputes and might make the trial shorter. We are told this very brief statement suggests Huntley will plead not guilty tomorrow.

There has been absolutely no point in Nicola and me going to bed these last few days. Sleep is impossible. As we are collected at 7 a.m., by Stewart and Trudie, we look and feel terribly drained. Oliver chooses to remain in Soham. Then, the fates pile stupid stress on top of desperate stress. We had meant to spend the train ride to London confirming arrangements and timings but the train is completely packed. We have to stand and then we're separated in the crowd.

Finally, the guard upgrades us all to the quiet of the first-class carriage. We get to King's Cross in comfort but this is not the end of the saga. Chris had better not apply to the Met for work because he leads us the wrong way round the underground system. Getting lost in the Big Smoke should make us all steam with more stress and pressure, but it doesn't. Everyone ribs Chris mercilessly. We arrive for our rendezvous with the Chapman family at Snow Hill Police Station, slightly fussed and late.

We are going to get more fussed. The police tell us there is an agreed press strategy. We will walk down to the Old Bailey, where we will pause for a group photograph. In return, the press have promised there will be no rogue reporters following our group or working a couple of paces in front of us. As we walk out of Snow Hill, the City of London police stop the traffic. The media watch us in unexpected silence, which only adds to the tension. We stop next to the first bank of photographers and, then, are asked to stop again outside the entrance to the Old Bailey. We had told the police we wanted our presence to be discreet. Now Nicola and I are shaking, and we don't stop shaking when we get past security.

We go into Court Number One for the 11 o'clock start and sit just in front of the dock. We have been asked to be meticulous in our behaviour and not shout out anything, offensive or otherwise, when Huntley or Carr arrive in the dock. Yes, we are on trial, too. If we behave, control ourselves and act civilised, this will help our request for the same seats for the main trial. If we do anything that might make life awkward for those sensitive victims Huntley or Carr, we'll be punished – perhaps they'll make us sit at the back of the court with paper bags over our head!

The court is packed – the media, a few family members, the lawyers. I recognise many reporters from the press conferences last August. As we take our seats, our legal team is in front of us. Now everyone begins to notice something. Huntley's legal team has not turned up, although no one knows why. At 11 o'clock there is still no sign of them. I start to fret. Is there a problem of some description? Is Huntley ill or feigning illness yet again? Has Huntley fallen out with his legal team? Is Huntley going to plead guilty now? More waiting, more pressure. Each and every time the Judge's Clerk walks through his door, the whole court looks for a sign that something is going to happen – but no, nothing. Something is clearly wrong. The silence becomes oppressive.

After 20 nerve-racking minutes, Huntley's legal team strolls into court. Then, Huntley is brought up the stairs into the dock, only to be sent immediately back down again as he has come up too soon. The form is that the judge takes his place first and, then, the accused is brought before him. It all seems slightly chaotic. As we finally all rise for Mr Justice Moses, Huntley sits down at the front of the dock. Then Carr enters court. A number of prison service officers stand between them – not that it matters today, as neither Huntley nor Carr ever glance at each other.

Huntley's QC, Mr Coward, apologises for the delay. The explanation is banal. The train one of his team was due to take was cancelled. You could not script this if you tried. Two victims' families have been left sitting in the most famous court in the world, confused, worried senseless, without a clue, and no one bothered to explain it was all down to the railways. No one could be fagged to send a message up to court. I hope this is not a sign of things to come. I glance at Nicola, shake my head in despair and see she is shaking. She is staring intently at Huntley. Her mind must be running wild as she tries to come to terms with the fact that the last person to see, or touch, Holly is sitting only 10 feet away. I also start staring at Huntley. After the hearing, Nicola would tell me that she remembers nothing about the legal exchanges. She just remembers staring at Huntley, hoping that her silent messages would somehow reach the man who robbed our daughter of her life.

The young female Court Clerk stands to read out the charges. Huntley's come first and the Clerk's voice breaks with emotion. It takes longer than I had anticipated, as the charges are duplicated; identical charges, first relating to Jessica and, then, to Holly. Huntley pleads 'not guilty' to both charges of murder in a barely audible voice. If a jury could see the look and body language of this pathetic individual, we could all be saved a lot of time and heartache. On the second charge of conspiracy to pervert the course of justice, Huntley pleads guilty. That takes everyone by surprise. If the reactions of his legal team are anything to go by, this includes them. People gesture and look at each other in confusion.

Carr pleads 'not guilty' on two separate charges of assisting an offender and conspiring to pervert the course of justice. So Huntley and Carr are pleading differently to the same charge, even though they were clearly working together. How is this going to develop?

Then all potential witnesses are asked to leave the court while points of law are discussed. As Nicola and I walk past the dock, Huntley arrives at the top of the stairs next to me. I stop immediately. Only the thick wooden dock and its glass shield stand between us. As I stare directly at him, he refuses to engage in any eye contact and just stares down at his feet. This moment will stick in my mind for the rest of my life, for I believe I am looking at someone so racked with guilt he cannot face the father of his victim. Then, we are chaperoned to a witness service room where we debate his guilty plea to one charge – and we all agree on one thing. Huntley appears to have spontaneously made his own mind up to plead guilty to the lesser charge. A little later, our QC, Mr Latham, informs us that every effort is going to be made to get the family evidence agreed by the defence teams. We are delighted to hear this. Not only will this mean that we can sit in the court from day one and hear all the evidence, but we can begin to receive information about the case and how it is progressing. We are relieved that Oliver seems unlikely to have to give evidence.

Before he leaves Mr Latham confirms two things: first, that in 15 years of murder trials he has not seen a police force work as hard as Cambridgeshire have over the last few months. Second, he thinks we have the strongest of cases. He adds a quick caveat of 'nothing can be guaranteed', but we are very grateful to him for sharing his positive perceptions with us.

At the end of this tense morning, our three FLOs, Nicola and I go for a meal in the pub opposite King's Cross Station before catching our train back to Ely. As we finish eating, yet again, Holly's favourite song 'Angels' comes on the jukebox. We all fall silent.

Our relationship with our FLOs has always been close, but now, for the first time, we feel close enough to tell them what the loss of Holly really means to us both. We wanted her to have the education and opportunities neither of us had. She was so talented. Now it's all a shattered dream. We know the public perception is that we are coping well, but we are still in turmoil and trauma really. We've learned not to show it too much, but we are very frightened of not gaining justice for our beautiful daughter. We have lost the one individual capable of rising above the mediocrity which surrounded her. We hoped so much for her and all that has been broken. I did not mean to cause any upset by my impromptu speech in the pub, but, as I run to the toilet, everyone is in tears.

There's another bomb scare on our way home. No trains are leaving King's Cross. So, we get a taxi to Liverpool Street Station to catch a train from there. The god of trains is against us again and produces a serious delay just outside Harlow. Everyone in the train seems to be reading the *Evening Standard* which carries Holly and Jessica's picture. Everywhere we look we see the girls. And it takes two and a half hours to get home.

We need a break and, late in April, we go to Scotland, staying with my cousin Fergus for the 40th birthday of his brother, Grant. Archie Steele, the piper from the Ely Cathedral service, is also a guest and pipes in the birthday cake.

While in Scotland, we receive an alarming telephone call. In London, our lead QC, Mr Latham, has been attacked. He has suffered a serious facial injury and a possible hairline fracture to the skull. As if that is not bad enough, DI Gary Goose, the Family Liaison coordinator, has also been attacked, this time in Peterborough. Gary has been stabbed in the head with a screwdriver and has injuries to his face. The police don't think there is a link, but it can't be ruled out entirely. What if they're wrong? Will we be attacked next? We have already received threatening letters and abusive telephone calls. These really are the most testing of times.

I am learning more than I ever wanted to about court procedure. The prosecution has to hand in the bulk of their case by 30 June, which means some evidence should start to be agreed and we should finally get a clue as to the nature of Huntley and Carr's defence. With the trial still scheduled for October, this will allow both defence teams three months to digest the final files of information. The police feel the trial should still start on time and we are relieved by that. The prosecution has kept to every deadline but will the defence teams be as uncooperative as usual?

Later we get formal notification by hand that Nicola, Oliver and I all need to be on standby between 6 October and 31 December to attend the Old Bailey as prosecution witnesses. We still hope that the defence teams will accept our evidence. But the letter is the first time we have seen a possible end date for the trial in writing. We may be able to go into 2004 with two successful convictions behind us, ready to plan ahead for the rest of our lives.

May 2003

Throughout this ordeal, it is odd how many details go wrong. On

Tuesday 6 May, Oliver and his class are meant to study some CCTV footage to see if anyone can identify a mystery cyclist, caught on the Ross Peer's Sports Centre's cameras on 4 August 2002. The police don't think this information is of major significance, but they do not want to have unfinished details. We discuss with Oliver how he would like to view the video. He is told he can:

- *Watch the video at home first and then at school.*
- *Watch the video at home only.*
- *Watch the video at school only, away from his classroom.*
- *Watch the video at school only, with his friends in a classroom.*

Oliver chooses to watch it at school in a classroom. He wants to be treated the same as everyone else. We remain very proud of our young son; he has never asked for special treatment; he has never even asked for a day off school over the last eight months. And school bores him. Even though he is more reserved than normal, this is his way of dealing with things and we have to accept that. Oliver seems happy that he has been asked to make his own decision.

When Oliver gets home, we ask if he recognised the cyclist. We are completely gob-smacked at his answer. 'Didn't see the video, Dad, the teacher made me leave the classroom and stand outside. I felt a complete prat.' Oliver seems put out, and rightly so. Although the police agree to drop round a video for Oliver immediately, maybe a different kind of damage has already been done.

The next day, the Home Secretary, David Blunkett, announces he intends to set out changes to the way murderers will be sentenced. The 'life to mean life' term will be imposed for those found guilty of terrorist murder, but will also apply to those found guilty of sexual, sadistic murder of children. The law may not change before Huntley is sentenced, but I welcome this wholeheartedly. If Mr Blunkett's initiative does 'give a signal to perpetrators that we will not tolerate their presence in our society' then bloody well done him.

Soham has quietened down once more after the brief flutter under the media-scope during the recent hearing. Everyday life seems to be returning to some kind of normal. We know we have everyone's support and best wishes, and that counts for a lot, but, in truth, it is now two families bracing themselves for the trial, not the community. We try to re-integrate into the community – the phrase, of course, makes us sound like criminals. We go to Sergio's Restaurant for a couple of meals and I attend the Soham Town Rangers dinner, where Vinnie Jones comes every year as Club President. Nicola and I go for a walk every evening and we usually stop and talk to a number of people. We hear stories of August last year as people explain the lengths they went to to avoid speaking with the media, for fear of saying the wrong thing. It's telling that everyone says that when they went abroad for their holiday, they decided not to mention they came from Soham. We understand why. Our small town has become a byword for evil.

At the Village College, the Vice-Principal Margaret Bryden has returned to work, which I am very pleased about. I visited her and her husband, Derek, straight after finding out about their absence from teaching late last year. I saw that Margaret blames herself for employing Ian Huntley, and so for the carnage that followed. I tell her again and again that neither Nicola nor I blame her. I can only hope that when the facts come out at the trial a clearer picture will emerge, so that Margaret can move on – she deserves that.

But it's easy to be knocked off balance.

On Thursday 15 May, while talking with Tim Alban Jones, I am completely stunned to be asked what Matt Tapp was doing in Soham with a TV crew yesterday. Was this official and allowed by the police? What is going on? The documentary was ditched, we were told. This has an exceptionally bad feel and I ring Chris Mead at once. Chris promises to investigate further. Within a quarter of an hour I am told that the film crew was recording a child safety video, which sounds about as likely as me winning this week's Lottery. It again makes me wonder about the senior management of the Cambridgeshire Constabulary and their priorities. By Friday teatime, Chris has met Matt Tapp and Temporary Det. Supt Chris Stevenson. Chris confirms that the filming was authorised by the police. True, it was 'definitely in relation to a child safety video', but I'm disturbed it was sanctioned at all. Couldn't they shoot a child safety video in a place where two girls were not recently killed? As we only found out by accident, what else is going on that we do not know about? We are relying on the police for so much that this clandestine development worries us. At least the footage has been embargoed till after the trial.

We've become so worried about the unfair trial issue that Nicola and I decline an invitation to see the Soham Rose unveiled at the Chelsea Flower Show. The *Soham and Ely Journal* carries a picture of the Soham Rose being held by Esther Rantzen which, given her association with children's causes, makes some sense.

On Friday 23 May, Frank Murphy, the Cambridgeshire educational psychologist, rings. Nicola went to see him to make sure we were taking the right decisions in relation to Oliver. He agreed that Oliver should be told the whole truth openly. Frank informs me he is interacting with the staff at the school who are keeping a close eye on Oliver – despite the recent slip-up with the CCTV footage. We know that Oliver is being looked out for. One of his form teachers is Maggie Loasby. She and her husband, Graham, used to live a few doors down from us on East Fen Common. Their youngest daughter, Alice, used to play with Holly. Every morning Holly would walk to school with Alice. We know Maggie will contact us if there are any problems with Oliver.

The end of May brings yet another twist. Maxine Carr's mother has been arrested and charged with intimidating a witness. Sixty-year-old Shirley Capp will appear in court after a woman who lives near her in Grimsby complained. Goodness knows what is going to happen next. We've long since given up hope that Maxine

Carr will do the decent thing. But, if she is like her mother, she may well not even realise she has done anything wrong in the first place.

June 2003

On Monday 2 June, Chris Mead updates Nicola and me about an 'expert's conference' chaired by another prosecution QC, Karim Khalil. The meeting was first class. The police are pleased, the barristers are making progress. Our team appears likely to hand over the entire prosecution papers before the end of this week. This is an excellent development and will be three weeks ahead of the original deadline of 30 June 2003. The inference is clear: the trial will start on time. We are grateful for all of the hard work everyone on our side has put in, and I am pleased that Huntley may well have a busier weekend's reading than he had first planned.

And after the trial? After we get justice, please God? We will need to get away, so we book a trip to New Zealand to stay with my cousin, Julie, Dean and my goddaughter, Sarah. Booking this holiday for January 2004 is almost defiant, a sign that we are beginning to recapture some control of our lives.

But control does not come easy. At 1.17 a.m. on 9 June, I wake with such a startle that I feel something is desperately wrong. I wake Nicola and get up to see if any intruders have broken in. I check our mobiles for missed calls or messages. Something is not quite right. Eventually I go back to bed, baffled. But the effects linger.

My 6.15 a.m. departure to Cambridge is normal enough but I am two miles past the Burwell turning before I realise my mistake. As I take a different route down the A14, I travel behind a builder's truck and can only watch in disbelief as a length of wood gets caught in the wind and hurtles towards my windscreen. Fortunately, the wood falls just short of my van but I can't help driving over it. A tyre has been punctured, I realise when I get to

Cambridge. I drop my colleague Paul Knighton off and drive to the nearest tyre and exhaust depot I can find. I am the first customer and wait for them to open. Another early bird customer drives in. The car park is huge but that does not stop the other early bird struggling to park. He tries to park by me three times and caps it by reversing straight into the side of my van. Lady Luck has definitely got it in for me today.

Worse, I forgot to take my mobile telephone with me when I dropped Paul off. By the time I retrieve it, it is past 10 a.m. There are two messages, and both sound urgent. The first is from Chris Mead and the second from Nicola. Nicola tells me she has been asked to leave work and head for home. When I return Chris Mead's call, I am simply asked where I am, and told that I will be picked up at once in the centre of Cambridge. I am told nothing else.

Stewart arrives with Chris and, once I am inside their car, they say that Ian Huntley attempted suicide in the early hours of this morning. He is on a life-support machine and on 24-hour monitoring. His condition is described as 'critical'. I am completely stunned. My initial reaction to Huntley's suicide attempt is to simply wish him good luck, and please try harder.

Chris and Stewart, however, have a different perspective. They warn: 'If Huntley dies, you will not have the opportunity of seeing justice being done for your daughter, Holly.'

Yes, but if he does die we will have access to all of the evidence anyway and can make our own assessment. Clearly this suicide attempt shouts the word GUILTY from the rooftops anyway.

'If Huntley survives it may well have an impact on the start date of the trial, taking its conclusion into 2004,' Chris adds.

'Oh, shit, we have just booked our flights to New Zealand for January 2004.'

'It may well be possible that Huntley will survive and live in a vegetative state. Although legislation is in place that would allow a trial to still take place, there would be a long delay in getting to that position,' Chris adds. This is the worst of all three scenarios. The thought of brain damage had not crossed our minds. Goodness only knows what level of service Huntley would then receive from the 'do-gooders brigade'.

We can but wait patiently to see what happens. By midday the news is on television and people ring to get a fuller update. Chris and Stewart are outside in the garden, pacing, making and receiving calls continuously. For a bizarre hour it is like being back in August 2002, when our troubles first started.

The police want Mr Justice Moses to make an order under the Contempt of Court Act to restrict publicity. There is already an order in place, but the feeling seems to be that if Huntley does die, the restrictions which applied to him would no longer be valid. The media could unleash whatever material they have about him, but with Carr still alive, the police fear her legal team would then press the 'unfair trial' button – and get somewhere.

With all this up in the air, I cannot believe Tim Alban Jones is on television, yet again giving interviews. He may not realise it but he is playing with fire, and playing, possibly, into the hands of the defence. The more publicity, the more chance they have to argue that there is no chance of a fair trial. The police contact Tim and request that he stop. Tim agrees at once but it's too late, of course. He has done the interviews.

By early evening we have some news which we are asked to keep strictly confidential. Huntley is deliberately being held in a state of unconsciousness with his breathing regulated by equipment. It is believed his condition is 'no longer critical but stable'. The prison guard who spotted him convulsing in his cell at about 3.30 a.m. acted quickly. We are told that Huntley is going to be revived at 8 a.m. tomorrow and that he took an overdose of pills, thought to have been prescribed for a heart condition.

Ironically, this could be a win-win situation for Huntley. If he really did want to take his own life and succeeds, the gutless bastard would not have to face the rigours of the trial. But if he survives, then yet more publicity could boost his unfair trial application. Again, we face the unbearable thought that Huntley may not have to face court at all.

Our FLOs return before 8 a.m. and tell us that Huntley has been revived. Not only is he lucid and coherent, but, apparently, very angry at his failure to die. Obviously he has not yet had the opportunity of speaking with his legal team to hear the potential benefits of his actions. In the afternoon Huntley is taken back to prison amid a blaze of publicity. But he is allowed to remain unseen, a blanket over his head. I find this bloody frustrating. Why can't people be made to face up to their responsibilities? He really is a fucking wanker.

Of course, the press wants to know what we think about this drama. Two reporters are hot-footing it to Soham. We agree to release a formal statement to stop the media calling us at home. We think it prudent to contact members of our family, asking them all to make no comment.

The police go, leaving Nicola and me to reflect on this tense start to the week. We are even more confused and frightened than before, as there are serious questions to be asked. How did Huntley, who was under 24-hour surveillance, manage to conceal enough pills to attempt suicide? Why did he choose to try and kill himself now? The Home Secretary has asked for a report from the prison. Whatever it says, we have yet again seen that the justice system, in which we as ordinary people have placed our faith, is far from flawless. As to why Huntley tried today, we can make an educated guess. On Friday, after the prosecution handed over the details of the case, Huntley's legal team went to see him. It would have taken him a while to read and assess the strength of the evidence against him, and then Huntley must have realised how strong it was. He decided to call it a day. The trial cannot come soon enough now.

On Thursday 12 June, our vicar – now a national figure – is in the media again, picking up his MBE. We knew it was coming and have braced ourselves for it. We're less worried about the defence using Tim's MBE as really it does not have any relevance to the case. I have sent Tim my best wishes.

On Friday 13 June, Chris Mead offers me a different perspective on Huntley's suicide attempt. It may help us. If Huntley can manipulate prison officers while he is under constant surveillance, with so sly and well-executed a plan, no one can argue that he is mad and does not know what he was doing. What chance did Holly and Jessica have against him?

As we near the anniversary of Holly's death, we continue to be annoyed – and that is putting it politely – by local community or 'Gold Group' meetings. At times we have been able to glean information from them that we felt the police should have given us. But being part of this Gold Group seems to have given some people a false sense of their own importance, and they continue to misrepresent this case as a community tragedy. And their egos are ballooning. Am I being oversensitive in thinking that these members of the clergy, educational psychologists, Council representatives, headmasters, etc. should discuss how to mark the anniversary of Holly and Jessica's deaths only after talking to the families? We prefer them – and their inflated egos – to shut up and do nothing.

As we get closer to the anniversary, I can't help but remember what we did on Saturday 14 June last year. Last year Holly was performing with the majorettes at the Church Fete. As I drive home past the churchyard, they are performing, and I realise I must tell Nicola before she goes out shopping. As I get home, it is obviously too late, for Nicola is in floods of tears, upset by this unexpected reminder of Holly's life. We don our walking boots and head off into the countryside to gather our thoughts and compose ourselves, hopefully away from prying eyes. In the early evening Nicola and I go to the annual church fund-raising event, which is a musical recital by a quintet. In a wonderful garden, it is a pleasant evening of music, food and drink – and there is even a dash of humour. One of our friends, Alison, tries to cut me a piece of bread, but hacks out a large, misshapen door wedge. We're well-mannered in Soham, and we don't laugh at those who have a loaf-cutting handicap. Not much anyway! It's nice to feel part of the group again, even if only briefly. After gaining justice for Holly and Jessica, we must reconnect with friends and family.

On Sunday 15 June 2003, I turn the television on in our bedroom to hear the two words 'Ian Huntley', before the picture appears on screen. The headline? The *News of the World* has pulled off an undercover 'trick'. Pictures of Huntley are all over the screen as, unfortunately, their hack infiltrated the prison he's being held in. We are terrified this will only help Huntley's defence team with their unfair trial argument.

I ring the police. Stewart Nicol is non-committal, though I sense some panic at Police HQ. One thing now appears certain. Huntley's defence will argue that no jury in the land won't have seen the story and the images and been influenced by them. We can only hope that the *News of the World* consulted their own legal experts before publishing the story. It is the newspaper we associate with Sara Payne and her campaign against paedophiles, after the murder of her young daughter, Sarah, so surely they would not publish something that would make it even harder for two families to gain justice.

The Home Secretary requests yet another enquiry from the Prison Service. I presume someone is going to be hugely embarrassed about the lapse in security. I suspect that, in the end, they'll say 'lack of resources and staff are to blame and procedures will be reviewed'.

The end of June brings another drama. Maxine Carr has also attempted suicide, trying to slit her wrists. I suspect she was not in too much danger when I hear that the only medical intervention needed to save her life was a single plaster. The psychologists call such attempts 'a cry for help'; this seems more like a whimper for attention. We have been imploring her to help us for months, by telling what she knows. And she hasn't. So I don't have much sympathy.

Nevertheless, Chris, Nicola and I all feel she is still likely to change her plea at the eleventh hour. Shockingly, the law actually encourages prisoners on remand to do this, I discover. While she is on remand, every single day Maxine Carr spends in prison will count for one and a half days of her sentence. So why should she change to a guilty plea and increase the time she has to stay inside? The whole system seems the wrong bloody way round.

July 2003

The beginning of July starts with a very upsetting piece of news. It seems we have been woefully misled by Chris Stevenson, as the police will be actively contributing to the documentary with the BBC. We are very upset. We really do have enough on our plate now. We repeat immediately that we will not take part in the documentary under any circumstances. I trust the police will have the courtesy to inform the BBC of our decision.

There have been many meetings between the police, the CPS and our own QCs. Encouragingly, Mr Coward, Huntley's QC, has said that he is 'live to the issue of all of the forensic tests'. But Huntley's defence team could still conduct their own forensic tests if they do not want to accept the results. So even now, the 6 October start of the trial has to be treated with caution.

In Soham it is now clear that Tim Alban Jones, Alan Ashton, Geoff Fisher, Howard Gilbert and Frank Murphy are likely to put out some form of anniversary statement on 4 August. Their theme will be 'Soham one year on' and they will all be recording their interviews later in the month; these will then be embargoed until the first week of August. At least it all seems to be organised.

By the middle of July, we see less of the police. Chris has been preparing papers for court over matters of public interest immunity information which will be given to the judge *in camera* when the jury are sent out. The jury too has to be kept out of the information loop.

Why is this legal system so one-sided? The road ahead seems rocky and we remain deeply troubled.

The *Sun* ran a story last week of a young lady who was awarded £178,000 compensation for sex harassment after one week at work.

They compare this with the £11,000 paid to Sara Payne following the murder of her daughter. We will get the same payout in the future. I have mixed feelings on this subject. No amount of money will compensate for Holly no longer being with us. However, given the emotional turmoil we have experienced and are likely to continue experiencing, if the state is compensating, then £5,500 per parent seems rather meagre.

Our concerns over Oliver's welfare remain as acute as ever. We continue to talk about Holly quite a lot and Oliver always acknowledges he is feeling okay about things when we ask. However, we both feel all is not well. We just wish somehow that we could find the key to open him up. It happens by accident eventually, and it takes me completely by surprise.

Oliver agrees to help tidy up Holly's grave. The soil has been sinking unevenly and the edges need defining and the area weeding also. I intend to dig down to remove six inches of soil throughout the grave and to refill with black fen topsoil, to give a more even, better effect. I am pleased Oliver is with me. Father and son, with a spade each, we begin the task in hand. I step back and admire Oliver's work as he carefully digs out along the top edge with his spade. He seems to be taking so much care that it is obvious he considers this task important. The sun is shining gloriously and no one else is there. Oliver fills the wheelbarrow and sets off to the tipping area. As he walks past me he simply says, 'I knew Holly would be found in a ditch, Dad,' referring back to what he said to the trauma specialist, Ruth Harrison.

When he gets back, he unloads the many questions that have obviously been troubling him since August 2002:

- *Was Holly completely naked in the ditch?*
- *How did the man know there was a ditch down there?*
- *How many people have seen Holly's body?*
- *Have you seen Holly's body?*
- *How were Holly and Jessica killed?*
- *Was Holly already dead before I searched on my bike?*

- *What will happen to the caretaker?*
- *Why did he kill Holly and Jessica?*
- *When do you think Mum will stop crying?*

I answer each question honestly. Many have already been asked and answered before but he has forgotten, and who can blame him? Things have been manic inside our house for months and I now feel that we should have made things clearer, more frequently, so Oliver could understand.

On Friday 11 July, Sonia Land, my literary agent, comes to lunch with another client of hers, David Cohen, who is an author and a film producer. Sonia is very open about struggling to find a publisher for my book due to the restrictions from the CPS. She feels it is best to leave the publishing contract until after the trial, which would also eliminate any risk of jeopardising the due process of law. I understand her predicament. David has come to sound us out about making a documentary after the trial about our experiences and to tell Holly's story. Nicola and I listen intently to him. After Sonia and David leave for London, Nicola and I discuss the theoretical offer. We decide not to formally decline David at this stage, as we have seen how our lives can change so quickly. However, we both feel it will be unlikely that a TV documentary will feature high on our priorities. For me, the book remains the only project – with or without a contract in place.

In the middle of July, Chris Mead asks if the vicar has spoken to me about his intentions for the trial. Tim has arranged for parochial duties to be covered. He has told the Cambridgeshire Police that, if it helps, he is willing to be based down at the Old Bailey. I got the impression that the police have serious reservations about self-promotional issues with Tim and worry about potential witness contamination. I suppose Tim has a different vision – promoting the good work of the church – but I am once again disappointed the vicar said nothing to me. As with most elements of my life right now, being kept in the dark causes my problems. Tim has become a high-profile individual and coverage of him attending court could mean yet more publicity and so might help the unfair trial argument.

At least the prosecution case is progressing nicely. We get brief details of three kinds of evidence. The case against Huntley will concentrate on vehicle movements, Huntley's movements and Holly and Jessica's movements. We are told nothing about a fourth strand, which I suspect consists of the increasingly 'strong' forensic findings.

Then, there is another one of these emotive 'how do you handle it' occasions. Donna Paxton Tomb comes 'home' from America to attend her and Nicola's 20-year school reunion. It is a very emotional night for Nicola, catching up with everyone for the first time since Holly's murder. To her credit, Nicola stays the night and puts on a brave face despite being acutely upset at times. Donna could not have come back at a better time for Nicola has had many emotional breakdowns over the last four weeks. The tensions leading up to the trial have slowly taken their toll on us both.

Towards the end of the month we have an unexpected visit from Chris Stevenson. The police have decided that three senior officers will be in court at all times, he tells us. They are Andy Hebb, Gary Goose and Chris Mead. I presume Chris Stevenson will be there too. We hear jury visits to Soham and Wangford will proceed. We are very pleased about this as we feel it desperately important that the jurors understand how close to our home the school is, and how remote the deposition site is.

Chris Stevenson tells us our side remains confident that the defence team will be unsuccessful in their 'unfair trial' application, but the police view is that the media have pushed the boundaries to the very limit. Nothing can be guaranteed. There could also be grounds for appeal and the appeal could go to the European Court. Our hearts sink as Mr Stevenson says this could take anything between three to five years. For Huntley it looks as if the system is there forever and a day. The irony is that the best outcome for us may well be for Huntley to be found guilty and for Carr to be found not guilty. Surely you cannot appeal on the ground it was an unfair trial if the same jury has found your co-accused not guilty? Our lives seem so contorted at the moment.

And then, it gets worse. For the first time Stevenson confirms Nicola and I will be required in the witness box by our own team. That takes our legs away rather. We both feel exceptionally apprehensive about appearing in court, though we will do anything to gain justice for Holly and Jessica.

August 2003

By the end of July, Nicola and I get the anniversary pieces for our approval. 'Soham – One Year On. A reflection by Tim Alban Jones' is first class. There is a short anniversary prayer from the Superintendent of the Newmarket Circuit of the Methodist Church, Alan Ashton. The prayer is fine, especially as I now know exactly who he is. But Ashton has also written a reflective piece, twice as long as Tim Alban Jones's. We didn't expect that, particularly as the text is not only rather self-promotional but includes a paragraph which riles me instantly.

'During these past months I have been reflecting on this tragic experience and I have identified a range of emotions and responses that I believe has enabled my discovery of finding faith at the heart of pain. The experience brought us through searching, hoping, praying, grieving, loving, caring, listening to the hardest issue yet to be faced – of forgiving.'

Well, I have news for Alan Ashton, we are still bloody grieving – every night and every day. If he thinks he is going to get on his soap box and bleat about forgiveness before we even have a verdict in place, then think again. Maybe he will find it in his heart to be forgiving when I kick him in the bollocks next time I see him.

The police agree to withdraw the piece. I believe they did so diplomatically, informing Alan Ashton that one reflective piece is enough and that, as he has written the prayer, then it is appropriate to use Tim Alban Jones's. I don't care how they manage to get to the end result, so long as it is achieved. In the same aggressive frame of mind, I ask the police to speak with Tim Alban Jones to make sure he does not attend the Old Bailey. I may be being unfair but I just feel all the clergy involved love to see themselves in lights, on camera and in quotes.

The last day of July happens to be a Thursday and is the day our local newspapers become available. The headline 'PLEASE STAY AWAY' grabs the eye. The ubiquitous Tim Alban Jones appeals to the general public not to visit Soham for the anniversary of Holly and Jessica's deaths. The piece is in a local paper, so what are people supposed to do? Leave Cambridgeshire? But it is really the rest of the article which upsets us. We learn Tim has decided to dispose of any floral tributes left in the church grounds at the end of every day. Men of God obviously don't need to consult anyone!

I'm glad we are going away to Ambleside in the Lake District for the anniversary. Before we go, Nicola and I head to Holly's grave to leave flowers. We stand and reflect together. Neither of us can believe it is almost a year since we last saw and spoke to Holly. We speak out loud to Holly, hoping she can hear us in our moment of need and we ask her to understand our reasons for not staying in Soham this coming Monday. Rob and Trudie Wright are going with us. They will be with us when 4 August comes round again for the first time, just as they were with us that fateful night one year ago.

Being out of Soham makes the anniversary a bit more bearable. Late afternoon we decide to attend the evening racing at Carlisle. Rob and I share a passion for the sport and Oliver is beginning to learn about and enjoy his horseracing. We miss the first race, so our first chance to have a look at the horses is for the 6.45 which hits us, for it is the time Jessica's phone was switched off (6.46) last year. Nicola bets on Blonde En Blonde, not only because of the obvious hair colour reference to Holly, but also because of the 'feminine' colours of the silks. As an outsider it's a brave selection and Rob and I confidently oppose

Nicola by backing the favourite. Well, only one of us troubles the bookmaker at the end of the race: collecting £80 is a very teary and emotional Nicola who wants to leave the course as soon as possible. Had we stayed for the fifth race Nicola might well have picked number 13, True Holly, and there is a horse called Old Bailey running. It doesn't matter, of course.

While we are away, the *Sun* reports on a play based on the deaths of Holly and Jessica. The director, Julie Bannister, says her inspiration 'had been drawn from real life abductions of young girls such as Holly Wells and Jessica Chapman'. My God, how low can people go? Perhaps one day Ms Bannister will be a mother herself; let us hope no one wrecks her life as a parent. Shame on her. Mr Westgate, our nuisance telephone caller and letter writer, also makes the news. He has been served with an interim anti-social behaviour order. Normally the police would have prosecuted him in court, but they were worried about publicity, and helping the unfair trial argument.

Life and death interweave as we wait for the trial. We hear of the death of Margaret Bryden's husband, Derek, and we hear that our third FLO, Stewart Nicol, and his wife have had a baby boy by the name of George. As senior management has decided two liaison officers per family will suffice for the trial, we won't see Stewart again professionally. He has been positive and played a big role in helping my family. We will always hold a place for him in our hearts.

On Thursday 14 August 2003, Nicola and I join Tim Alban Jones and his wife to travel down to Gloucestershire for a tour of the grounds of Highgrove. It's a wonderful day – good weather, great location – but what is most important is that it gives me time to talk with Tim once more. And to listen to his different views. By the time we get back, he has promised he will no longer talk with the media without informing me beforehand of his intentions. I appreciate his courtesy.

The defence statement from Huntley's legal team failed to materialise again last Friday. Again the police feel the judge will be displeased, but why isn't something being done about this? To me the lack of a defence statement has an underhand feel to it and does nothing to instil any confidence in the legal system for the near future.

On Monday 18 August, we get a shock that will feel much worse for the Chapmans. The CPS are dropping the case against Brian Stevens. The police let us understand that the case against him was strong. If something can happen at the eleventh hour to torpedo a strong case and get it dropped, what twists and turns await the start – or not – of our trial? Also, it will mean a return to the media spotlight; it will mean the smiling photograph of Holly and Jessica will illustrate banner headlines about a police officer who was once accused of indecent assault and possession of child pornography. This really does make me feel sick.

When Brian Stevens does appear on TV we find his posturing quite repellent. There are many unanswered questions. His arrogance almost defies belief. We believe something is not right about this whole business, and so do his former police colleagues. They are very angry at the CPS who decided not to let a jury judge. The whole debacle makes one think the system is protecting one of its own. I wonder how the Chapman family is feeling about this decision.

So how did Brian Stevens's credit card details get used to download child porn? How did pornographic images appear on his personal laptop, the one he uses for work? Perhaps we will never know officially, but I suspect the answers are rather simple and could be given by every adult in Britain. Standing alongside Brian Stevens is his wife, Jane, a social worker. Like many others, I am surprised she is willing to play the happy doting wife. Many people in Soham know her. She was the social worker who was called in to advise the young girl who was caught up in the saga which eventually led to the previous caretaker at the school, Mike Curtain, leaving. Huntley replaced Curtain. How life moves full circle!

The unexpected Brian Stevens's twist makes August even busier, and there is more bad news waiting just round the corner. On the 26th of the month, Chris Stevenson and Gary Goose ask to meet as a matter of urgency. They come straight to the point. Cambridgeshire Police have received a letter from Huntley's QC requesting an adjournment of the trial until January 2004. Nicola and I sit in stunned silence.

The prosecution will oppose the request on a number of grounds but Chris Stevenson and Gary Goose's tone of voice and body language suggest the defence will get their way. We agree to explain to the court how the delay will have a devastating impact on us. It may help and it is the least we can do.

When the police go, Nicola and I discuss the emotional issue of having a second Christmas without justice for Holly. We hoped we would see some end, but what we have just been told reminds us that our destiny remains in the control of others.

By the end of the month, I decide to stop work totally in order to focus on writing my book, which is not going particularly well. Scott and I agree to sell my part of the business to a mutual friend, Robert Wadsworth. I respect them both but, sadly, what Robert can pay falls woefully short of the market value. This is not an accusation, Robert, merely an observation. To get the best price, I would have to advertise my business for sale, potentially drawing publicity and headlines once again. So I don't have much choice but to sell privately and accept 'the loss'. I could not live with myself if somehow I contributed to publicity which helped Huntley and Carr escape trial. After signing the contract, Robert and I share a drink. As he goes in his delightfully upbeat and bullish manner, I ponder the bloody irony bloody again. For five years, I have worked seven days a week, slowly but surely building up my business, with one main aim in mind. To place ourselves in a financial position where we could afford to send Holly to the King's School at Ely, a school that would allow her musical and artistic talents to develop. That dream was wrecked last year, but it does not stop me thinking about it now. Nor does it stop me thinking about the time I did not spend with Holly during those five years, as work took so much of my energy. I have now under-sold my only asset and I am not sure how we will cope finan-cially.

September 2003

The Chapman family, Nicola and I are scheduled to meet the CPS and the West Midlands Police to hear why the case against Brian Stevens was dropped. Apparently the West Midlands police are seething at the decision. Then, the meeting is abruptly cancelled by Cambridgeshire Police. We are not told why, of course, and we can only assume the plot has just thickened somewhat.

The trial judge is not due back from holiday until 19 September, so we will not know the answer to Huntley's request for an adjournment till then. Strangely, it appears we have an unlikely ally, as Maxine Carr's legal team have made it clear they are ready for the trial and do not want the delay either. But Gary Goose still feels it will be put back to allow a 'fair trial' to happen. If a defence team asks for more time to prepare and doesn't get it, then there is an obvious appeal point if the verdict goes against them. I resign myself. The adjournment request will succeed. I try to understand why Huntley's team wants the delay. Is the evidence so compelling that no explanation can be put forward to defend Huntley? Are they struggling to disprove any forensic results? I am going to assume the answer to both my questions is – yes.

Although Gary has just informed me that Carr's team is ready for the trial, they also want something which suggests otherwise. 'Kevin, Maxine Carr's defence team has requested a copy of your writings completed so far,' Gary says. My heart sinks at the thought of handing over my observations. I have no concerns over my work being scrutinised by Carr's lawyers as they will soon realise that we have been kept out of the police information loop. What angers me is handing over details of my trials and tribula-tions, for the likes of Carr and Huntley to read before my friends and family do. The situation feels utterly wrong. Gary is surprised

I refuse to comply. I am sick to the back teeth. For the last 13 months, I have been forced to react in a negative manner as twist after turn affects my personal and family life. Don't people realise my daughter has been murdered, for fuck's sake? Yet, I have to hear why Carr's legal team has the right to access this information and what may happen if I do not comply. The system is completely insane. What about the right to a fair trial for the family of the victim? Enough is enough and although there is nothing to gain by shooting the messenger. I feel a great deal better for offloading a couple of barrels in Gary's direction.

As ever, Gary talks me round and, in the end, I agree to supply my notes to allow him to judge which points are relevant and need sharing with Carr's legal team. Gary feels the rest of the information will be withheld through an application to the trial judge under public interest immunity, which is a compromise at least.

On Sunday 7 September, new revelations about Brian Stevens. The *Mail on Sunday* run a story which suggests that his 'crucial alibi', Louise Austin, may be a former lover. She claimed Brian Stevens had travelled from a police convalescent home in Goring-on-Thames to her home in Cambridgeshire to spend the night innocently on the couch. Stevens could not possibly have downloaded child pornography images. So a mystery porn-freak must have hacked into his computer. I am a sceptical beast now and I wonder why Stevens did not travel back to his own home which happens to be in the same county as Louise Austin's. Kevin-the-sceptic suspects the journey to Ms Austin was all in the man's imagination and it is no wonder the West Midlands Police are fuming about the decision to drop the case against him. Ms Austin also worked for the CPS.

It is, however, the *News of the World*'s front-page headline that really grabs our attention as it reports the split between Michael and Sara Payne after the murder of their daughter, Sarah. There is not a comment made that we cannot relate to; the article is a desperately sad read. Sara Payne said, 'I think Mike and I both focused so hard on trying to build normality back into our family, we ended up forgetting we had a marriage that needed looking after too.'

I know what she means. Nicola and I have become more than distant over the last few months. No longer do we go to bed at the same time together. No longer do we sit down and eat a meal together. We both drink far more and I am by far the biggest culprit. Clearly, we have no fun in our lives. I am, perhaps self-ishly, bent on writing a book as a way of dealing with my feel-ings. Nicola does not share that. Of course, we talk every day, especially about our worries for Oliver, but it just may be that if we do not address our own relationship difficulties we may well create more problems for our son. Under any circumstances that would be unforgivable.

Two mediums said Tuesday 9 September would be a big, posi-tive day. Dennis predicted we would receive some money that day. Well, it is one up to the paranormals. We are asked to meet with the Marketing Committee of the Cambridgeshire Darts Organisation, at the Carpenter's Arms, to be presented with a cheque following a fund-raising competition. We appreciate the gesture and we stay and socialise for the most of the evening. It is a close to home reminder that the world is full of many caring people. But, because I now know the legal rules, I ask them not to give the media any details. I feel quite bad about their well-intended efforts not receiving any publicity.

Two days later the *Cambridge Evening News* confirms that Brian Stevens and Louise Austin have been re-arrested, this time on suspicion of perverting the course of justice. This offence carries a higher sentence than the earlier charges against Brian Stevens, so I cannot help but wonder how he is feeling today. The West Midlands Police are dealing with both the accused, so no incriminating stone will be left unturned. The front page also has a story first run by the *Daily Express*, which 'reveals' I am writing a book. The police, like me, are confused as to where this leak could have come from.

On 19 September, Chris Mead tells me that the trial has been put back four weeks and will now start on 3 November 2003. Clearly it is not unexpected. What is unexpected, however, is that Huntley's defence team have asked for their apologies to be extended to the families over the delay. A little bit of courtesy does help, and we accept our new position as gracefully as we can. But courtesy does not mean they have abandoned the unfair trial argument. Dealing with these issues pre-trial will take place on 27 October. The fact that we are only five weeks away is enough to set my nerves jangling. The rest of our lives depends on the result of this 'trial within a trial'.

The 22nd of September is my 40th birthday. And it brings good news. Chris Mead tells me that the defence teams have accepted our statements and that no member of my family will have to give evidence in court. It has taken 13 months to get here. Now, finally, we have been given the green light to hear all the details of the case against Huntley and Carr. There are so many questions I need answering and now this is actually going to happen. No excuses, no half answers, no deflecting tactics, no refusals. I can ask what I want and the information will be shared with me. I am glad it fell to Chris to give me this good news. Goodness only knows what pressure I have placed him under during the last year.

We set a date for the briefing and I cannot wait. As Chris leaves, I am left alone to reflect on today's unexpected twist. I am so relieved that Oliver will not have the ordeal of appearing as a witness that I start to cry. I annoy myself for being so sensitive, but then it dawns on me that, for the first time, my tears are tears of joy and relief, not of sadness. I have already received the best birthday present imaginable.

On 24 September, a number of high-ranking police officers walk round Soham to assess the logistics of the impending jury visit. The law has its quirks when it comes to this. First, both Huntley and Carr have the right to come along. I suppose that's reasonable, but the rules allow them to keep us all in suspense to the very last moment. On the morning of the visit, they can insist they want to be there. The potential security risks are obvious.

October 2004

Saturday 4 October would have been Holly's 12th birthday. I can still picture and remember her excitement on her 10th birthday and it is the energy and twinkle that Holly brought to our home that is still missing today. Perhaps it will never be the same again, I just do not know. For Nicola, as with all key dates over the last 15 months, the build-up has been the most difficult of times.

However, with the trial now fast approaching we have to focus.

Next Friday we will both, for the first time, get to hear the case against Huntley and, as we go to Holly's grave, we talk about it. In the weak morning sunshine, we take a seat and we confess all our fears as we brace ourselves to re-enter the public arena.

As we wait, there are a couple of flash points to contend with. The BBC has returned to Soham, which we knew was in the pipeline. Bizarrely, Nicola and I see a film crew outside the jet wash at Downfields Service Station, which seems very specific. Why would anyone film a jet wash? The police must have pointed them to it as a key area in the forthcoming trial. Chris Stevenson has spent a lot of time over the last few weeks with the media. I have no evidence to support my gut feeling, but, as we have been misled on a grand scale from beginning to end over this bloody documentary, we feel entitled to raise our deep concerns. We ask when Mr Stevenson and his fellow officers will start their interviews with the BBC. Presumably, they will be talking about the case against Huntley. Presumably, areas of evidence will be discussed before the trial starts. Why can't people just be honest about their intentions from day one? I am extremely disappointed in Chris Stevenson. Maybe in a few years I will look back and fail to understand why I am so upset about it. For now, though, I cannot understand why the police are helping the BBC just so the TV people can have a scoop on the night of the verdict.

As the trial nears, as being allowed finally to hear the details of the case nears, we find it hard to sleep. On 10 October, Chris, Trudie and their coordinator, Gary Goose, sit down with Nicola and myself. First, we have to read, digest and sign a detailed written undertaking. It says that as a result of our evidence being agreed an opportunity has arisen to:

'provide the parents with more detailed information in relation to the disappearance and deaths of their daughters, furthermore to provide to them an overview of the evidence against Ian Huntley.

The main objective to us all remains that Ian Huntley and Maxine Carr receive a fair trial. The Police therefore, in considering the above, have to take into account a number of factors to ensure that this objective is not in any way risked or compromised.'

The two main risks are that such information and the detail of the evidence reaches the public arena before the trial, thus risking the integrity of the trial. And, second, that one of us has to give evidence because of some last-minute change. The undertaking continues:

'It is therefore a matter for the Police to balance the understandable need of both families for information against preserving the integrity of the trial.'

To fulfil their legal obligation, the police must ensure the following:

1. The detail at this stage is one of an overview and does not go into detail as to the identity of witnesses or the detail of the evidence that they provide.
2. The information provided is restricted only to Sharon and Les Chapman and Kevin and Nicola Wells.

The two main risks are precisely the risks the police are taking by working with the BBC, but now is not a time for scoring points. It has taken an eternity to get here, so we simply sign our undertaking and as we sit in silence, the laptop presentation begins.

Huntley you are a fucking, conniving coward. Holly had more qualities than you will ever possess. May you rot in hell.

On Monday 13 October, Huntley's legal team disclose their unfair trial argument. Reassuringly, we are told it contains nothing that is not expected. I hope that this is a good sign for later in the month.

The last few days have been emotionally very tough. Reflecting on our newly acquired information has been soul-destroying. Our thoughts cannot move away from Holly and Jessica and their suffering. Never before in my life have I felt such anger and repulsion. Life is unfair and I feel so lost. The sooner that bastard is sent down, the sooner we can begin to rebuild. I also think about the many weird, cruel people who have contacted us. Where now are the scum who have been turning up to my home over the last year, when I feel ready for them? Where are the crazy people who ring my doorbell to ask if I will support their warped campaign to release Ian Huntley? Where are the people with their anti-American theories, posting their audio tapes through my door? Where are the international paedophile ring chasers who insist Holly and Jessica are moments from being rescued? Come to my fucking door now, you wankers. Knowing what I know now, you will receive more than a polite fuck-off.

On Wednesday 22 October, Chris comes to what surely must be my final pre-trial meeting with Sonia Land, my literary agent. This time roles are slightly reversed, for now I want Chris to protect my integrity. Over the last four weeks, I have received many offers from television and newspapers, some very substantial. It is becoming quite a scary position. My instructions to Sonia are simple:

1. My writing project is the be all and end all for me; I only need a publishing contract.
2. If a newspaper features in your planning because of

serialisation rights, please select a paper that you feel will represent my family and me fairly. Money is not the key issue.

3.   In terms of finance if you can negotiate a fee to compensate for the underselling of my business, the two years I believe I will need to complete my book and a three-year period of reduced earnings whilst I rebuild another cleaning business, I will be most grateful.

I agree with Sonia that I will not be in touch with her again until the trial is over. To date, this remarkable woman has epitomised business integrity and I trust her as my future lies in the balance.

Two days later, Chris and Trudie give us both an overview of what we can expect to happen at the pre-trial and what problems could occur. We hear that the lead QCs for Huntley and Carr will dominate the opening day. We are told to prepare ourselves mentally for only hearing one side of the argument, which is going to be very hard. Our QC Mr Latham will reply, of course, but we know that to hear highly intelligent, skilled advocates plead for Huntley and Carr will be monumentally tough. The defence teams will leave no stone unturned to obtain their right result: for them it is a matter of professional pride. The phrases 'beyond reasonable doubt' and 'on a balance of probability' sound rather hollow when your daughter has been murdered.

Mr Coward will obviously harp on every aspect of the excessive media reporting. The judge will be shown endless examples of stories on Huntley and Carr's background, Huntley's mental state, paedophile references or sexually abnormal references from Huntley's former partners, the claim that both Huntley and Carr gained jobs by deception and so on. It is very difficult to think of the media in positive terms at the moment as their work will be used to argue it is impossible to find 12 men and women who have not been influenced by all the reporting.

As a counter argument we hear Mr Latham QC will speak of 'the fade factor' in that sufficient time has passed, meaning that details are no longer in the forefront of people's minds. (Suddenly

I am grateful to Huntley's defence team for requesting an adjournment.) He will also mention that Huntley put himself in the public eye by courting the media. Chris's final comment captures, at long last, my longing for justice. He knows our lawyers will say that 'some cases are just too serious not to be tried'. He could not be more right.

But that need not be the end of it. Chris and Trudie highlight negative scenarios that could affect the process:

1. Huntley could be declared medically unfit to stand trial.
2. Huntley could sack his legal team, even at the eleventh hour.
3. Huntley could make an admission to his legal team, leaving them 'professionally embarrassed'.

Finally, Chris and Trudie discuss the possibility that Huntley may accept he did kill Holly and Jessica and plead guilty to manslaughter on the grounds of diminished responsibility. Our legal team will not accept this plea, as they feel the case against him is just too strong, thank God. For all of us the only successful result is the conviction of Huntley for double murder. Nothing less will allow us to move forwards as a family.

The weekend before Monday's Old Bailey start, Nicola and I work out how to best deal with appearing in public while the country gets to hear every harrowing detail of our daughter's last moments. We decide to see the trial process looking through the eyes of the jury. How will they perceive events, evidence, procedure, pressure? Will they understand legal protocol? Will they understand the legal tactics? This is virgin territory for us too, as well as for 12 members of the public, no different to ourselves.

Oliver wants to stay at home for the trial. We will come home every evening to share developments with him. The trial will dominate the media, so it's best he hear the details from his parents. Nicola and I also decide not to attend all of the days together so sometimes one of us will be at home for him. Equally, I do not intend to go to court when friends and people from Soham give evidence. It is going to be a very tough experience for some and I do not want my positive images of any of them tainted by some barrister ripping them to bits to make a point.

Tomorrow, we will confront the court system, the media and our own anxieties and fears. We have the support and best wishes of family, friends and local community, and also, I suspect, most people in the country wish us well. Two brilliant girls were murdered and their bodies burned. That must not be forgotten.

The Trial before the Trial

27–29 October 2003

The walk from Snow Hill Police Station, despite the phalanx of press, does not seem so stressful, but we are in a little bit of a daze as we make our way to the Old Bailey. As we walk through two sets of wooden double doors into the court, we take our seat at the very back, facing the empty dock. The press are in front. We are unexpectedly at the back solely because Mr Coward asked for us to be tucked away so we can't make any eye contact with the jury. If we cry because something is upsetting and the jury sees it, it might prejudice his client's right to a fair trial.

Unbelievable really!

It is even more unbelievable because there is no jury yet. The pre-trial deals with questions of law rather than of fact.

As Huntley and Carr are brought separately into the dock, they fail to spot where we are seated, although I suspect their legal teams have told them. As they both take their seats, we realise we can see the reflection of Huntley and Carr's faces clearly in the protective raised glass screen. It is almost as good as sitting in the front-row seats as we had asked. I hope we will have an opportunity to see them squirm later in the week.

By lunchtime we are getting very frustrated as we listen to Mr Coward embellish his argument with example after example of what was in the press. I start to believe the man is going to read out every story. But Mr Justice Moses interrupts, rather curtly, to say that as he has already read the examples, Mr Coward does not have to declaim them all to him.

Twenty minutes into the afternoon, Mr Coward sits down. The police are pleased, and surprised, that the application is over so quickly. Mr Hubbard, representing Maxine Carr, adds only a couple more examples. Then our QC, Mr Latham, replies. Tomorrow at 2 p.m., we will find out whether our prayers will be answered.

The drive home is painfully slow due both to the traffic and having a former policeman – the delightfully named Ringo – driving and keeping meticulously to the speed limit. But by 8 o'clock we join Oliver and update him. He does not seem very concerned about the specifics of the day but, before going to bed, he does ask one question, 'Will the trial happen?' We can't give him an answer.

If only we knew!

Neither Nicola nor I get any sleep. We're both too anxious about that very point. We hardly talk as we drive to London late the next morning for the 2 o'clock start. Justice for Holly and Jessica now lies in the hands of one individual. The thought that the judge might allow the defence applications to succeed is just too harrowing to think about – but I can't help thinking about it.

Court Number One fills but the place is hushed. Many people mouth 'good luck' messages as we sit behind the media representatives again. Bizarrely, although seats are not reserved, people seem to be sitting in the same seats. It is almost as if an unwritten agreement exists after yesterday's first come, first served melee.

The judge is sharp on time. I can feel my heart quicken. I sit down and Nicola slips her hand into mine. The moment is upon us. It's not a long moment. Within seconds Mr Justice Moses dismisses both applications. It is a moment of pure euphoric joy to hear this simple sentence. In front of me, their heads bowed, sit Huntley and Carr. I hope their hearts (if they have any) are beating as fast as mine. As I have seen an overview of the case against Huntley, today's decision means one thing and one thing only: a guilty verdict will be forthcoming. Huntley, your days are numbered.

Mr Justice Moses explains the reasons for his decision and then we go back to the witness service area where we can celebrate properly, and noisily. But even then I feel we have to be careful as we are aware that, yesterday, the judge gave Mr Coward permission for Huntley to be absent from court in order to have a psychiatric assessment. It must be very reassuring for Huntley to have so much medical expertise at his disposal. If the doctors decide Huntley is not stable enough to instruct counsel, the trial will probably be delayed again. What makes all this harder is that this hidden threat is likely to be with us throughout the trial. Nevertheless, it is not all doom and gloom. Yesterday Huntley regularly signalled and wrote notes to his legal team. He cannot have it both ways. By being so involved in his defence, I hope Huntley may just have shot himself in the foot.

We get back to Soham quite confident. Little did we know what Mr Coward had in store for us.

29 October

We thought the prosecution and the defence had come to an understanding about some aspects of the conduct of the trial. We would find out otherwise. As Mr Coward rises, there is a swagger in his body language. He is going to make an impact. He is ahead of the rest in grasping how crucial the next few minutes are. He says, 'What I am about to say has been the result of many months of deliberation. To the best of Mr Huntley's present knowledge and recollection.'

Before Mr Coward can finish, the judge interrupts: 'Why do you need to say this in court?' He adds that Mr Coward is under no pressure to say anything. My God what is about to be said here? Surely, it cannot be that important. I do not know if I am in a state of panic or confusion. Arrangements are supposed to be in place to warn us when any sensitive material is going to be introduced in evidence. Within seconds, our unwritten agreement is exposed as worthless rhetoric as Mr Coward prepares to read a list of admissions, which Huntley accepts:

1. *The deceased girls came into 5 College Close some time after 6.28 p.m.*

2. *The deceased girls died upstairs at 5 College Close.*

3. *The death of Holly Wells was in the bathroom and was accidental.*

4. *The death of Jessica Chapman occurred after Holly Wells on the threshold of the bathroom.*

5. *Huntley laid hands on Jessica Chapman in order to stop her screaming.*

6. *Huntley is unsure where exactly he placed his hands and at no stage did he intend to kill or cause grievous bodily harm to Jessica Chapman.*

7. *Huntley placed the deceased girls in the Ford Fiesta and drove them to the deposition site.*

8. *Huntley cut the clothing off the deceased at the deposition site.*

9. *Huntley set fire to the bodies.*

10. *Huntley brought the clothing back to the college.*

11. *Huntley attempted to burn the clothing outside the Hangar in the bin.*

12. *Huntley moved the clothing inside the Hangar.*

13. *Huntley changed all of the tyres on his Ford Fiesta; however, this is unconnected to the events in issue.*

14. *Huntley never returned to the deposition site.*

(The above list is not an exact copy of Mr Coward's words. However, it is an accurate representation of the notes taken by two police officers in the courtroom.)

Nicola and I sit aghast, completely shocked by the revelations. Members of the press stare at us to gauge our reaction. So does the crowd in the public gallery. The two key admissions are those that say Holly died accidentally and that both the girls died upstairs. We become extremely distressed but we are in court, stuck among many reporters, and we don't want it to show. It takes an immense effort to maintain some composure. Somehow, Nicola and I both manage to stop ourselves crying out loud, but Nicola cannot stop silent tears from falling. As she struggles to maintain her dignity, I can only reflect on Mr Coward's work, this morning.

Lawyers have to defend their clients, of course, but we could have been warned and the Chapmans could have been warned – to be prepared for something momentous. I'm afraid it leaves me feeling bitter towards Mr Coward. The road ahead is going to be a long one. Our return to the witness service area is emotional. We're bewildered and in some disarray. This was not what we expected. After what feels like an eternity waiting, FLO coordinator Gary Goose joins us and we hang on to his every word. First, the good news. Today's admissions have come out, because of the strength of the case against Huntley. The police feel that over the last 3 days the case has moved forwards more than it did in the last 14 months. Mr Coward will not dispute vast chunks of material, so the case will probably finish this side of Christmas, which is excellent news.

But to get two murder convictions we must prove Huntley's state of mind was that of a sane, calculating individual. We wonder just why these admissions have been put forward today. The answer may well be linked to Mr Coward's new application. In light of the admissions the defence cannot see the purpose of the jury visit to Soham and Lakenheath! Mr Latham opposes this vehemently because he knows how damning those visits will be. Judge Moses rules the visits will take place.

We're sick as we realise what is *not* in the admissions; there are no specific references as to how Holly or Jessica died. But the defence don't have to explain; it is up to the prosecution to prove guilt 'beyond a reasonable doubt'. The police believe Huntley will retain his right to silence and not go into the witness box, which is a great shame, as our legal team would love the chance to cross-examine him.

At home, Nicola and I settle down to share our own thoughts

far removed from the intense atmosphere of the Old Bailey. Next week, the pressure will really be on because a jury will have been sworn in.

The Trial

3 November–31 December 2003

With the benefit of hindsight I realise that the last year has taken its toll on Nicola and me. We have both become aggressive, mistrustful and suspicious of everyone and everything that may affect Holly and Jessica's right to justice. We have stopped trusting people and this is totally out of character. We need to reclaim our characters, our personalities, as they were before we lost Holly.

Nicola and I know that we have stopped doing 'the little things' for one another that make our marriage a happy and sponta-neous one. As we share some observations and criticisms, I slowly begin to realise that I have misjudged Nicola's emotional recovery. I have assumed that her brave face and outward strength repre-sent her real feelings. I could not have been more wrong. Nicola is as broken-hearted now as she was in August 2002. I've been so self-absorbed, trying to deal with my own pain through the book, that I have completely overlooked the well-being of the one person who deserves so much more. With Nicola still desper-ately trying to adjust to life without Holly, I feel such a bloody fool.

I only very recently explained to Nicola my reasons for wanting to write this book and it means a great deal that she is supporting it. For the first time since my writing became serious at the beginning of the year, Nicola is reading some of my notes and manuscript. Writing has forced me to confront some tough issues. I only hope she can deal with these, if they hit her as she reads.

I also feel a fool about my son. Oliver is still quiet. Margaret Bryden, Vice-Principal of the Village College, rang us to discuss him. At a recent parent–teacher meeting teachers mentioned how subdued he seemed. It hasn't helped that we have not exactly shown a great deal of unity in front of Oliver recently.

Oliver's birthday is in the first week of December and will almost certainly fall during the trial, which is unfortunate, but there is a little positive development for him – at my expense. Back in the spring Oliver asked if he could have a quad bike. We couldn't afford it, but I did not want to rule it out entirely. I promised Oliver that if he could somehow save half the purchase price, I would match him with the other half. To my complete shock he has managed to do just that, so I now have to keep my promise and order the bike. I shall be more careful in future!

We finally feel able to think about our memorial to Holly. That brings Nicola and me into contact with the local stone mason, Jeremy Reader. It seems many years ago now that Jeremy was a young lad playing in the Isleham youth cricket team I coached, so circumstances apart, it is good to see him again. It does not take long to realise that his artistic talents far surpass his sporting ones – fortunately. It is a huge step for us to begin thinking about a lasting tribute. Jeremy quickly grasps its importance. We do not have to explain that we will never have the chance to celebrate Holly's 18th or 21st birthdays, engagement or wedding. This is it, our final parental contribution to Holly's life. We trust in Jeremy's abilities to design and create a fitting headstone for our little soul-mate; it will include the images of the Soham Rose and Winnie the Pooh, Holly's favourite character. We ask only that it is in place before Christmas.

We also have to make domestic arrangements for the trial. Members of our family will care for Oliver while we are at the Old Bailey. We will be driven to a basement car park to avoid the press scrum, and this car park is only a couple of minutes' walk from the centre of the Old Bailey. The system has granted us exemptions from security checks when entering the building. If our daily commute becomes too arduous, the police will book us into a hotel for the evening, another small example of the level of service and care we continue to receive.

There has been a quite extraordinary desire to obtain justice for Holly and Jessica amongst ordinary police officers. To acknowledge their work and commitment, we agree to take part in a post-trial press conference, already planned by the police. Of course, we won't contribute if Huntley is found not guilty.

Finally, now that Huntley has admitted so much, we can give a little thought to Maxine Carr. The police continue to say that the case against her is strong, so we take them at their word and expect a guilty verdict on all charges. But what if this does not happen? Our position is simple: so long as Huntley goes down, we don't give a damn about Maxine Carr.

5 November to 20 November

First day of evidence in court. Like the jury, we concentrate as Mr Latham methodically outlines our case. Certain details are very harrowing, and we are glad when the lunch break comes round. As we get to the witness service area, we are told that our nuisance writer and caller, Mr Westgate, has turned up outside the Old Bailey and caused a commotion. He's now under arrest. Perhaps a spell in a London jail will give him time to think clearly about the consequences of acting in this preposterous manner.

By 3 p.m. on 7 November, Mr Latham completes his opening statement. The cases against Huntley and Carr appear over-whelming. I can't help but wonder what the jury are thinking. Over the last three days, Huntley became visibly agitated as he listened to the evidence against him. I've never sat through a court case before and I'm amazed how Huntley's legal team keeps inter-rupting proceedings, requesting adjournments for their client.

Some sanity is eventually restored by the judge, who tells Mr Coward: 'The Court will not revolve around Mr Huntley. There are other parties' interests that need to be considered.' We are really frightened when Huntley and his legal team disappear from the courtroom, to return with not one, but two psychiatrists.

Before the jury is brought in each morning, Huntley and Carr's legal teams complain about press reports of the previous day's evidence. It becomes a routine: court rises, sits, and then the day starts with a fine display of whining and self-pity by the defence. I'd naïvely thought the unfair trial issue had already been resolved, but it seems to just drag on. Messrs Coward and Hubbard hand over the offending tabloid articles with a good deal of dramatic posturing. These two impressive advocates will try every trick they know in defence of their clients.

Happily, all Mr Justice Moses does is to tell the media to 'dampen down emotions so the defendants can get a fair trial'. The police, like Nicola and I, feel very positive about the judge and the way he has overseen the proceedings so far. He has the most extraordinarily dismissive tone of voice. No wonder one of the newspapers referred to him as a 'headmaster' type.

Mr Latham's opening speech dwells on an irony. Huntley is arguing that he can't have a fair trial because of the press – yet for 13 days, while we searched for Holly and Jessica, he did nothing but talk to the bloody media. He spun lie after lie, particularly on television. The prosecution needs to show that his actions were deliberate and carefully planned. But what's more planned and deliberate than telling lie after lie to cover your guilt?

It does a lot to change our feelings towards the media, and the journalists sitting in front of us here in court. They are, essentially, allies, and we salute them: because of their exhaustive coverage, no one can claim that Huntley did not know what he was doing.

By the end of the day, Mr Latham has set out the prosecution case. Huntley's defence team may have two avenues, we are told. First, Huntley may claim that Holly and Jessica were killed in self-defence, which is almost comical and can be dismissed out of hand. Second, Huntley could argue that Holly and Jessica were killed by accident. Only time will tell.

For the past few days, family members have joined us in court. Nicola's parents are here and they say they want to come regularly; my mother and Aunt Sheena are present but they don't want to return, which I am pleased about, for they have witnessed 'the positive' part of the trial, with Mr Latham presenting our case. From now on, Mr Coward and Mr Hubbard will be having their say. We all brace ourselves for a difficult journey as they try to discredit the prosecution's witnesses and evidence.

On Monday 10 November, the jury is due to visit Soham. The jury will be driven past Jessica's house on the way to my home where the ill-fated last walk started and end up at the Village College. The area must be press-free and 'sterile', in police jargon, with no one able to communicate with the jurors. We decide to leave Soham and head for a walk in the grounds belonging to Simon Gibson in the nearby village of Exning, a walk we have enjoyed many times because the grounds are private.

As we travel out of Soham, we pass the convoy of police motor-cyclists, the judge's car and the coach transporting the jury members. It is a surreal moment. Late afternoon we return home and touch base with the police to hear how the jury visit went. Smoothly, it seems. For the senior members of the police, today is also a busy day, as they are completing their interviews for the BBC documentary. The assumption is that two guilty verdicts will be returned against Huntley. Let us hope that Mr Coward's advocacy skills do not force them to eat humble pie.

On 11 November the jury will travel to visit the deposition site in Wangford. And we will be quietly visiting 5 College Close, the scene of our daughter's murder.

Before we visit the former caretaker's house, Nicola completes yet another statement for the police. She confirms that Holly never suffered from fainting, blackouts, fits, convulsions, epilepsy or any other condition that might cause her to suddenly fall over. It's the first clear sign we have that our side is preparing to counter a possible explanation Mr Coward may put forward for Holly's death, supposedly in the bathroom. Our side is trying to close any potential loopholes that might make the jury think there was a 'reasonable doubt'.

We are only allowed into College Close after the area has been swept for press. Then, suddenly, the moment is with us. Nicola and I slip quietly inside the house with our FLOs and Detective Inspector Alan Gill. The supported wall structures and what looks like temporary flooring is all there is. There is not a single thing left in the house, even the doors have been removed.

We head for the bathroom, which I want to see because of my recurring nightmares and Huntley's admission. I am shocked by how small it is. We fail to see how Holly could come to any harm by falling here: if the bathroom furniture were still present, there would only be a few feet of empty space. She just couldn't have fallen far – or hard – enough in here to sustain a serious injury. What is Mr Coward going to suggest?

One unexpected thing hits us. Huntley had a panoramic view from this house. Looking through his bedroom window, he could see the Hangar, the very building where they found the girls' clothing. Downstairs, at the front of the house, a window over-looks the Lodeside part of the school. Huntley could see Holly and Jessica from the moment they left the Sports Centre. They walked past his house and into College Road, before completing the fateful U-turn. Witness sightings confirm that the girls, for whatever reason, turned back, just after passing Huntley's house. I do not believe for one second that this was their idea; more likely they were called back. By Huntley. Two ten-year-old girls couldn't possibly imagine his evil intentions. Forget Huntley's ramblings about being outside with his dog and 'suddenly noticing Holly and Jessica standing next to him'. Forget every word the man utters. His lair was ready and waiting.

Before we go, we tell ourselves to take something positive from the visit; twelve jurors have seen what we have today. Unlike us, they are not aware of Mr Coward's attempts to get the jury visit cancelled. This is held back in case it affects their view of the proceedings – or maybe because it would reveal so much about Huntley's character.

We hope that the jury will remember the details and significance of what they saw.

After this visit we are off to the Marriott Hotel, to meet Tom Lloyd, Chief Constable of Cambridgeshire. There's a second meeting scheduled with David Westwood, Chief Constable of Humberside. We have been told these meetings will cover issues relating to Huntley's past, and will explain how he got a job as a caretaker. There seems to be a grey area relating to background checks. Chris has warned that the meeting with Mr Westwood is going to be difficult.

The meeting with Tom Lloyd is straightforward enough. Background checks on Huntley were completed on his 'other' surname of Nixon, so no link was made with Huntley's 'record'. Even if it had been completed correctly, this check would not have turned up anything other than a domestic burglary incident, 'lying on file'. This suggests that the Cambridgeshire Police did not mess up. But we also learn that there was some confusion over the sending and receiving of a fax between Cambridgeshire and Humberside Police. It does not really matter much to us where the error lies, if the fax would not have brought any new information to light.

We also discuss issues that have caused us trouble, such as police cooperation with the BBC and the seating at the Old Bailey. Mr Lloyd promises that he will ask if we can sit in the Corporation of London seats, in front of Huntley and Carr, on verdict day, at least. Mr Lloyd also mentions that Her Majesty's Inspector of Constabulary and the Home Secretary are showing interest in the questions of vetting and how intelligence is held. There may be an enquiry after the trial. At first this strikes me as a rather extreme measure, and I can't see the justification for it. But my view would change after our second meeting, with the second chief constable.

As we meet the Chief Constable of Humberside, David Westwood, we are presented with a formal letter and an appendix, outlining the contacts between Humberside Police and Huntley and Carr, over a number of years. The letter reads:

'I wanted to see you today in order to inform you personally of a number of previous contacts that Humberside Police had with Ian Huntley and Maxine Carr in the years before 2002. It has not been possible for me to give you these details earlier, in order to protect the trial process, but in seeing you today I have sought to ensure that you are fully informed at the very earliest opportunity.'

The letter concludes:

'It is very important that the trial of Ian Huntley and Maxine Carr is not in any way prejudiced and clearly the information contained within this letter has the ability to do that, should the content become common knowledge prior to the verdict being announced. I would ask therefore that the content remain confidential to yourselves until the verdict.'

The last sentence is like a breath of fresh air, with someone placing some trust in the parents, at long last. However, upon turning over the page to read the appendix, we are completely engulfed in shock:

Contact One   Allegation of Unlawful Sexual Intercourse with
                  a Girl of 15 years of age. (1995)
Contact Two   Allegation of Burglary and Theft – dwelling
                  (1995)
Contact Three   Allegation of Unlawful Sexual Intercourse with
                  a Girl of 13 years of age. (1996)
Contact Four   Allegation of Non-payment of Fines/Arrest
                  for Failing to Appear at Court. (1996)
Contact Five   Allegation of Rape on Adult. (1998)
Contact Six   Allegation of Rape on Adult. (1998)
Contact Seven   Allegation of Indecent Assault on a Girl of 12
                  years. (1998)
Contact Eight   Allegation of Rape on 17-year-old Girl. (1999)
Contact Nine   Allegation of Rape on 17-year-old Girl. (1999)

Each contact carries a summary of details and a short breakdown explaining why the police took no further action. As Mr Westwood continues to read to us, he offers more information about vetting, information technology and criminal 'intelligence' issues. Although we follow his well-meaning breakdown of the document, we are not registering the points very well. I can only focus on the contact list and its implications for Holly and Jessica. Despite the serious, serial allegations of sexual violence against Huntley, the information was routinely removed from the Criminal Intelligence System by a process known as 'weeding'. It beggars belief.

Each and every time a police officer had to deal with Huntley there was no information retained on the system to provide a snapshot of his past. The police lost the opportunity to establish a pattern of behaviour. Ironically, 'the system' has contributed to the deaths of Holly and Jessica.

Mr Westwood's correspondence shows that Maxine Carr provided an alibi for Huntley, for contact nine – the alleged rape of a seventeen-year-old girl, almost a bloody child. We suspect there were even more allegations that went unreported, so Maxine Carr must be aware of Huntley's brutal history. As his parents must be. Mr Westwood's letter shows many contacts with Social Services and confirms that a then 12-year-old victim (Contact Seven) lived in the same street as Huntley.

In a small community people talk and word gets round; therefore, if our assessment is true, between them Maxine Carr and Huntley's parents have all stood back and thus allowed their partner and son to work as a caretaker with direct access to many children. He was a time bomb waiting to go off, and they should have been aware of the risks. We go home deeply troubled.

These revelations change our attitude to Maxine Carr. She has chosen to stand by her man, knowing his past. We feel this to be despicable, and guess the general public and media will agree.

On Wednesday 12 November, I find it impossible to attend court, after yesterday's shocking news. It's always sickened me to see Huntley when he comes into the dock, but now, knowing his past, I harbour too much anger to be sure I can control myself.

A number of friends feel the same way and are anxious not to say the wrong thing as witnesses. On Friday 14 November, my young friend and fellow cricketer, Mark Abbott, calls me at home to talk about his experience in Court Number One. It has been a deeply stressful time for Mark, and he was worried about coping with the pressure. His father, Andrew, travelled with him to London to support him, but even Dad's presence could do nothing to calm his nerves as he went into the Old Bailey. Mark had an unenviable wait before they called him to give evidence at 3.37 p.m. Once on the witness stand, he could not bring himself to look at the two accused. Mark began to fidget and decided to hold his hands behind his back. During cross-examination, Mark rejected Mr Coward's suggestion that each statement he'd made had become embellished with time because he wanted to help. Mark felt this was legal talk for accusing him of dishonesty. Mark does not lie, let alone commit perjury. He is as straightforward, uncomplicated and trustworthy a young man as you could ever meet. Mr Coward went after him, hard, and Mark could feel the sweat run down his back. No one deserves to be treated that way. But that was not the end of Mark's ordeal. After giving evidence he was announced to the photographers outside the Old Bailey and advised to stand for a short period of time.

This is what happened next. After the flashbulb intrusion, Mark walks to the top of the road, turns the corner into the relative quiet of the next street and breaks down. Mark cannot stop himself from worrying that somehow his evidence will damage the fight for justice for Holly and Jessica. He cries down the phone, relating his ordeal, and I cry with him. I have felt every detail and walked every step with him. Murder reaches and wrecks far beyond the immediate victims.

20 November to 30 November

Over the last week I have become completely disillusioned, observing the methods of Messrs Coward and Hubbard against almost every witness. My heart goes out to all those who have endured their onslaughts. Mr Coward has a pattern of questioning witnesses' evidence. He either suggests that their memory is at fault, or claims that, given the awful nature of the crime, they may have subconsciously embellished their statements to help the prosecution.

Furthermore, woe betide any individual who Mr Coward feels should have made written notes earlier than they did, as they are in for a merciless ride. In Mr Coward's paper-mad world, it does not seem to matter that police officers were spending every second desperately searching for two missing children. That is made to seem insignificant – even irrelevant. They should have been writing it down in triplicate. Mr Coward is trying to convince the jury that any written notes not made immediately after the events they describe carry an element of uncertainty. Mr Coward may have deftly sown doubt amongst the jurors. At this moment I despise him for his skills.

Mr Hubbard, for Maxine Carr, has a very different courtroom style. He shouts at witnesses, and aggressively queries notes and statements. Several times, he demands why certain witnesses did not make any written notes during August 2002. Even when a witness insists on the accuracy of their testimony, Mr Hubbard tries to pick holes in the facts as stated and suggests an alternative scenario for them. It's a very clever technique. Even when the witness stands their ground, Mr Hubbard makes the jurors doubt them. It is sickening to see this whole process, day after day.

Throughout the proceedings, Huntley comes and goes to his heart's content. But, at least, the court is no longer forced to adjourn whilst he takes a break to compose himself. Instead, Mr Justice Moses simply grants permission for him to leave and Huntley is taken down into the holding cells. It is extremely strange to keep seeing this.

Huntley is now interacting with his legal team much more frequently, writing many messages while witnesses give evidence. He sports a suit and new haircut, and his image has been 'made over' to try to make him appear respectable. Significantly, the two psychiatrists are no longer in court. Maybe, at long last, the penny is dropping for Huntley. We can now all dismiss his previous mental health antics for exactly what they were – a figment of his overactive imagination. For me, this is a defining moment; I sense Huntley realises he has been painted into a corner by the build-up of evidence. His only remaining option is to come up with a plausible explanation of how Holly and Jessica died, something he has failed to do for the last 15 months. The scales of justice appear to be tipping in our direction.

As if there is not enough stress in the courtroom, Nicola and I are subjected to yet more pressure by Cambridgeshire Police. It is the subject of the ill-advised television documentary again, and whether or not we will reconsider our decision and contribute to it. The BBC is keen for some input from one or both of the families involved. Well they can be as keen as they want, but we repeat our refusal. I also begin to suspect from the tone of the BBC's request that Mr Stevenson has failed to inform them of our earlier, unambiguous 'no', and I am not sure why. Like Mr Blunkett, the BBC do not like being told no. After we refuse, certain witnesses, once they have given their evidence, are telephoned at home by the police, and asked if they will take part in the documentary. So the police are now working for the BBC! For example, my former business partner, Scott Day, is contacted by DCI Andy Hebb. I'm disappointed, as we all hold Andy in very high regard. However, Scott knows my position and his decision not to take part is immediate. Thank you, Scott. I resent the way the police have gone about this whole documentary affair. It is even beginning to poison our feelings of gratitude to the FLO team. As I sit in the courtroom facing Mr Stevenson, he writes down every moment of the day's proceedings. I wonder if he is working on a book. If it transpires to be true, this may explain not only why he is scribbling so furiously, but also offers a rather sad insight into some past decisions. I also wonder if Mr Stevenson is planning ahead to his retirement in 2004. Perhaps we are just unlucky that the senior investigating officer is at the end of his career. What I do know is that the pressure some of his decisions have caused my family and me, and the poor FLOs, caught in the cross-fire, is inexcusable. But, at least, he got his man.

On Friday 21 November, we hear that next week may well be the end of live evidence. We are asked to prepare ourselves for a key witness about to take the stand, the pathologist. It seems appropriate that today is the moment Nicola and I receive a copy of his report on the deaths of Holly and Jessica.

Please believe me when I say nothing can prepare you to read a pathologist's report on your own daughter.

Once we have done so, we analyse the lengthy document with the help of our FLOs, to see what Huntley's defence team may come up with. We are told that the defence will not be calling their own pathologist, which means they accept the Home Office pathologist's report. We read and re-read it, and find one point the defence may use to sow doubt. It concerns a small fracture on Holly's skull, thought likely to have been caused by heat haematoma, when Huntley set light to the bodies in the ditch. Although there is no evidence of any substantial bleeding to support the argument that there was an impact fracture – which would suit Mr Coward – I am sure that listening to his dissection of all possible causes is going to be harrowing.

We are not the only ones speculating. We are told that a theory of Huntley's dog somehow being involved in the death of one or both of the girls is likely to be introduced. I had not given the dog any thought for a long time now, but clearly the defence may put anything forward to justify the thesis of 'accidental death', which is the only possible way Huntley can escape conviction on both counts of murder. We remain worried senseless that he will evade justice.

Monday 24 November and our 'big' week starts with a morning of forensic evidence being explained to the jury by Mr Latham. We become aware of technical terms such as primary, secondary and tertiary transfer of fibres and the conclusions that can be drawn from them. After lunch we are asked, rather unexpectedly, to have an immediate meeting with Chris Stevenson.

Mr Stevenson is accompanied by Hywel Jarman, Head of Media and Marketing for Cambridgeshire Police. At once, we are told that the pressure of handling endless media enquiries about both families' post-trial intentions has become so great that the police cannot continue passing on these messages. They advise us to seek independent legal advice, especially as the media are offering large sums to the Chapmans and ourselves. The police clearly don't want to be accused of cashing in, or taking commissions, if we accept a specific newspaper offer at some stage. I understand their predicament but I'm not too happy. Since the start we have conducted our business with the media through the police.

It seems to me that Mr Stevenson and other senior officers have encouraged this growing pressure, through their dealings with the media during the trial. I suppose if we did intend to deal with the media and compare offers, then this change of position would make life yet more difficult, right at the crucial stage of the trial. But Sonia Land is dealing with the only contract I have any interest in – for a book.

On Tuesday 25 November, Nicola and I are graphically reminded how fresh facts hit hardest when Keith Prior's statement is read out in court. Mr Prior discovered Holly and Jessica's bodies and we feel his personal agony as he describes finding them.

It is a timely reminder that the twelve jurors are hearing information and evidence for the first time. What are their thoughts right now? I can see most of them from my none-too-panoramic vantage point, and they have all been attentive over the last few weeks. Do they know or understand the importance of what is about to happen with the pathologist's evidence? Have they realised the significance of Huntley's state of mind not really being an issue any more? Bizarrely, although we all know Huntley has made 14 admissions, these have yet to be formally introduced to the jury by Mr Coward. Why has this list of admissions not been forthcoming sooner? Is the timing tactical? I can only raise these questions to myself for now.

As the morning proceedings continue, Huntley is given permission to leave, as apparently he is feeling unwell. Immediately afterwards, Maxine Carr passes a note over requesting the very same. For one moment it looks like the case against Huntley and Carr is going to proceed without either of the defendants in the dock, which can only be described as farcical. Before this happens the judge sends the jury out and addresses both defence teams. He is more concerned at the absence of Huntley, as the evidence in question primarily relates to his case. He says that Huntley, in the absence of any medical evidence, should return to the dock and asks Mr Coward to speak with his client. The silent cheers can be felt all around the court. But the cheers do not last too long for me, as the judge suddenly says that later in the day there is likely to be evidence which will be difficult for the families to hear. We are also told that if we wish to hear this evidence, we must remain in court throughout as our leaving might distract the jury. We have been forewarned. We had no idea what lay in store from Mr Coward.

The court proceedings resume at midday. Carr and Huntley have recovered in record time and are present. There is no time to settle properly before Mr Coward hands over the all-important list of admissions to the jury. The list is rather more exhaustive than before, with 21 admissions in total. New admissions accept that various materials, schedules and interviews are accurate. This must be making a huge impact on the jury as they quickly scan the document, before the next witness, Patricia Wiltshire, takes the stand. She is an expert on pollen and the ditch at Wangford was full of that.

The next moves are bizarre, given the list of admissions. Wiltshire claims there was a second track leading into the ditch at the deposition site and the prosecution say this shows Huntley went back to the site. The police are holding two sets of footwear covered by pollen from plants like those in the ditch. Mr Coward tries to shake this expert evidence. But if Huntley only went to the deposition site once, then who wore the second pair of pollen-covered footwear? I think back to the medium, Dennis Mackenzie, and his claim that three people were involved. Dennis has repeated that to me often since, but this is the closest I have come to hearing any evidence which supports him.

At 3.04 p.m., Dr Nat Carey, the Home Office pathologist, takes the stand. Mr Latham questions him and together they set the scene, Dr Carey describing the state and position of Holly and Jessica's bodies when they were found. Mr Latham explains to Dr Carey that he does not want to go into too much detail about the state of the bodies, but what is said is heart-rending enough. This moment might have been too much to bear if we had not already studied the pathologist's report.

The evidence takes less than an hour, but it feels more like a decade.

Then Mr Coward rises. I'm very anxious. After questioning Dr Carey on rigor mortis, strangulation, drowning and smothering, suddenly the moment is upon us. Mr Coward is about to put forward Huntley's account of how Holly and Jessica died in his home. It is an account which has never been put forward before. Everyone knows the importance of the moment. There is absolute silence as Mr Coward begins.

'I am going to put to you my client's case of what actually happened on 4 August last year. At the material time, Holly Wells had a nosebleed and because it wouldn't stop, she, Jessica and the defendant Mr Huntley, went up to the bathroom at number 5 College Close. Holly sat on the edge of the bath at the tap end, which is the end furthest from the door and next to the bath is a washbasin. Jessica sat on the other end of the bath, nearer to the door.

'Mr Huntley was getting pieces of tissue or toilet paper, putting them under the cold tap to cool them and handing them to Holly. On one of his turns from getting the wet tissue to give to Holly, he slipped and it seems he may well have banged into her as she was sitting on the edge of the bath and she went backwards. He has no recollection of a bang but he does remember a splash when Holly went in the bath which had roughly 18 inches of water in it because Mr Huntley was going to wash the dog.

'Jessica stood up and started screaming, "You pushed her, you pushed her," and he then turned towards Jessica and either with one hand or two, he is not sure, put his hands out towards Jessica – his memory is over her mouth – to stop her screaming. For how long he was in that position he cannot say, but he was then conscious that Jessica was no longer supporting herself on her feet. He let go and she went to the ground.

'He then turned round to the bath and Holly was lying in the bath, apparently dead. He lifted Holly out of the bath, put her on the floor, looked for signs of breathing, found none, turned his attention to Jessica, looked for signs of breathing and found none. That is the whole account.'

Dr Carey says he wants time to consider the defence version and to refer to other forensic experts. The judge accepts this, along with Dr Carey's request that the defence put their position in writing. Then, the judge adjourns proceedings.

As we gather in the witness service area, no one can really believe what has just been said. If it were not so deadly serious, one could easily assume the explanation was a joke. But it's nothing of the kind, and I remember that it is up to the prosecution to prove beyond a reasonable doubt that Holly and Jessica were murdered. My God, what will happen if Mr Coward somehow gets Dr Carey to concede that Huntley's explanation of events is even vaguely plausible? This nightmarish thought churns through my mind as we travel back to Soham.

For the first time, we phone home to ask if Oliver can be kept away from all news coverage until our return. As justice for Holly stands or falls on Mr Coward's argument, we want to explain the day's proceedings and our perceptions of them to our son alone, and in private.

As soon as we get back, we sit down together and we explain Mr Coward's account. We also explain to Oliver we believe that the account will not stand up, but that we cannot be sure at this stage. We tell our son the implications if the jury accept Huntley's story. Oliver is very quiet and heads off to bed, under no pressure from us, presumably to mull over this new information.

For the next half-hour Nicola and I call friends and family. Some of them have been reading the transcripts of court proceedings all day on the rolling news channel. Everyone we speak to shares our concerns at this afternoon's developments and many express their frustration. They too perceive the whole legal system to be unfair and one-sided.

Then Oliver suddenly bursts into the living room triumphantly. 'Mum, Dad, it cannot be true. Holly could not have drowned in the bath. Let me explain . . .'

For the last 20 minutes or so, our son has been busy experimenting in the bathroom. We listen, amazed, as he tells us there is no way Holly could have fallen backwards into the bath. If her legs were under the washbasin, they would have got caught up underneath. And even if they did become free, Holly would have fallen backwards across the width of the bath, with her backside in the water and the lower part of her legs still dangling over the edge. The likelihood of Holly falling backwards, lifting her legs over the bath, twisting sideways and then falling into the water is a non-starter. Oliver adds, 'Dad, if Jessica saw Holly fall into the bath, she wouldn't have screamed, she would have laughed.' Out of the mouth of babes! Let us hope Dr Carey can demolish this absurd defence story tomorrow.

We get no sleep and a delay to the start of court proceedings doesn't exactly soothe the nerves. But finally, late morning, Mr Coward recommences his cross-examination of Dr Carey. Dr Carey is professional, clear and does not allow Mr Coward to dominate. Step by step, Dr Carey blows apart the theory.

I can't feel anything like happiness in this court, dealing with Holly's death, but Dr Carey is a joy to behold and we feel less anxious. By the time he leaves the stand, our fear that Huntley may fool the jury into accepting his account of the deaths has completely disappeared. In less than half an hour, Dr Carey has given two families not only an instant sense of relief, but, more importantly, a belief that justice for their precious daughters is edging nearer.

The FLO coordinator, Gary Goose, asks Nicola and me if we would like to meet Dr Carey at lunch. It is a wonderful idea and we accept the invitation immediately. As we slip into a side room to meet and thank Dr Carey for his expertise, it is an emotional moment. My handshake and thanks are as heartfelt as any I have ever given.

I'd like to go back in time now. Just before we broke for lunch, there was yet another shining example of the way Carr's QC, Mr Hubbard, deals with witnesses. This time the hapless victim was a bus driver, Paul Walmsley, who picked up Maxine Carr as a passenger. Mr Hubbard 'suggests' that the bus driver has got his facts wrong about the route he was driving, which seems unlikely: a bus driver knows his route all too well. Then, Mr Coward asks if Walmsley made any notes of his conversation with Carr during the journey. This is getting ridiculous. A bus driver does not write and drive at the same time! For one thing, it would be against the law – for another, bloody dangerous. Why should he even think about recording a conversation with one of his passengers? Is this really the great British Justice system at work? After Mr Coward abruptly sits down, the judge offers an apology to Mr Walmsley: 'Sorry you have been dragged all the way down here.' I would have preferred a few words to be added, such as, 'to listen to such nonsense'. But however nonsensical the law may be, you can't say so in court!

We go home in a much lighter frame of mind than yesterday. We also get a boost because we get a card from David Beckham and the England squad, saying that their thoughts are with us all. It is something positive to give to Oliver. The police have also given Oliver a photograph of the caretaker's bathroom, complete with bath, sink, and toilet. He sees that his own theory was spot on and gives us a small, knowing nod. Good lad.

Tomorrow, Friday 28 November, Nicola and I are staying at home, as we are exhausted. I am doing a little writing when at 10.48 a.m. I receive a text message from Chris Mead in court. It reads:

> 'Stop press – Huntley is going to go in the witness box. Probably Monday. Will update you later.'

I am totally taken aback. Our legal team must be rubbing their hands at the very prospect. Are there problems between Huntley and Mr Coward? The 'devil' and his advocate not getting on? Does Huntley now believe his only chance is to conjure up another fabrication about what happened in his tiny bathroom? No one predicted this. What the hell can he say after his account of what happened to Holly and Jessica has already been torn apart? Does the legal system really allow 'another bite at the cherry' once your original story has been disproved? The reality appears to be that yes, it does. I feel very anxious again.

1 December to 31 December

On Monday 1 December, the court is as busy – and packed with journalists – as it's ever been. We are told that the 'overflow' press-room, which receives a relay of Court Number One's proceedings, is also teeming with reporters. First, the judge warns the media they must not get up and leave while Huntley gives evidence. At 11.32 a.m., Huntley is escorted to the witness box and takes the oath which is, in my opinion, his first lie of the day. He is Mr Coward's witness and counsel for the defence gives his client the softly-softly treatment. Mr Coward eases Huntley into confirming his account of what happened from 4 August onwards. Nothing is missed. Oh, this Mr Coward is good. Thank God we have an overwhelming case against his client. By lunchtime, Huntley has made some new points. Following the pathologist's observations that he could not see how Holly could have drowned in 18 inches of water when the overflow is at 11, Huntley now says the water in the bath was between 6 and 8 inches deep. It's hardly the first time Huntley has changed his story after hearing evidence that contradicts it. Perhaps the most graphic example of this was when Huntley first mentioned, many months ago now, that it was 'the dark-haired girl' (Jessica) who had the nosebleed. After we and the Chapmans had given statements, and we'd confirmed that Holly used to suffer from nosebleeds when she was younger, Huntley simply changed his story to best fit the facts. Suddenly it was Holly with the nosebleed, he said.

The police believe that Huntley felt he had to introduce a plausible explanation for any blood found in his house. So he concocted the nosebleed scenario. Huntley also mentions a green mat in the bathroom, which kept slipping. This wobbly mat made him lurch and knock Holly into the bath, while he tackled the 'difficult task' of passing her a wet tissue. How desperate this man is to save his neck. Huntley also explains how blood came to be on his quilt, which takes us all by surprise. Jessica wanted to use the toilet, he claims, so he and Holly left her in the bathroom and went into his bedroom. There Holly's nose dripped blood on his quilt.

All we can do is sit and listen to this tripe. Yet there may be certain elements of truth in Huntley's observations, though of a very twisted kind. His earlier statements claimed Maxine Carr was in the house having a bath, which was a wholesale lie. Yet Nicola and I believe that this would have been the very line used by Huntley to entice the girls into the house, to see their 'teacher'. By the same token Huntley's account of Holly being in his bedroom may have an element of truth to it, minus the blood-dripping scenario. This may indicate where Holly lived the last moments of her life. I'm no body language expert and I can hardly be objective, yet I notice Huntley's manner. He speaks much more freely when he is confirming facts that seem true. We can see the difference from the rear of the courtroom and I am sure the jury see that even better as they are next to the witness box.

It can only go downhill for Huntley from now; the easy ride

from his own legal team will not last for ever. Richard Latham QC is waiting round the corner for you, Huntley; just like you did for two little girls, you sick, pathetic, wretched bastard. May he be as ruthless with your freedom as you were with their lives.

One small piece of information comes out which links directly to an observation made by the second medium, Ron Moulding, back in August 2002. Ron spoke of 'Keeper's Cottage' before Huntley had become a suspect, which I translated to 'Caretaker's House'. Again, I become impressed by gifts I did not believe in earlier. Huntley confirms that, on the night he drove to the deposition site to dump the bodies, he ended up on a grass verge by a turning to his father's old house, near to Keeper's Cottage. It is quite a spooky moment.

On Tuesday 2 December, Richard Latham QC is to enter the fray. Today, for the first and probably only time, we journey to the Old Bailey with an air of excitement and expectancy. We would not be disappointed.

Mr Latham pulls no punches and wastes no time, launching into Huntley at the first opportunity.

'You are a liar, Mr Huntley,' Mr Latham says.

Then, he adds, 'You were inventing a defence to fit the facts, weren't you?' If the accused was confident that he could handle Mr Latham's cross-examination, it takes about two minutes for him to learn otherwise. With a gap in the dock where Huntley normally sits, we have a better view of Mr Latham in action and we all revel in Huntley's collapse as the prosecution takes him back to Sunday 4 August. Not even a 10 minute break will help you now, Huntley, there is no hiding place. You, and you alone, have put yourself in this position. For the first time in your life, you are going to have to face the consequences of your actions.

Just two minutes before the lunch break, Huntley cracks in the most dramatic fashion. Mr Latham dismisses his account of how Holly and Jessica died accidentally as 'absolute nonsense'.

He repeatedly accuses Huntley of murdering both girls. Why, Mr Latham asks with total disdain, did Huntley not reach out to

Holly after he knocked her into the bath? That would have been normal. Ian Huntley's rage stuns every person in the courtroom.

'In *these* circumstances it is very rational to know what you are doing,' Huntley tells him sharply. He sounds angry and offended.

'In those circumstances,' Huntley continues, 'it is not so rational. Believe me, I know.'

The importance of these 25 words – and the fury in Huntley's voice as he spoke – cannot be overstated. Mr Latham knows it: he has just landed his catch.

Then he whispers:

'You can be perfectly assertive when you want to, Mr Huntley.'

'Yes.'

'You can get angry, can't you, Mr Huntley?'

'Yes.'

'You just lost your temper with me, didn't you?'

'That's because you . . .' there is now a long pause. 'You have your opinion.'

Slightly louder, Mr Latham repeats, 'You have just lost your temper with me, haven't you?'

'Yes.'

'Did you lose your temper with one of these girls on that Sunday evening?'

'I had no reason to lose my temper.'

'Did you become the assertive individual you became two minutes ago?'

Mr Latham's meaning is stunningly obvious. We all rise for a remarkably well-timed lunch break, hoping that the jury will decide the true answer to that final question is a 'yes'. Today, with this defining moment in the bag, even the food at the Old Bailey canteen tastes okay.

Today is also Oliver's 14th birthday, so Nicola has stayed at home. It is a shame that she missed Mr Latham in full flow, but her priorities, as ever where the children are concerned, lay elsewhere. As I touch base with her by phone, she is completely unaware of the drama in court this morning and makes the point that this could turn out to be Oliver's best birthday present. I think, and hope, she's right.

On Wednesday 3 December, Huntley looks like hell. I guess it has been a sleepless night for the accused. Once more, Mr Latham's intellect, rhetoric and timing prove too much for Huntley, who again struggles to keep his cool. After Huntley's fury yesterday, I am sure that his legal team spelled out the consequences of his seeming such an angry young man.

Then Huntley leaves the box.

Before Maxine Carr can be called, there is a long debate, without the jury present, about the summing-up stage of the trial. The issue is details of the case pending against Huntley and Carr on charges of benefit fraud. The prosecution would like to refer to their little scam-against-the-state, as it demonstrates that Carr has a history of lying with Huntley. It is a matter of record that Maxine Carr has already admitted these charges against her. However, her defence team would like to overlook that, to portray her as an individual of good character with no previous convictions. Mr Hubbard does not want his client cross-examined on matters for which she has not been convicted, while the prosecution argue it is one thing to say Carr had no convictions, but quite another to claim she is a model citizen living blamelessly. The judge rules that the subject cannot be introduced as the jury needs to focus on important issues and should not be diverted. It is not a full-blown victory as the judge indicates he will re-visit this ruling if the defence asserts anything beyond 'no previous convictions' for Carr. We are very disappointed that this ruling has gone against us.

At 2.25 p.m. Maxine Carr is called to give evidence. Mr Hubbard now repeats the softly-softly approach and guides Carr. It is a very interesting moment. The police believe Carr will distance herself from Huntley. If she does say something to help the prosecution's case against Huntley, we would like to know why she did not do so earlier, when two distraught families desperately needed her help. However the key point is that Huntley has been and gone with his evidence – he has no automatic right to reply to any contentious points, if they are introduced now.

Mr Hubbard tells the jury that details of the girls' deaths had been 'harrowing', but had nothing to do with his client. He goes on to say that, 'within two weeks of her arriving back in Soham, the course of her life had changed for ever. She had done no wrong whilst events were unfolding in Soham.' They are not there to judge her morality as an admitted liar, but to decide if she committed a crime. Mr Hubbard points out the irony of someone as fond of the two girls, as Carr claimed to be, finding herself in the dock with the man accused of their murders.

By the end of the afternoon, Mr Hubbard has finished guiding Carr through her version. It's a slick performance, giving the impression that they worked hard on the script. Still, however good the writing, the plot doesn't convince. There are only so many times you can say you lied because you loved someone, or say that you chose to believe Huntley when he said the girls left the house alive, when so many facts point to the opposite. Carr and her team are simply going to keep repeating the same claims, almost as if they expect the jury to believe these implausible assertions if they're repeated often enough. It is a bit like listening to a party political broadcast!

Tomorrow Mr Coward will have first shot at Carr in the morning. It is a complete role reversal for Nicola and me, as we find ourselves suddenly welcoming, instead of dreading, his advocacy skills. Now that his own client is all but doomed, we hope Mr Coward will nail Carr.

Exhausted, we spend the night in London. The next morning, we head off for our hotel breakfast, unaware the surreal is about to strike again. We walk to a small table at the far end of the dining room, through an orchestra of chattering and clinking cutlery, and sit down. As usual, we've been recognised, and it leaves us feeling deeply uncomfortable.

Sitting to my left is a large man of Mediterranean origin, who rises and walks towards Nicola. My first thought is that Mr Med is going to offer his condolences, as this happens frequently at the moment, but no. Suddenly, he knocks into our table and falls forward in Nicola's direction, so that they are face to face. The noise grabs everyone's attention, and I have to admit my second thought about this person: he is too big to hit.

Then, the penny drops.

The man is not being rude or aggressive. He is choking and fighting for his life. By the time he turns to me, his face is beet-root red and he looks terrified. I step to one side to allow one of the staff members watching to help.

But none of the staff seems to realise it's an emergency. The man is fighting for breath, gesticulating in panic, there is no time to lose. I have to do something as everyone is just looking. I know I cannot attempt the Heimlich manoeuvre, because he is too big to get my arms around. I can only think of slapping him in the back to see if I can dislodge whatever is stuck. If there was anyone still tucking into their eggs and bacon, unaware of the drama, then the first slap must have caught their attention. Unfortunately, it does not work. Slaps two, three and four don't expel the food either. As the luckless victim begins to lurch downwards, desperate to draw a breath, I realise he might be about to die. There's time for one last attempt; so with a small jump to give extra height and momentum, I punch him in the middle of his back with my every ounce of strength. I could not have hit Huntley any harder. In the nick of time, his food finally becomes dislodged. There is the smallest show of thanks from Mr Med and the hotel staff, as I sit down, shaking profusely, to await my poached eggs.

As we arrive at the Old Bailey, word has already reached the police. Chris Mead meets me with the opening line of, 'May I take your cape, Mr Wells?' Many of his colleagues add to the mickey-taking, but I get no chance to act the life-saving hero – and I don't have much inclination to do so once we walk into Court Number One.

Mr Coward does not disappoint. He leads with a clever opening question that forces Maxine Carr to admit that she lied.

'Are you conscious of the fact that what you told the jury is different to what you told the police?'

Mr Coward dissects Carr's comments about finding a duvet, sheets and bathmat in her washing machine when she got back from Grimsby. He asks her why she did not tell the police? It is an innocuous-looking question, but the response, like Huntley's loss of temper with Mr Latham, completely takes the whole court by surprise.

'I am not going to be blamed,' she says, 'for what that thing has done to me or those children.'

The look of horror on Huntley's face is priceless. The love of his life has just spurned him in public – and done it with what sounds like feeling. I suspect it's a 'good' script and a good actress.

'That thing' is an apt description of Huntley. But it is an amazing moment and the court is stunned. Almost on cue, an elderly man faints and is carried away from the public gallery. Mr Coward presses on. He asks Maxine Carr to think about some of the facts she knew, when she 'believed' Huntley as he said the girls left the house alive.

You knew, Mr Coward says:

- *The girls had been in the house.*
- *There was blood in the house.*
- *A girl sat on the bed.*
- *Huntley was the last person to see them.*
- *The car boot had a new carpet.*
- *The interior of the car had been cleaned.*
- *Huntley wanted you back from Grimsby.*
- *There was bedding in the washing machine.*
- *The house was clean and smelled of lemon.*
- *The bathmat was missing.*
- *Huntley was really scared.*
- *Huntley wanted you to lie.*

I believe Mr Hubbard's claim, made yesterday – that Carr did not know or believe Huntley had killed the girls when she lied for him – is wrong. It is wrong by a country mile.

Carr now admonishes Huntley, placing more daylight between them. Carr has claimed that Huntley was 'very controlling' in their relationship, but we believe she will fall short of saying he was violent towards her. Both Mr Coward and Mr Latham would have a field day adding, 'I knew he was violent' to the extensive list of things that were wrong in the house on her return. It places a very different perspective on events and that is why Carr and her legal team will not introduce it. Under cross-examination, Carr uses a number of phrases to describe Huntley and their relationship; they include that he was abusive, controlling, that she was scared of him, 'you don't know the kind of person Ian Huntley is towards me' and 'he (Huntley) had a very controlling attitude towards me'. No specific mention of violence though.

Late afternoon, when the jury has been sent out, Mr Justice Moses suggests to Mr Hubbard that Maxine Carr has admitted conspiring with Huntley to lie. The option of asking Carr to plead guilty on this charge is given but declined. Once more we find ourselves witnessing strategy at play. I wonder if her team thinks the jury will be more likely to give Carr the benefit of the doubt on the more serious charge, if they choose to give a guilty verdict for the lesser charge. It is a mind game with very high stakes.

Mr Latham's cross-examination of Carr is biting and thorough as he repeats many points for the jury. One of the strangest is that Carr was with Huntley, in their car, when they picked up a hitch-hiker. Huntley told the hitchhiker that he had been 'the last person to see the girls alive' which conflicted with the news, then being reported, of a sighting of the girls in Little Thetford. Mr Latham drills home the point, 'As soon as you heard him say that, that must have rung alarm bells.'

All afternoon, Carr turns on the crocodile tears for the jury's benefit. Nicola and I both know that when you are really upset, you don't have tears on tap, you can't switch them on and off at will, regain your composure and answer a new question. But that is precisely what Maxine Carr has been doing. We are watching an actress at work in the witness box.

The last word goes to the judge, who tells the jury they are approaching 'the most important and sensitive stage of all – reaching their verdict'. He expects them to be listening to speeches from the three QCs into Tuesday of next week, and then he will sum up.

On Friday 5 December, Nicola and I stay at home while legal points are argued in court. Trudie Skeels is there for our family and updates us on a complex day. Mr Coward asks the judge for three counts to be suggested to the jury for Jessica's death, namely: murder, manslaughter or accident. For Holly, Mr Coward requests murder, manslaughter by gross negligence or accident. The gross negligence part of the manslaughter count stems from the fact that Huntley had a duty of care to look after Holly, because of her nosebleed.

All these possibilities make us more anxious. We know that Mr Coward will try to persuade the jury of the least serious charge – and persuasively so. Mr Hubbard will ask the jury to assess what Carr knew and believed, explaining it is their duty to try and work out her state of mind and whether or not she was putting two and two together. The jury are likely to be told that it is not up to them to try and assess what Maxine Carr should have been thinking. It all seems rather complicated.

We do not waste our day at home. Nicola and I approve the copy layout for Holly's headstone and are delighted by the end product. It really is a fitting tribute. The all-polished Bahama Blue granite headstone and kerb set, specially imported, will have pink lettering. Jeremy, the stonemason, feels the memorial will definitely be in place for Christmas and we are most grateful. As we walk to place some flowers on Holly's grave, we are pleasantly surprised to see the most glorious bouquet of flowers. They have been sent from the ship's company of *HMS Vengeance* and it reminds us that so many people's kind thoughts remain with us.

On Monday 8 December, a juror is absent due to illness. So

nothing happens and, for the same reason, nothing happens the next day. It adds to the sense of drama as we await the closing speeches.

Finally, on Wednesday, Mr Latham stands up. You can feel the tension in court. We know he is not going to labour every point as he feels that if the jury have not grasped the significance of the main issues by now, they never will. He gives a robust, factual summary; the prosecution believe the jury should find 'guilty' on counts 1 to 4 respectively. Ahead of me, Huntley sits in the dock, his head slightly bowed. Like the rest of us, the accused has to listen as Mr Latham reaches his damning conclusion. I believe I'm watching Huntley count down, second by second, to the moment he goes to jail for life. There is a sense of relief that the end is in sight. That end must conclude with two verdicts of 'guilty' on two charges of murder. Nothing else will do.

After Mr Latham, Mr Coward responds. He tells the jury that acquitting Huntley is not an option, before pleading with them to convict him of manslaughter over both Holly's and Jessica's deaths. Although we were forewarned of Mr Coward's approach, it is still immensely hard to remain calm. Mr Coward even refers to cases of multiple cot deaths, suggesting that although the deaths of Holly and Jessica could be classed as 'rare events' it would be very dangerous to think two rare events could not happen. This is the defence's last desperate roll of the dice.

On Thursday 11 December, Mr Hubbard surprises us as he pleads for the jury's empathy. He uses the card that Holly wrote to Maxine Carr last year as a prop. He waves it around to get sympathy, taking advantage of my daughter's affectionate nature. I hope Holly isn't watching. In an almost comic twist, Hubbard quotes crooner Engelbert Humperdinck: 'Please release me, let me go, for I don't love him any more.' (At least he doesn't sing it!) The QC turns on Huntley and all but stamps the word 'Guilty' on his forehead. Hubbard's quiet, caring manner today contrasts sharply with the high-decibel aggression he used against witnesses for the prosecution. Surely the jury will judge this transparent attempt to save Carr's neck for exactly what it is?

As we travel home, I can only hope the jury heed the judge's words. He told them, 'It isn't a defence to say, "Hasn't she suffered enough?"' Which is what Mr Hubbard said.

But we also know – and it hardly reassures us – that another major case here at the Old Bailey has just been thrown out on appeal, because the judge gave a flawed summing up. From day one there have been so many factors which could affect the trial process: what an awful thought that having come this far, it is still possible to fall at the final hurdle.

Nicola and I get no sleep. We are tired as we return to court the next day. We expect the final summing up will not last too long and that we will then witness the jury being sent out to consider their verdicts. That will be a huge moment for us. The jury can take all the time they want; all we know at the moment is that the police feel the verdicts for both cases will come down swiftly. Because a verdict may be reached today, Oliver is with us for the first time, accompanied by our nephew, Thomas.

It is this morning, of all mornings, that our normally smooth passage into the underground car park goes awry. No one is at the access gate to let us in. As we wait for the gate to open, our car is surrounded by photographers. Ringo, our driver, drives around the block once more. For Oliver and Thomas, their first experience of the Old Bailey is a most bizarre one.

Just after 11 o'clock, the jury retires to consider their verdicts and the waiting game begins. Once they've left the courtroom, the judge addresses all those who remain. When the verdicts are announced he wants absolute silence in court. He will not stand for any shouting. If there's any kind of a disturbance, he will simply rise and recommence the rest of proceedings with no one in court. We're also told that our request to sit in the Corporation of London seats in front of Huntley and Carr, for the verdict, has been turned down. It's another small reminder that the families' thoughts and feelings are at the bottom of the priorities.

At 12.45, our hearts miss a beat when the barely audible tannoy system calls for all parties connected to the Huntley and Carr trials to return to Court Number One. The sense of foreboding and dread is immediate. Is this it? Only an hour and a half or so of deliberation? Can this really be the moment when we get justice and can start to move on to the next step of our lives? We feel very unsure as we walk down the stairs, round the corner and into the marbled corridor leading to Court Number One. Nicola and I hold hands. But it turns out to be more surreal stuff.

The judge announces that the jury have asked to see the bath. It was taken from Huntley's house. Apparently, although they will view it in total isolation, such a request must be conveyed to all the legal teams first.

We walk back to the witness service area rather gloomily and debate the ins and outs of this request. Surely the jury don't believe Huntley's account of Holly drowning? It is more likely, we tell ourselves, that the jury wants to make a token effort to measure the bath before writing off Huntley's version. But it is extraordinarily difficult to be positive about this development. After all, the pathologist, Dr Carey, demolished the drowning theory. He confirmed that there was no secondary transfer of blood through water onto Holly's clothing, which would have been the case if she had a nosebleed. Have the jury missed this point?

Later in the day, Nicola and I have a short meeting with Sir Ronnie Flanagan of Her Majesty's Inspectorate of Constabulary. Sir Ronnie informs us that there will be an immediate announcement of a Public Inquiry after the verdicts. After our recent meeting with the Chief Constable of Humberside, we understand the importance of such a decision. We know that we will continue to be in the public eye once we return from New Zealand, which is the last thing we want. But if the Inquiry leads to changes in the law and in police practice, then this could be the best and most lasting memorial for Holly and Jessica. It has always been a desperate thought that Holly's death would be in vain – a beautiful wasted life. But just maybe our daughter's early death will make a difference to other families. It was always our belief that

Holly would somehow do just that, bring benefits to others' lives. We tell Sir Ronnie we will attend the Inquiry, not because we think we are so important, but just because we think we should be there. This has been the worst time in our lives; we just hope something good comes out of all this suffering.

On Sunday 14 December, I get an unexpected call from the medium Dennis Mackenzie. As ever, his observations are thought-provoking. He is adamant that Huntley will be found guilty of murder on both counts. His view on Carr is not so reassuring.

'Kevin, don't expect Maxine Carr to serve much more time than she's already done now. She is not going to get the full house against her and she definitely will not spend much longer in prison,' Dennis says.

It is an interesting time to get a call from Dennis, as we are now aware of a couple of pieces of factual evidence which corroborate some of his earlier observations further. Back in August 2002, Dennis said that looking out from inside the house (College Close) he could see the number eighteen, and that the letter J featured. It now dawns on me that my then business partner Scott's vehicle, in which we searched together, carried a registration plate beginning J18.

Then, when Dennis revisited us in the spring of 2003, he highlighted two dates. The first was spot on. The second date, which fell during the trial, seemed to pass uneventfully. We now learn otherwise from the police. Behind the scenes, it was the day our legal team found out about the impending list of admissions from Huntley. It is difficult to think of a more defining moment in the case.

But it is Dennis's last piece of information which is the most extraordinary. Back in August 2002, Dennis drew attention to the very spot where I first met Nicola, although I did not explain its importance at the time. He then felt this spot, next to the river, was linked to Jessica's missing mobile. In spring 2003, I 'came clean' and told Dennis what I believed to be its relevance (i.e. that Nicola and I had first met there), only to be told that was not why it mattered. It was to do with a phone, Dennis insisted. Today, I realise why Jessica's mobile was not what Dennis 'sensed'.

On the Sunday Holly and Jessica were killed, Huntley phoned a local woman, to try to meet her while Carr was away. Although there is no suggestion that the woman encouraged Huntley, she was the same woman who sat next to my wife, as her friend, some 22 years ago, when Nicola and I first met. Dennis does indeed possess an extraordinary gift.

Tuesday 16 December – and still there are no signs of the jury reaching a unanimous verdict. This is the third day they have been out and everyone feels that they must be having trouble agreeing on the Carr verdict. The police make optimistic comments – like 'it is good the jury are taking their time deliberating, it will hope- fully negate an appeal point' – as we wander aimlessly around the canteen. By late afternoon there is a rumour that the jury do not just disagree on the verdict for Carr, but for Huntley as well. We are completely distraught at this idea, even though it is only a rumour – and who knows where this rumour comes from? Chris is quick to explain that if a jury cannot come to a unanimous decision within a certain time, the judge will allow a majority decision, i.e. if ten out of the twelve agree, then their verdict will be accepted.

The fact that we are still waiting is a very real reminder that our lives hang in the balance. Nicola and I have to face the possi- bility that Mr Coward may just have instilled enough doubt in the minds of some jurors for the verdict to go horribly wrong. We don't sleep at all that night.

On Wednesday 17 December, when we get to the Old Bailey, palace of justice and chamber of rumours, yet another whisper is doing the rounds. The judge is going to direct the jury to take a majority decision. As he enters the court at 10.30, it feels like everyone is willing him to say it, but the judge just invites the jury to retire to consider their deliberations further. We trudge back to the canteen.

At 11 a.m. the tinny, poor-quality tannoy system, requests all parties attached to the case to return to Court Number One. We all look nervously at each other as we descend to hear what we believe may be the verdicts. Again, we are mistaken and frustrated. But now Mr Justice Moses does direct the jury to take a majority decision. Out we go once more.

The police believe we will be back in court in the next ten minutes because Chris Stevenson saw an expression of relief on the foreman's face, after the judge ruled a majority verdict would do. I hope he is right. But Stevenson gets it wrong. Time ticks: 10 minutes, then 15, then 20 pass; half an hour, 40 minutes come and go. There is not a smile to be seen anywhere. Rob, Trudie, Nicola's parents, Uncle Peter, Oliver and myself are all immersed in our own private thoughts. What can the jury be debating?

At 11.45 a.m. the tannoy sparks into life once again and we all sense this is the moment. The butterflies return to my stomach as we walk into the courtroom. My God, you really can cut the atmosphere with a knife. Everyone's eyes focus on the judge as he makes himself comfortable. The moment is upon us.

The charge of Huntley murdering Jessica is the first one put to the foreman. He speaks the one word we all wanted to hear – guilty! We all look at one another and offer a silent fist clench, conscious as we are of the judge's demand for silence. There is a pregnant pause before the charge of Holly's murder is read out. I stare down at my shoes praying for the same simple answer – and it comes, loud and clear – guilty! To my right, Chris Mead is in tears; to my left, Nicola is also crying. Further down the back row Nicola's mother and father are also in tears. I look at Oliver and mouth a silent 'Are you all right?' and get a small nod 'yes' back.

It has finally happened. Justice has been done. Nothing else matters now.

The sense of relief is indescribable. Finally, we have a decision that, God willing, will never allow this vile man to surface in the real world again. If the wind were in the right direction the judge might well hear the cheers coming from Soham at this moment!

There is no time to absorb the verdicts. The charges against Maxine Carr are read out next, and Dennis Mackenzie's predictions come true as she is acquitted of the more serious ones. We are most surprised at the not guilty verdicts. She is found guilty on the conspiracy charge only, but all that is insignificant compared with Huntley's conviction, and always will be.

Before I know it, Huntley and Carr are taken down to the cells and the courtroom empties, as fast as it filled earlier in the day. We, like the Chapman family, remain and we all embrace and release some pent-up adrenalin. There is no joy, just relief. Many members of the Cambridgeshire Police seem to feel it as strongly as we do. Even though we have had issues with the hierarchy and the higher ups of the investigation, there has never, ever, been a moment when the level of commitment, and of desire to secure justice for Holly and Jessica could be questioned. We will remember that for the rest of our lives. For Chris, Trudie and Gary there are extra-special hugs to acknowledge their fantastic and very personal help to us.

Fittingly, our friends Rob and Trudie stand by our side. They were our guests at the very beginning of this time of trouble on 4 August 2002 and they are here now at the end. Nicola and I will be calling on their strength of character in the months ahead and perhaps they will call on ours. Like many others they have stood up, stood with us and been counted and we remain deeply touched. Never will we underestimate the value of true friendship in our lives.

Before too long the judge is back to pass sentence. Now finally, we are allowed to sit in the Corporation of London seats, in front of the guilty two. We appreciate the gesture immensely. As Huntley and Carr are brought up into the dock, they make no eye contact with us, instead choosing to stare at the judge. There is not a flicker of emotion from Huntley, as Mr Justice Moses instructs him to stand up and listen. His words could not be starker:

'Ian Kevin Huntley, on 4 August 2002, you enticed two 10-year-old girls,

Holly Wells and Jessica Chapman, into your house. They were happy, intelligent and loyal. They were much loved by their families and all who knew them. You murdered them both. You are the one person who knows how you murdered them. You are the one person who knows why.

You destroyed the evidence, but you showed no mercy and you show no regret. It is plain that once you killed one you had to kill the other in your attempt to avoid detection. On 10 August, six days later, you told the BBC that you thought you might be the last friendly face that these two girls had to speak to. That was a lie which serves to underline the persistent cruelty of your actions. On the contrary, one of those girls died knowing her friend had been attacked or killed by you.

After you had murdered them both, you pushed their bodies into a ditch, stripped them and burned them, while their families searched for them in increasing despair. And as Kevin Wells called out their names, you pretended to join in the search. Three days later you demonstrated the extent of your merciless cynicism by offering that father some words of regret. Your tears have never been for them, only for yourself.

In your attempts to escape responsibility, in your lies and your manipulation up to this day, you have increased the suffering you have caused two families. But it is not just those two families whose lives you have sought to destroy. Your crimes are those for which the community suffers. The children you murdered were children whose lives brought joy to the community and whose deaths brought grief.

There is no greater task for the criminal justice system than to protect the vulnerable. There are few worse crimes than your murder of those two young girls.'

I am genuinely stunned by the speech and it is immensely difficult to remain calm and composed. I hope every word of every sentence stays with Huntley until his dying day. With two life sentences now beginning, may your nights be long and arduous,

Huntley. You deserve nothing more.

A shorter speech dwells on Carr's ability to lie all too glibly, and Mr Justice Moses sentences her to three and a half years' imprisonment. Our legal team told us they expected about 6 years. Later, it would transpire that Carr's legal team told her to expect 8 years. We disagree with the 'not guilty' verdicts on the more serious charges, and feel she's been very lucky with the jury and the judge. However, at least for now, we really do not care one jot about her. I wonder if the jury will have the same view of her when they become aware of all the facts about her past. The same goes for the one juror who incomprehensibly chose to give Huntley the benefit of the doubt. Tomorrow, the newspapers will be full of stories about his past and his history of violence.

As Huntley and Carr are sent down, Mr Justice Moses turns to us and the Chapmans and offers some unexpected words of encouragement before disappearing. We leave the courtroom to watch Chris Stevenson, Andy Hebb, Gary Goose, Marion Bastin and John Goodier gather to give a post-verdict speech to the media. Chris Stevenson reads the statement outside the Old Bailey. He is not just surrounded by all forms of the media, but also overlooked by a helicopter! There is a moment when Mr Stevenson's emotions nearly catch him out, before he recovers to complete his task admirably. It reminds us that we will have to keep our emotions in check as we leave to contribute to a post-verdict press conference. Nicola and I are chauffeured to face the press. Although very nervous, we take our places at the front of a packed room and try our best to answer questions honestly. As we stand to leave there is a nice touch from these 'hardened' hacks, a small ripple of applause. It means a great deal.

Within minutes, Nicola and I are out of a side door to meet with Martin, our police driver. Fortunately, or unfortunately, as the case may be, Martin is an aggressive driver and he has to follow two police motorcyclists, as we have been allocated our own escort through East London. Martin smiles the broadest smile imaginable as he tries to keep up with the bikers. With lights and sirens at full pelt, Nicola and I sit in terrified silence as we go through red lights, drive on the wrong side of the road, set off every speed (sorry, safety) camera and attract the attention of pedestrians. Sometimes it has taken us two hours to get from the Old Bailey to the outskirts of London. Today it's taken 14 white-knuckle minutes.

The rest of the journey home is less Formula One. Nicola and I are in contact with family and friends to let them know we are relieved. Obviously they all know the verdicts. We only hope that we never return to observe the criminal justice system again. It has been a truly shocking experience even with two guilty verdicts in place, but it is clear that the system is about winning and losing in court, not searching for truth. With the defendant having to prove nothing, this inequitable system leaves us many questions that will remain unanswered for the rest of our lives. How just is that?

Once home I discuss my book contract with Sonia Land. I have spoken to her twice over the last couple of days, after the jury went out, so I know the general details. Sonia has negotiated with the *Mail on Sunday*. They will serialise my book, which is the integral part of the publishing package, allowing me to complete my writing project without financial worries. I will always be grateful for Sonia's input. As the offer is higher than I was expecting, it not only covers what I need to balance the books and restart in business, but will also allow us to make a chari-table donation at some stage in the future. But as part of the contract, the *Mail on Sunday* requires an exclusive interview for this Sunday's edition.

On my dining-room table, I have details of huge financial offers from other newspapers also asking for the first, exclusive inter-view. One of them has actually offered £500,000 – half a million quid! It is a staggering amount of money; it is actually the equiv-alent of my completing 45,545 window-cleaning jobs, which, believe me, is a great deal of glass. Both Nicola and I will always be grateful for the scale of this offer, but we cannot accept it. Just as I know in my heart that writing my book is the correct way for me to cope with this part of my life, I also know I do not want Holly's death to be a spring board for family riches. By the end of the evening Nicola and I have signed the *Mail on Sunday* contract. Tomorrow morning, we will welcome one of their reporters, Sarah Oliver, into our home.

On Thursday 18 December, tough new sentencing rules come into force which ensure that 'life means life' for those convicted of multiple murders. Unfortunately for us, Huntley has missed this new legislation by one day, as he was sentenced on the 17th. For now, we will have to wait for yet another judge to consider the case and set the tariff for Huntley. It is a desperately uncomfortable thought that even now, after all we have all been through, Huntley may not receive his full comeuppance. As no one can give us an expected timescale or even confirm if Huntley's two life sentences will run concurrently or consecutively, we pray his sentence will not be as lenient as Maxine Carr's.

Sarah Oliver arrives early and that proves to be the start of an intense day's work. Nicola and I feel that, as we have signed a contract, it is only proper to commit to being completely honest and open. We place our trust in Sarah to represent our viewpoint fairly and accurately. But she is not alone this morning. To protect their 'exclusive', the *Mail on Sunday* have three additional employees present. Craig, Alistair and Ross form our team of minders and leap up every time the front doorbell or phone rings! Craig Hibbert is really a photographer and he keeps Nicola busy, locating and sorting out various photographs of Holly, while Sarah and I talk and discuss the strength of various adjectives along the way. By the end of the first evening, my reservations and fear of being misrepresented have all but disappeared, and Sarah has gained our trust and respect for her sensitive, compassionate approach.

On Friday 19 December, I am in contact once more with Sonia Land, this time to speak fully about David Cohen's offer to produce a TV documentary. Nicola and I hold the same reservations about television as we do with newspapers: the risk of misrepresentation. I am also very confused as to the potential negative impact such a film might have on my book. Sonia quells my initial concern, explaining that the audience for a primetime documentary, and likely readership of my book, are very different. This seems to be confirmed by the *Mail on Sunday* being aware of the documentary, yet happy to agree a long-term contract, serialising my book. Of course, the crux of Sonia's call is to ask if we will take part in such a documentary.

In trying to decide what is best, we list what we know or believe to be the crucial factors. At this moment, Huntley's family members and past girlfriends are doing interviews with newspapers. Huntley's history – most of all with Lincolnshire Police and Social Services – is the subject of much press activity. With the Public Inquiry starting early next year, the New Year won't bring much by way of quiet. And Maxine Carr may be released in early 2004, which I'm sure the media will seize on.

In our opinion, all of these factors deflect from Holly, Jessica and the family victims, still very much trying to cope and adjust in the glare of the media. Why shouldn't the victims' story be shared? Maybe the police and other authorities can learn something from seeing the effect Holly's murder has had on us as parents. It is also clear that some friends and family members would welcome the opportunity to make a positive contribution to a defining project in Holly's memory, perhaps even find it therapeutic. After much debate, we decide to accept David Cohen's offer and make the film.

It would be ridiculously naïve to assume that everyone will support our decision to tell our story, so we brace ourselves for some criticism. That will be difficult to handle. We know that we have no one to blame but ourselves if it hurts too much.

On Sunday 21 December, the *Mail on Sunday*'s front-page headline simply says, 'Holly's Story – by her parents'. We're happy with the article and its presentation. During the day, family and friends express their approval and support. We do not tell them how worried we were over the last three days, working with Sarah Oliver. She was a stranger but she kept her personal pledges and integrity. For that, we will always be grateful to Sarah. Tomorrow, David Cohen will come to start the documentary and I hope that working with him will not be different,

Three days later Nicola and I are completely shattered. David Cohen arrived with his colleague and cameraman, David Carr-Brown, and between them they have completely taken over my home with their presence and equipment. It has been strange meeting David Cohen again as, at first, he seemed to be blissfully unaware of much of what we'd been through over the last 16 months. I was not expecting that. Suddenly my notes, the chronology, the observations and the record of emotional issues proved of the utmost significance.

The documentary will be shown on ITV, as a *Tonight with Trevor McDonald* special, which takes us full circle back to the same programme, on which we did our appeal for Holly and Jessica in 2002. What is clear to me now, just before we break for Christmas, is that my early reservations about David not being aware of the important issues, as I see them, are misplaced. To Nicola, our families, our friends and me, he has been kind, caring and sensitive. No one is left in any doubt that David's agenda mirrors our own in wanting this documentary to reflect our love and deep sense of loss over Holly. That matters immensely. His attitude has helped quell my own reservations about the end product. In short, David has gained our trust.

With our house now empty and quiet, Nicola and I leave to visit Holly's newly erected headstone for the first time. The finished memorial is wonderful and Jeremy has excelled in his delicate artwork. I don't think it could be bettered. Of course, it is a poignant visit and despite the cold, we sit down together, to talk about the last few weeks and how our lives have changed so dramatically since August 2002. In a few days' time we will be flying off to New Zealand for four weeks of anonymity, peace and much needed space. And, most important, we will have the chance to spend uninterrupted time with Oliver. That is the right way to bid farewell to 2003.

There is one last thing in the pipeline for Nicola, however. She wants to meet, face to face, with Maxine Carr. Although we do not know if Carr will agree to such a meeting, Nicola has told the police. When the time is right, they will broach the subject with Carr and her legal team. For now, we will give no more thought to it. If she says 'yes', it could be an explosive welcome back in February.

New Zealand

January 2004

If there is a better way to start the New Year other than being present in a slice of God's own country, I cannot wait to experience it: New Zealand is incredible.

Our flight with Singapore Airlines started rather well as we found ourselves being upgraded to business class for the first leg of the journey from Heathrow to Singapore. We remain grateful to Singapore Airlines for their kindness.

As we travel past Auckland Harbour and over its famous bridge up to the East Coast bays, in glorious sunshine, the month ahead could not be more different to the one we have just left behind.

We stay in Murray's Bay with my cousin Julie, Dean and my goddaughter, Sarah. Our first days are spent visiting the local beaches, enjoying some hot sunshine and warm sea water. Dean regularly brings his small boat down to Brown's Bay and it is great fun being pulled along on the calm sea waters. But Oliver is still very unsure about getting into the sea, in case there are sharks. It bothers us, as we were rather hoping the change of scenery would help him find his former happy-go-lucky character. Nicola tells me she intends to have a quiet word with him when we return 'home' to Murray's Bay.

I deliberately stay behind to allow Nicola a little time to chat things through with Oliver. As I go into our bedroom, Nicola looks completely crestfallen. She can't speak for a long period as she breaks down and sobs on my shoulder. Although I am used to seeing Nicola upset, this is different. There is an intensity present which I have not witnessed since 2002.

'Oh, Kev, it's Olly . . .'

I listen, in silence, as Nicola explains and it is heart-rending stuff. For the first time, Oliver has 'broken down' and told her he is frightened he, too, will die. He reminded Nicola of a conversation she once had with Holly, after watching a news item relating to a child murder. Holly wanted her mum to reassure her that nothing similar would ever happen to her. Oliver remembers this conversation and remembers Nicola's comforting reply. In his mind, those parental reassurances have a horrid hollow feel to them. Over the last 16 months we have done nothing but try to dispel Oliver's fears. It is with a sinking feeling we realise that we have missed the point. Clearly Oliver does not want to hear words of comfort; they are the very things he associates with the death of his sister. We are extremely confused as to what to do next.

Oliver's fear of sharks in reality is anything but. The fear of Jaws is simply his way of expressing his deep-rooted anxiety that something dreadful is going to happen to him next. Nicola sensed enormous relief from Oliver once he had said these things out loud, but that does not stop us feeling desperately sad. Oliver will be the brother of 'murdered schoolgirl Holly Wells' for ever, and that could cost him dear.

Nicola and I agree on a plan of action. We feel it is important to try and coax Oliver away from thinking that every family incident is a threat or prelude to something sinister. His life will never be the same but we need to instil in him the belief that it is acceptable to carry on, look forward and be positive. Nicola and I decide to try some 'risky' leisure activities, throughout the rest of the holiday. If Oliver can see his parents overcome some fears of their own, it may give him the lift he needs.

On Sunday 4 January 2004, we are all guests of Dean's parents, Malcolm and Shirley at Omaha Beach, which boasts the most wonderful stretch of sand. It is virtually devoid of people, which does take some getting used to. There is hardly anyone in New Zealand. Really! Today the wind is blowing in towards the beach from the sea and the waves are absolutely perfect for Oliver to try body boarding. Dean leads the way and Oliver watches from the shore before reluctantly being persuaded to 'give it a go'. After half an hour, no more terror of sharks. Oliver has taken to his new-found sport like a fish to water. For the rest of the day he hones his skills with a wonderful smile and laugh on his face, just like the Oliver of old. We have not seen him this happy since before August 2002, and that makes it a joyous day.

Over the next few days, we continue our 'take a risk' therapy. We travel down the side of a mountain in a plastic go-cart, horse-trek on ridiculously steep paths, take jet-boat trips, go quad-bike racing and accompany Oliver in a bungee-type ride called The Swoop. All this shows Oliver that life, with all of its inherent risks, does go on.

On 16 January we go to Brown's Bay. As the afternoon drifts along, down the beach there is a commotion. Bystanders gather. From far off it seems to involve a large fish and Oliver asks if he can go to have a look. As he runs off, we hear the siren of an ambulance and our hearts miss a beat. When Oliver gets back he explains in a very matter-of-fact manner. Two children are dead and one adult may also have drowned. He describes watching people on the beach try to revive the young children. But what can we say? For the last 12 days we have tried to show Oliver that life is for living and that everything will turn out fine for him and his future. We did not see this coming, and it brings back some of the recent hell. Oliver did not view the body of his sister and, now, he has seen the dead bodies of two children. We feel that life has just smacked us all in the face as we gather up our things to head back to Murray's Bay. Our thoughts and prayers can only now go to the heartbroken New Zealand family. We're worried about the emotional impact this incident may have on Oliver, but they have lost two children on a sunny afternoon. It puts our dilemma in perspective.

On Wednesday 20 January 2004, there are developments back in England. Gary Goose and Chris Mead are meeting Maxine Carr and her solicitor, Roy James, in Holloway Prison. The aim is to assess if the proposed meeting between Nicola and Carr will prove beneficial. Nicola and I respect Gary and Chris and their judgement. It is nearly as good as being present ourselves.

Nicola and I have produced a list of questions we would like Gary and Chris to get some clarification on. These include:

- *Was Maxine Carr aware of Huntley's past?*
- *Were Huntley's parents aware of his past?*
- *Why did Carr take the course of action she did since August 2002?*
- *Was there any violence in Huntley and Carr's relationship?*
- *What were Carr's first thoughts when she knew Holly and Jessica were missing?*
- *Why did Carr not confront Huntley about the washing being done upon her return to 5 College Close?*
- *What did Carr really think about the state of the bathroom and the alleged water damage in the dining room?*
- *Why did Carr not challenge Huntley on his irrational behaviour?*
- *What did Carr think when Huntley told her that one of the girls had sat on their bed?*
- *Why didn't Carr tell the police earlier that the girls had been inside the house?*
- *Why did Carr wait until the trial 'to tell all'?*
- *What does Carr really think went on in her house on 4 August 2002?*
- *Does Carr think that Huntley will ever tell the truth about the events leading up to and beyond Holly's murder and if so, who to?*
- *Is Carr aware of the fact that if she had spoken up earlier, potentially two sets of parents may have had an opportunity of recovering their daughters' bodies before the advanced level of decomposition set in?*

We are not sure if Maxine Carr's solicitor will allow some of these questions to be raised. Nicola and I count down every second, waiting for Chris Mead's call, to update us on the meeting.

But the outcome proves to be disappointing. Carr did provide some answers, but Chris and Gary agreed a confidentiality clause. It prevents the contents of the meeting becoming public knowledge. We will respect and uphold their undertaking, given on our behalf, not to divulge any specifics, even if it is about someone we both despise.

At the end of a long three-way telephone call, my wife's hopes of addressing issues with Maxine Carr in person have disappeared. There is nothing to gain by meeting the woman in the near future, indeed perhaps the very opposite. Nicola dismisses the idea the moment Chris finishes his call. We decide not to discuss this again.

At the end of January, David Cohen comes to New Zealand to film a final sequence for the documentary. I suppose David wishes to portray some form of 'happy ending' for his and our programme, perhaps seeking to convey a sense of moving on. Whatever his intentions, they are certainly thought-provoking, for he has inadvertently touched upon our own hidden goal: the chance to have a final, defining say about Holly's all-too-public death and the hope that we will adjust and become a happy family again.

For now, we bid farewell to this stunningly beautiful country, having recharged our batteries and enjoyed four weeks of anonymity. We know there are issues in the media which will affect us when we get back to Soham, so we can only hope that our resolve holds out.

The Bichard Inquiry

When we get back to Soham there is much catching up to do, not least in terms of addressing the huge volume of post that built up in our absence. Even the overwhelming evidence of the trial and the exposure of Huntley's past are not enough to convince some oddballs of his guilt. Their half-baked ideas and theories as to what may have happened are frankly ludicrous, but it is not good for the soul to receive this kind of material. It is agonising to read letters telling you to take comfort from the fact that, at least, your daughter did not die a virgin. I find it excruciating, and more than a little surreal, to learn that some madman thinks it's his role in life to tell us that strangulation may have helped Holly to achieve an orgasm before her death. This is the cruel reality of being in our position – we're magnets for the drivel of the desperate and depraved.

Of course, these obscene and crazy letters are far outnumbered by positive ones, much more representative of normal society. The written word is a very powerful tool and often a well-meant letter strikes a chord. On Thursday 5 February one such letter humbles me. The writer is a former paratrooper, who confirms that every year he visits Arnhem to pay his respects 'to the lads who are still there'. So do many other veterans. He adds, 'many other chaps who think they are tough' find the visit very emotional and the sense of tragedy is made more intense by watching hundreds of Dutch children place flowers on the graves of English soldiers. After the Service of Remembrance, the children often approach the veterans for a little keepsake, such as a badge, which they are happy to pass over to these 'special people'. The letter continues, 'My friends and I at the Parachute Regiment Club think that Oliver and yourself, Mr Wells, are special people and we would be pleased if you would accept the two caps enclosed.' It is a wonderfully warm gesture. The letter concludes, 'Oliver has a signed Manchester United ball – so do I. The United team are called "The Red Devils" – so are the Paras. The Germans in North Africa called the Paras "Rote Teufel" (Red Devils) because of the red caps and the courage they showed in adversity. And Mr Wells, your family certainly did that. May I wish you all the best in your future lives?'

This letter and the caps are enormously uplifting. When I stop to think about the level of suffering individuals from that era endured, it becomes more than a boost. It's an inspiration.

Huntley and Carr have been in the news again. As different headlines and stories break, they seem to take on a life of their own. The news has covered the length of Huntley's sentence; Carr allegedly writing a book; a debate over restoration of the death penalty; the re-examination of the death of one of Huntley's former neighbours; Carr's application for early release and the Bichard Inquiry. All make it a very busy month.

In February, the press reports on the compensation of £11,000 (£5,500 per parent) that we will receive from the Criminal Injuries Compensation Scheme. Both sides of the debate (i.e. 'Not enough' and 'Why is there money at all?') are aired. The coverage acts as a catalyst for me to complete the outstanding paperwork for the claim. This means that I am going to have to apply for Holly's formal death certificate. Even though I know it is only a form, completing it proves to be as difficult emotionally as anything I have done. At some stage in the future, we will receive a cheque from the compensation scheme, as we will for our contribution to the television documentary, but Nicola and I will not be the ultimate beneficiaries. When Oliver is 21 there will be a small trust fund at his disposal. We feel that is the right thing to do at this stage. In 2010, Oliver will be able to agree or disagree with our decision. Whatever he chooses will be fine by us.

By the end of February, the newspaper twists and turns relating to Huntley and Carr spiral on. The big issue has been Maxine Carr's attempt to gain an early release. She failed, which we are pleased about. We were disappointed she applied in the first place. Her sentence was lenient in the extreme. Surely someone close to her could suggest that she serve the rest of her term without grandstanding. It is bloody bad enough that every day she spent on remand counted for a day and a half of her sentence. That's why she admitted nothing, I suspect. The more I think about the legal system, the angrier I become. But, at least, Carr will spend the rest of her sentence in the right place, the right place for someone who can chillingly say 'the girls are out of the equation', in between bouts of cruel deceit and lies.

Behind the scenes, meetings and activities dominate February. The Village College has been praised by Ofsted following a visit from their inspectors, which reflects very highly on all of the staff and pupils. Along with the Chapman family, Nicola and I have met with Village College staff to discuss the demolition of Huntley's house, the 'hangar' building and Huntley's garage. It does not take long to reach a unanimous decision to remove these painful reminders from our community. We worried the school would somehow lose out financially, but we learn there will be government funding for both demolition and redevelopment.

At the end of the month, the newspapers report that Huntley has received a smack in prison. We are surprised it has taken this long, given the number of letters we've had from ex-convicts predicting what is likely to happen to the man. This unexpected twist leads to an amusing moment, as one member of the public forwards me a copy of an email which he sent to the Governor of Belmarsh Prison. It reads:

'Sir,

Would you kindly commend the gentleman who went some way towards giving Huntley what he so richly deserved and tell him that when you let him out, it will be my privilege to buy him a drink (or three).'

I wonder if the Governor did pass on that message.

In February I get an important letter from Shelley Gilbert, who lives in Totteridge, London. She also sent a proof of her soon-to-be-published book, which she has written to raise public awareness of children's bereavement issues and to encourage conversations about loss between kids and adults. Shelley is well qualified to write about this and she was also bereaved as a child. The contents really do hit home. As I read about the spiral of grief, whirling through happiness, sadness, confusion, anger, guilt, fear, shock, relief and disbelief, it dawns on me that I have felt every one of those emotions. By the end of my first read, I realise the importance of the project and accept Shelley's request to help promote *Grief Encounter*. The decision would eventually lead to my becoming patron of this charity and has put me in contact with many caring, informed people who want to make a difference. It is refreshing to be part of something positive.

Two other messages in Shelley's book hit home. First, she writes 'pain is the price we pay for having loved someone'; second, she says *Grief Encounter* aims to 'dispel the myths about acceptance and moving on'. Shelley could not be more right.

On 13 January, while we were in New Zealand, Sir Michael Bichard defined the terms of reference for the Inquiry into the deaths of Holly and Jessica. They are as follows:

'Urgently to enquire into child protection procedures in Humberside Police and Cambridge Constabulary in the light of the recent trial and conviction of Ian Huntley for the murder of Jessica Chapman and Holly Wells. In particular to assess the effectiveness of the relevant intelligence-based record keeping, the vetting practices in those Forces since 1995 and information sharing with other agencies; and to report to the Home Secretary on matters of local and national relevance and to make recommendations as appropriate.'

On Thursday 3 March, I go to Holborn in central London, to attend the Inquiry. I have been in regular contact with Sir Michael and his secretary, Jim Nicholson. Chris Mead, Gary Goose and I walk through the press – again – and into the building. Inside, we regather our composure to meet with Sir Michael before today's proceedings get under way. He gives us the warmest of welcomes; he is a very open, uncomplicated and matter-of-fact individual.

By the end of the day, I possess a sense of inner peace that some good eventually may come from the death of my daughter. Today I saw Counsel to the Inquiry, James Eadie and Kate Gallafent, use their considerable intellect and skills in a manner very different to their counterparts in the Old Bailey. This Inquiry is open and has a positive feel about it. Witnesses leave having been heard properly and without having had their dignity shredded. This is the right climate to encourage honest debate between all parties and to arrive at a useful set of recommendations.

Gary, Chris and I head back to King's Cross Station, and we pop into O'Neill's Irish Bar once again. As we sit down 'Angels' comes on the juke box. Coincidence or not, it serves as a sobering reminder of why we are all in town in the first place.

Thursday 11 March proves to be one of the most testing days we have experienced since Huntley's conviction. The Chief Constable of Cambridgeshire, Tom Lloyd, gives evidence at the Inquiry and Nicola and I feel it only proper to attend and show our moral support. But it does not start well. Counsel for the Inquiry, James Eadie, asks why the second statement of the Cambridgeshire Police was only signed this morning. The legal team representing the Cambridgeshire Police reply that it was not possible to get a signature earlier. The inference is that the report was amended in light of other evidence. It reminds me, I am sorry to say, of the tactics used by Huntley's defence. I am genuinely confused as to what areas need to be changed or protected. If there had been no vetting errors relating to Huntley and his employment at the school, no trace of his past record would have been found due to Humberside's flawed intelligence records. That is public record. So was Mr Lloyd perhaps being a little defensive and overprotective of his force?

Today, also, the Crown Prosecution Service confirm that Maxine

Carr will be charged with a string of fraud offences as well as lying about her qualifications to get work at St Andrew's Primary School. Is that a complete coincidence? The news will grab headlines. When you start to wonder, you start to wonder. So I do wonder; *has* that announcement been cunningly planned to deflect media criticism from Mr Lloyd? Even now, despite the best efforts of our FLOs and their coordinator, Gary Goose, we, the surviving victims, seem to remain at the very bottom of the senior officer's priorities. Mr Lloyd knows we will be at the Inquiry today and he knows we will be dramatically exposed to the media as a direct result of this announcement. It appears that no lessons are being learned. Despite our very public support of Cambridgeshire Constabulary, it seems, rightly or wrongly, that careers come before care.

But Gary Goose manages to get a delay of the announcement of the charges against Carr. And it is not all doom and gloom at the Inquiry. Chief Constable Tom Lloyd has done the right thing, held his hands up, and accepted responsibility for the mistakes and failings of his force. He promised he would 'personally ensure that any recommendations of this Inquiry and indeed any other recommendations that come to my attention are fully implemented and responded to positively'. That is the very message we needed to hear and we feel reassured by his pledge. Nicola and I are not here to apportion blame, other than to Huntley, for Holly's murder. But it is important to us both that some form of better procedures comes out of the tragedy. Lloyd's promise should help.

Tonight at 9 p.m., ITV are showing our documentary, 'Our Daughter Holly', under the *Tonight with Trevor McDonald* banner. There will be no commercial breaks, which is a gesture we neither expected nor requested, but appreciate deeply. Before getting to this stage, I have had many meetings with the producer, David Cohen, viewing various edits as the programme gradually took shape. David has kept his promise of allowing me to view the edit at every stage and together we have amended a number of inaccuracies, leading to a truthful depiction of Holly's story and ours.

After the broadcast, Nicola and I get many wonderful supportive letters from members of the public. Some touch on how our 'public bravery' has inspired others to confront personal problems in their own lives. Some comment on how important it is for a man to be seen expressing his emotions. Others reflect on the necessity of victims speaking of their pain and loss, showing that crime is not some abstract matter of statistics and legislation. Others simply thank us for allowing them into our private world. As parents, we just hope that people can see Holly was the most extraordinary of daughters, whose loss we will feel for the rest of our lives.

I also hope the film sent a message to Huntley: that although he has shattered our dreams and changed the course of our lives, he will not break our family spirit. With this documentary now behind us we feel focused and more positive than at any time since August 2002. Although I did not expect to be saying it, thank you for coming into our lives, David Cohen.

At the end of April 2004, we and the Chapman family meet the trustees of the Holly and Jessica Fund. Everyone agrees that the balance of approximately £70,000 should be distributed to local causes and should finance a suitable memorial to Holly and Jessica. The first donations will be paid sooner rather than later with approximately £30,000 set aside for established groups, clubs and organisations. Many children and adults will now benefit from the hard work of the trustees, Nadine and Coral, and the generosity of the public. Nicola, Oliver and I have received £6,000 each. We could not have afforded to go to New Zealand without this help, and we could not have imported a very special piece of granite from India for Holly's memorial. We remain extremely grateful. Nicola and I hope that by using the bulk of the funds to support the community we do not cause any ill feeling to those who wanted to make a direct contribution to the families. We can only apologise if we have inadvertently done so.

Nicola and I also complete a 'Victim Impact Statement' letter, which forms part of the dossier the judge bases his decision on when setting the tariff for Huntley. There seems no point in holding back at this stage, so in a very matter-of-fact letter, we detail the scale of our loss. Then, we learn that Huntley's legal team have the right to see our letter, which means Huntley himself can read it. There is no getting away from this position if we wish the judge to hear our viewpoint. A letter from the National Probation Service makes this clear: 'If you have a particular reason you do not want the prisoner to see your Victim Impact Statement then you can make an application to the Judge that your state-ment is not seen by Ian Huntley or his legal representative. In that situation the Judge will not be able to take the views expressed in your Victim Impact Statement into account when setting the tariff.'

It is almost grotesque and the logic – or lack of logic – defies comment.

I also get some police statistics from Gary Goose. They are a very real reminder of the scale of the investigation. Amongst a very long list are the following:

Nominals identified (people/names)	14,555
Police officers	1,539
People who know the victims	707
Number of exhibit items	7,351
House-to-house enquiries	4,352
Documents	23,914
Telephone contacts	9,796
Statements	6,825
Police actions raised	11,365

On 31 March, Chris Mead and I travel to visit the Home Secretary, David Blunkett. It must be quite bizarre for Chris, as a sergeant, to meet the elite of his profession, such as Sir Ronnie Flanagan and, now, David Blunkett. I am being given a platform, I suspect.

The first thing I notice inside the main building is how busy everyone is. The rooms are packed with desks and civil servants, some of them barely visible behind huge piles of paper. Even when we find a clearing with a couple of settees, it feels more like a waiting room in a corporate headquarters than the historic, grand and opulent Home Office. Chris and I voice our concerns to David Blunkett and Hazel Blears MP, the Minister for Policing. Although we did not hear or see a signal indicating to David Blunkett that our half-hour slot was up, he called it to the minute, which was most bizarre. He promised he would seek answers on all of my points. However, there is one point that I felt Mr Blunkett was not expecting and it concerns the Bichard Inquiry. I stress that I do not want the Chief Constables of Cambridgeshire and Humberside to be held personally responsible for historic errors. Instead, Nicola and I would like both of them to be given the opportunity to focus on implementing the changes Sir Michael recommends. I really am a political innocent.

Once out into the streets of London, Chris and I manage a wry smile. Neither of us had the courage to mention one coincidence to Mr Blunkett; namely that his dog has the same name as Huntley and Carr's – Sadie. Perhaps another time!

In the same way that small negative things continued to crop up throughout 2002 and 2003, small positive ones now make a guest appearance. On Saturday 3 April, in just 38 minutes, 5 College Close is flattened to the ground. Nicola and I will no longer have to drive or walk past this awful reminder. Every brick and every piece of the building will be taken away and ground down into dust. There will be no trophies for the ghouls who covet such items. The fall of the house is symbolic not only for us, but for our friends and family too. The flattened area will be laid to turf in the near future and may well be used as a bus shelter for the children. Whatever happens is fine by us and ultimately lies in the hands of the Village College. We know Howard and Margaret and we know that their decision will be an appropriate one.

In April we get news of the premature death of the second

medium who visited us during 2002, Ron Moulding. I will never forget the complete look of surprise on the face of the FLOs when Ron uttered the words 'Keeper's Cottage'. May you rest well, Ron.

There is much better news, too, and this time it relates to Oliver. Child Victims of Crime is a police charity whose aim is to provide surviving children with a gift once the trial is over. Oliver has chosen some gymnasium equipment, after fully grasping the ethos behind the charity. It was very rewarding to see our son look so pleased at his impending windfall. Somehow, Nicola and I would like to try to help this charity because we know first-hand how it has helped our son. We decide that, as well as Grief Encounter, Child Victims of Crime will receive some of the proceeds from the sale of my book. That feels good.

May starts. It is my favourite time of year. It's not just the warmer weather, it is also the beginning of the flat racing season and the cricket season. Nicola has already said she is happy for me to return to playing league cricket. So I find myself opening the innings for the Ely and Haddenham Cricket Club at the Paradise Ground.

As my opening partner, Jon Peacock, raises his bat to acknowledge his half-century, my miserable score is two. Jon reminds me of my total at the end of each over, just in case I had forgotten. But then he is the first batsman dismissed on the day. As other partners come and go, my own half-century eventually arrives. It's odd. I feel a sense of purpose and self-belief. Suddenly I realise I could score a century on my return league debut as our captain, Mark Abbott, joins me at the crease. (Mark, of course, was a witness at the Old Bailey and was the person with whom I shed a tear, when he told of his experiences over the telephone.)

Out on the field, suddenly it dawns on me that life must go on. Other things do matter – cricket matters, friendship matters and competing again matters. For me, the 'nervous nineties' simply become the 'emotional nineties' as three figures edge ever nearer. And then it happens. I get my century.

My team-mates cheer. My whole body tingles with emotion.

As Mark and I meet in the middle of the square, we embrace and cry. This time they're tears of joy, and we both understand the significance of the moment. It is priceless.

Our lives are back on track. Nicola feels settled and strong enough to start shopping again. Oliver is socialising with his mates and I am back playing the sport I love with friends I treasure. As for Holly? She is in our hearts and always will be. It has taken an eternity to be able to say this and mean it, but I accept that life must go on. Holly will remain in my thoughts every day for the rest of my life, but that is not the issue now. Today, I have seen, felt and experienced the bigger picture. If upholding Holly's memory means embracing life and its challenges from now on, that is what I will do. I hope that things will turn out positively for Nicola, Oliver and me in the years to come. That means Holly will play her part, for just as she inspired us to review our lives many years ago, she can be our inspiration for the years to come. I do not need any better motivation than that.

On Tuesday 15 June, together with the Chapman family, Nicola and I meet with Sir Michael Bichard, at the Quay Mill Hotel. We are to be briefed about the conclusions and recommendations of his Inquiry, ahead of next week's public release. But Nicola and I cannot concentrate totally, as my father's health has deteriorated at an alarming rate. As we leave Addenbrooke's Hospital to meet Sir Michael, my father remains unconscious and the prognosis is desperately poor. I try my best to understand the key points of the Inquiry report, but my thoughts are with Dad. My family and I will always remember today for very different reasons, because my father has lost his last battle. It is a strange day to become 'head of my family' and even though his death is not unexpected, it is still tough to take on board.

I mourn his passing and I also mourn what did not pass between us. At no stage have Dad and I taken the time to discuss August 2002 or the events that followed. That is just how things are between us. On Saturday 17 August 2002, Dad came round for his only visit as we all paced outside for news waiting to hear if the two bodies that had been found were those of Holly and Jessica. After we knew that Holly and Jessica would not be coming home, he never mentioned Holly's name again.

Over the last few weeks, apparently Dad told Mum that he felt his time was nearly up, and he finally broached the subject of losing his only granddaughter. It was a little sign that despite his pragmatic exterior, Dad died with a depth of pain that equalled the loss felt by all of us left alive. I have a funny feeling that when the two of them meet up in the afterlife, Holly will keep him more than busy.

The following day, Wednesday 16 June, Sir Ronnie Flanagan, Her Majesty's Inspector of Constabulary, is due round to discuss his report into how the Cambridgeshire Police ran the investigation. I have met him on a number of occasions over the last few months and he has always filled me with confidence. Sir Ronnie always does something which simply breaks down any potential barriers that may exist between officials of his rank and members of the public such as me – he gives a hug. Before we speak. This gesture is remarkable and shows his great empathy for the victims of crime and their families.

Sir Ronnie's report details both good and poor practices in the police investigation. The police started well but failed to carry on the good momentum of the night the girls went missing. They allowed Huntley 13 days of unusual behaviour and constant interaction with the media until his arrest. The only benefit was that Huntley's behaviour helped to establish his all-important state of mind for the trial. Only a sane and cunning bastard would have acted as he did.

Sir Michael's report states:

- *'Huntley alone was responsible for, and stands convicted of, these most awful murders. None of the actions or failures of any of the witnesses who gave evidence to the Inquiry, or the institutions they represented, led to the deaths of the girls.'*

- 'However, the Inquiry did find errors, omissions, failures and shortcomings which are deeply shocking. Taken together, these were so extensive that one cannot be confident that it was Huntley alone who "slipped through the net".'

We agree with both statements, even though the extent of 'systematic and corporate' failures at every level was shocking to hear earlier. Even now, it seems incredible that there was no information technology system that allowed police forces to share information on sexually dangerous men and other suspects unless there was a conviction. Whatever happened to prevention rather than cure? At various stages of the Inquiry, Nicola and I have had to dig deep to reaffirm our belief that the blame lies with Huntley alone for the murder of our daughter and yes, this has been pushed to its outer limits. Because nothing can change what has happened to Holly or Jessica, our approach to the Inquiry from day one has been to show our support and to hope and pray that recommendations can be agreed to protect other children. Sir Michael was right to comment that he could not be confident that Huntley alone 'slipped through the net'. His 31 recommendations should make it as difficult as possible for paedophiles to slip through the system and gain access to children.

Finally, there is one last message from Sir Michael. In six months' time, he intends to reconvene in order to assess progress. That can only be a good thing. My work on this book will be finished long before then and by the early part of 2005, when its conclusions become public, I will be ready to return to window cleaning. I believe I can do so in the knowledge that Sir Michael and his team will have created a practical and suitable memorial for Holly and Jessica.

Over the last few months there have been frenetic media reports on both Huntley and Carr, many of them speculative. The hacks are fascinated with Carr's future (Where will she live? Will she adopt a new identity? Be given 24-hour police guard?) Then, there's the inmate prison revolt against her, and Carr's admission of twenty charges of benefit fraud and lying on job applications. There is comment on Carr's lenient sentence, her release date, a security blunder on the eve of that release. It goes on – crucial documents stolen, death threats, 'draconian' high court action preventing any details of Carr's new life being published. We learn there is a race amongst prison gangs to murder Huntley, that Carr will become a nun, that Huntley will lodge an appeal. A former trial witness now believes that Holly and Jessica's bodies were in the boot of Huntley's Ford when he collected Carr from Grimsby. So the list continues.

But there is also the positive news that a second person linked to the 'Soham Murders' has received formal recognition. This time, Marion Bastin has been awarded an OBE for her work as the reviewing lawyer in the case. During the trial, nothing was too much trouble for her as she took time out to explain thorny points of law. Marion always warned us whenever our legal team was going to introduce any sensitive information into proceedings.

But there are knock-on effects of all these twists and turns. Each development brings calls and visits from the media, requesting comment. When Nicola and I refuse, the media ask extended members of our families. Even when they refuse, it sometimes becomes a story. We will all be glad when things get back to how they used to be, if that is possible.

After the Inquiry, the Home Secretary announces that he requires the Humberside Police Authority to suspend Mr Westwood as Chief Constable. Back in March, we told Mr Blunkett that this would be a mistake. The Home Secretary's decision leads to an enormous amount of press interest. I become involved because of a comment I make to the *Mail on Sunday* which becomes a front-page headline. However, I maintain my stance that individual blame is not the way forward. When I met with Mr Westwood for the first time, he was open and honest. He trusted us with confidential information. That meant a great deal. Mr Westwood has kept the pledges he made to us to make sure personally that the Humberside force improves. In the last few months he has written many times, keeping us up to date with progress. This is the attitude that is needed from all parties if any lessons are to be learned. For these reasons, I maintain my support for the man. There are no politics and no hidden agendas in my home. In our opinion, Mr Westwood deserves the chance to put things right.

An Ending of Sorts

This book needs an ending – and I am not sure what it should be. But I believe enough time has passed for me to give an honest assessment of our position. Today is Saturday 6 November. It is also the day that I first met my future wife 22 years ago; so it is a good date to reflect on two very different chapters of my life.

Over the last few months, the media coverage has been relentless. We have had press on: the possible resignation of both chief constables, the suspension of the Chief Constable of Humberside, Maxine Carr being confronted by members of the public, Carr's 'pampered' new life, Ian Huntley admitting to his mother that he deliberately killed Jessica, Carr's mother jailed for 6 months for intimidating a witness, Carr speaking to the *Mail on Sunday* – in person, media comment on how Carr speaking out conflicts with the media ban in place against her, 'new man' in Carr's life, Carr to meet her mother in prison, Brian Stevens found guilty of conspiring to pervert the course of justice, potential review of allegations against Stevens of downloading child pornography onto his police laptop, Carr breaking her curfew, Carr dumped by boyfriend, Stevens formally sacked from his job, Carr wants a 'boob job', one of Huntley's former victims speaks out, Huntley likely to be interviewed in prison over an incident in the past and the Chief Constable of Humberside returning to work. It runs and runs.

Since the summer, though, Nicola and I have radically changed our attitude. We have accepted that various aspects relating to Holly's murder will always be in the public eye, but that does not mean we have to cower at every headline or become upset at every story. We will do our best not to focus our thoughts on Ian Huntley or Maxine Carr. Writing this book has enabled me to accept, understand and embrace the circumstances and changes forced on my family and me. Feelings of anger, frustration, upset, shock, hatred and aggression no longer dominate my daily thoughts and that has to be a good thing. This book, we feel, has allowed us to reclaim Holly: and that goes for our extended family and for Holly's friends. Writing a truthful account of what happened has been good therapy. I hope we all can now accept the new direction our lives have taken and not dwell on what might have been.

During July 2004 I was able to play a small part in the launch of the Grief Encounter project in London. I still do not like public speaking and giving interviews, but what I like to do does not matter in the bigger scheme of things. It was an enormously uplifting evening and my first opportunity to contribute positively to Grief Encounter. I remain committed to the charity. If it can continue the hard work, vision and ethos that Shelley, Emma and the committee have in abundance, then I will be a lucky man.

For us as a family, the way forward is to reflect upon the many good things that have come into our lives since August 2002. Throughout this book, I have touched on examples of people's kindness and generosity; there are many hundreds more that have not been mentioned. Everyone's positive contribution has more than played its part in our emotional recovery and we remain eternally grateful. Although this grieving journey is going to be a lifetime one, we owe it to Holly's memory to make it as smooth as possible and that means focusing on something that we do have some control over – the rest of our lives.

On Friday 5 November 2004, two positive things happened. First, Chris Mead was honoured for his professionalism and level of support given to my family by being named 'Family Liaison Officer of the Year' in the first National Police Awards. It is richly deserved. The accolades have poured in for Chris, including one from Lord Brian Mackenzie, who presented Chris with the award:

'One of the most demanding tasks was in protecting the family from unwanted intrusion. To do this he displayed exceptional personal reserve, making sure that the best possible levels of service were available from the police and other agencies. He sacrificed his own time, energy and emotion in providing a service and maintaining this high level of contact for the 18 months leading up to and post trial.'

Every word is true. You will not find Chris doing interviews or making television appearances, as that is not his style, so it falls on me to offer an assessment of the man who started out assessing me in the darkest of days. No one has made a bigger contribution to the future well-being of my family than Chris Mead. Through the worst times, he has been stoic and resourceful. It takes a special person to be able to begin with the end in mind. At our lowest ebb, in total misery, Chris provided us factual understanding, realistic options and hope. At no stage did he flinch from his duty; at no point was he not honest. He is a man of great integrity and a credit to his force, his family and himself. Nothing – and no one – outranked the needs of my family. Thank you – Mr Mead.

Second, good news about Oliver. He has got a carpentry apprenticeship, pending examination results and we are delighted. Oliver has always said he wanted to become a carpenter and, given his considerable practical ability, he will do well in his chosen field. Now he can work towards his future. Is it coincidence that he is doing what Ruth Harrison so long ago suggested might be best for him? In a month's time, Oliver will reach the ripe old age of 15. From our perspective as his parents, it has been desperately sad to witness our son's confusion, unhappiness and fears over the last 2 years. Oliver has been a shadow of the energetic, outgoing, full of fun 12-year-old we loved – but not any more! Ever since his return from New Zealand, Oliver has started to regain his confidence. There is a spring in his step and a smile on his face as he dashes home in between playing football, snooker, badminton and table tennis. Oliver only sees the good in everyone and we are proud of him for that. His welfare has always been paramount for us and, ultimately, his resilience has been our salvation. There can be no greater joy than to play your part in educating and nurturing children along life's path so they can embrace their own independence. Nicola and I will have the privilege of doing that for our son. Yes, our life has been full of tragedy and unrequested intrusions, but, as a family, we are back on track.

I now have a sense of balance and that has allowed me to request the publisher to proceed with this book; a task made easier because David Cohen has stepped forward to take on that role. In David, I have someone who has already proved his integrity, and that allows me to place my trust in his guidance and stewardship of my defining project. Despite the manic twists and turns of the last couple of years those key values of integrity and trust hold true, I am pleased to say, in so many of our friends and acquaintances.

This book represents the full stop at the end of a very long sentence. Now I can rejoin those closest to us to embrace the future, and I feel that despite Holly's death, despite all the traumas I have described, there is a future which will still have some brightness to offer.

Thank you for taking the time to read my story.

One Year On

Today is Monday 16 May 2005. It has been just over a year since I completed the then-final chapter of my book – 'An Ending of Sorts'. Today is a very good day to be back at my desk, as I am in no great shape for window cleaning! With my aching joints, stiff muscles and a torso peppered with bruises, it is almost a relief to work with only my fingertips and brain once more. What put me in this sorry state? A dust-up with the paparazzi? Nothing so glamorous. I was one of three well-meaning but ill-prepared adult volunteers to go with Oliver and his Under-15 football team-mates to an end of season paintball 'fun day'. But it meant far more than a simple day's outing.

When our world was turned upside down, Oliver withdrew into himself. I could never have foreseen that only a few years later, he would display such a confident, outgoing, and competitive nature. It is a very positive sign that life continues, with all of its challenges. We decided we would not let Holly's murder be the end of our lives. Oliver is now very much back to his old self, as proved by the bruises which testify to my advancing age (yes, they do still hurt when you press them, Oliver!). Nicola and I will always hold our son's well-being to be the most important factor in our lives. When he collected the 'Most Improved Player of the Year' award this season, it meant much more to us than just a sign he'd learned some lessons on the field. Well done, Oliver.

The last year has had its twists and turns, with continuing regular updates on Huntley and Carr coming from our tireless friends in the media. Most of the reporting focuses on Maxine Carr and her various alleged exploits. Before too long, the attentions of the tabloids won her a permanent anonymity order, but it no longer matters to me or my family. We have all stopped reacting to the likes of Carr and Huntley. It seems the media have finally accepted this, since they no longer contact us for comment on each new development. As we have faced our share of media intrusion it seems ironic that the court should grant Carr a lifetime order to prevent the press reporting any details of her whereabouts. Having seen her legal team protect Carr from questioning, shield her from photographers and arrange for certain of her 'court appearances' to take place by satellite link, I am almost not surprised that neither she nor Ian Huntley seem to understand the depth of hatred that most principled, family-orientated people in this country have for them.

Ironic is the word. Could it be that Maxine Carr's successful 'day's work' in the courtroom, though it led to her acquittal on the more serious charges, has left her without any chance of clearing her name and reputation, or knowing real liberty? Well, in my opinion, you only deserve the former if you possess honesty and integrity.

There was, however, one newspaper report that did catch our attention, and no doubt also struck the jurors who gave Maxine Carr the benefit of the doubt back in December 2003. Huntley apparently now alleges that Maxine Carr told him to burn the bodies of Jessica and Holly. Carr denied that during her trial. But if, for once, Huntley is telling the truth, then everything else that is a matter of record, such as the intensive cleaning of the house and car, takes on a rather different light.

You have to believe me when I add that as Nicola and I cannot change what has happened, we will not allow any new developments to affect our emotional well-being. That is the right way for us to move forwards. The publication of this book in March 2005 helped us regain a sense of balance and feel we had reclaimed our daughter's memory. There is no need to comment any further about those two wretched individuals.

Meanwhile, there has been another violent death in Soham. A resident of the very street where the Chapmans live, just around the corner from my house, stands accused of murdering his former partner. Though this bears neither the slightest relation nor any resemblance to the deaths of Holly and Jessica, the media respond, predictably enough, by demanding a comment. The phones ring again, and for a terrible moment it seems the circus will be back in town. Even if we had a comment to make, we wouldn't, but as it happens, there's nothing for us – or the Chapmans – to say. Our thoughts go to the surviving members of the woman's family as they prepare to face the trial process and come to terms with their loss.

Twice in three years, my home town has been thrust into the spotlight. We hope this will be the last such incident for a while.

We have not moved out of Soham, and we don't intend to. The town has been deeply affected by our family's loss, from the earliest days of the search, and we are in some ways more connected to the community than ever before. Everyone I've written about in this book, from Holly and Jessica's schoolmates to the Police Family Liaison Officers who became so important to our lives, and the local vicar who all but became a celebrity, has been marked by these events. In general, life in Soham rolls on, but there have been some changes.

I have been very struck by the resilience of the local children and the positive way in which they have all performed. Holly and Jessica's 2002 St Andrew's year group are now in Year 8. I know they have been closely monitored over the last couple of years and the vast majority have coped and settled down extremely well. Unfortunately, there are always some exceptions. Nicola and I can only hope and pray for the children who still receive professional help. Their continued pain is a powerful reminder of the ripple effect from one man's evil actions. Now and then, usually by accident, we bump into boys and girls who were Holly's close friends. They all seem so much more grown up now, and from time to time, Nicola and I check with their parents to find out how they're doing. When we see these young people growing up, as Holly and Jessica should be, we can't help but wonder what Holly would have looked like today. Holly's image will always be that of a young girl just a few weeks shy of her eleventh birthday. Do any of Holly's friends still think about her? The gifts, flowers and messages which they regularly leave on Holly's grave answer that question, loud and clear.

The school has also seen some staff changes. Headmaster Geoff Fisher has moved to Little Thetford School, eight miles away from Soham. Little Thetford Village, of course, was the setting of the false sighting of Holly and Jessica in 2002. Geoff will be sorely missed at St Andrew's and his successor will face an enormously difficult task. They will need not only to maintain educational standards, but to earn the respect and affection that so many parents, like ourselves, hold for the departing Head.

The Principal of the Soham Village College, Howard Gilbert, is also about to depart. In September 2005 he will take charge of a larger college, closer to his home. I know that everyone wishes him well. Along with his fellow staff members and vice-principals, Howard had the unenviable task of nurturing, guiding and educating children in unprecedented and traumatic circumstances. At some stage soon, we are likely to be in contact with the Village College administration again. This time our meeting will have a positive feel to it; hopefully, the residual £37,000 from the Holly and Jessica Fund can be put towards some new changing rooms, a facility much needed by the many girls' and boys' football teams that play there most weekends.

From the moment in 2002 when both families declined to engage with the media, the mantle of the 'voice of Soham' fell upon the vicar, Tim Alban Jones. Over a long period of time, Tim represented my home town admirably, before finding himself overwhelmed with interview requests. Once you have placed your head above the parapet, there's no way to win with the media. There were times when Tim's media appearances created conflict. As a father whose one thought was to secure justice for his daughter, I was concerned by the risk that Tim's many interviews might lend weight to the 'unfair trial' applications that Huntley and

Carr's legal teams repeatedly argued in front of the court. In the end, nothing Tim said or did caused any harm to the prosecution, and all such issues are completely in the past. I feel comfortable occasionally joining the St Andrew's congregation and watching Tim do the work he was trained for, as he happens to be a first-class clergyman. I have seen him many times over the past few years and it is obvious to me that Tim's true vocation is as a man of God. I suspect that when the church authorities believe Soham is ready for a change of face, Tim will be quietly bumped up the ranks. If and when his promotion comes, he will be sorely missed.

Dennis Mackenzie's part in the search has brought widespread recognition of his special talents. He's been busy ever since and now writes a weekly column for a national magazine. I am sure he will excel in this new role, and hopefully bring a little comfort to the many people who seek the services of a genuine medium.

Going public about our experience with Dennis has led to my learning much more about the paranormal than I ever expected to. It's not that I've become 'a believer' – I've *heard* Dennis predict fact after fact that at the time he could not have known by any normal means. Later, many of those same facts not only proved to be true, but were essential to the case against Huntley. I don't fully know what I believe: but where I used to scoff at the notion of psychic powers, now, the evidence of my own senses has taught me there's much more to this life than science can explain yet. In some ways, that comforts me.

The detailed notes I kept on our consultations with Dennis are said to have intrigued some police, as a contribution to the ongoing debate as to whether 'psychics' can be of use in their investigations. I've since learned that an agency exists in Florida, teaching cops to develop extra-sensory perception. It's enough of an issue in the USA for some people to have suggested that the government should license psychics, and crack down on the charlatans.

I've been reading about this through the year, out of interest: I wondered if other police forces had achieved breakthroughs by using mediums. The Los Angeles Police Department had a study done, which found that psychics were no better at identifying guilty parties than random guesswork. On average, they said a psychic could be expected to 'get it right' about once in their lifetime!

But there are other experts who have found that mediums can sometimes be useful. Vernon Geberth, in his book *Practical Homicide Investigation*, describes how officers can and do work with psychics. Of course, the police – like me, to begin with – are always sceptical, but Geberth seems fascinated by several mediums. One of them, Noreen Renier, says that after touching an object from the scene of a crime, she can 'see' the crime take place and identify the offender.

I also read of Ken Charles, a British police officer who used his psychic abilities over a 32-year stint in the Met, doing all manner of police work including fraud, burglary, murder and Royal Family Protection. The Queen Mother is said to have consulted mediums, so they must have had plenty to talk about.

Charles's autobiography, *Psychic Cop*, claims that he used his remarkable powers of intuition to 'read' a suspect, tricking them into making a mistake and leaving clues that would reveal their guilt. Before I met Dennis, I would probably have thought this *Psychic Cop* either a liar or a little bit mad. Now I just can't say.

And Dennis himself contributed to another murder hunt. He recently came back from across the pond, where his work with the police department in the Midwestern city of Wichita, Kansas, is a matter of public record. Dennis was brought in to assist with the investigation of nine murders that took place over a 31 year reign of terror, at the hands of the 'BTK Serial Killer'. Working with the former lead detective on the case, Dennis made a number of observations about the person responsible for the carnage – observations very different from those provided by the 'professional psychological profilers' used by the Wichita PD. On 26 February 2005, as Dennis had predicted, a man was arrested and charged with the murders. He will stand trial soon. As if further proof of his talents were needed, Dennis confirmed to the police details of the monogram 'signature' used by the killer, which were never made public. It is, indeed, a very strange world we live in, much of it hidden from most of us.

I have written a great deal about the very mixed blessing of being recognised as Holly's Dad by strangers, which brought both touching expressions of sympathy and hurtful 'cold shoulders'. Since 2004, there has been a good side to my slight celebrity. It has allowed me to become active in promoting some of my favourite causes. First at Pride Park, the home of Derby County Football Club, Nicola and I became Ambassadors for the Football Association's Child Protection and Best Practice programme. I was hoping that as an Ambassador, I'd be addressed as 'Your Excellency', but maybe that only happen in films. The title – even if it was only ours for the day – did have to be earned. Giving interviews and speeches will never be my strong point, but I was glad to play a part in publicising the FA's forward-thinking intentions. The theme of the annual conference on child protection was 'Doing the Right Things' and both of us left Derby awe-inspired by the commitment of so many professional people to improving children's lives.

At the end of the conference, Nicola and I had our picture taken with a talented group of schoolchildren who had closed the proceedings with a couple of songs. Nicola was quick to point out that these children were in the same year as Holly was in 2002. It was a very poignant moment.

Soon after, I gave a short speech on behalf of the Care and Education team of Cambridgeshire County Council, to support the launch of 'Staying Safe in the Foundation Stage' a ground-breaking programme for children aged 3–6 years. The programme seeks to lay foundations for healthy, assertive and confident children by encouraging conversations between adults and kids. This echoes the key message of Grief Encounter, the charity of which I have become a patron. The founder of Grief Encounter, Shelley

Gilbert, and her committee are busy planning for the next stage of the charity's development. I hope to be of help to them in the near future.

On 23 February 2005, Nicola and I, along with other family members, attended an awards ceremony held by Cambridgeshire Constabulary to recognise the many officers and members of the public who contributed to Operation Fincham. The ceremony began with the handing out of Senior Investigating Officer's Good Work Certificates before moving on to the Chief Constable's Letters of Recognition. Finally, the evening ended with the Chief Constable's Commendation award, reserved for those who displayed exceptional service, over and above that expected in the normal course of duty. We were delighted that all of the Family Liaison Officers, for both families, and indeed their coordinator, Gary Goose, received this highest of awards. Of course, the atmosphere was rather muted and I am sure that all of the recipients had mixed feelings, particularly as both the Chapman family and ourselves dominated the front two rows. We were a very real reminder of Holly and Jessica.

Gary Goose had the sensitivity to ask both us and the Chapmans about what to say in his remarks. His opening speech was spot on. Gary told the audience that the night was a celebration of the successful conviction of Ian Huntley, and an opportunity to commend those who'd played a part in bringing him to trial. Gary also pointed out that thanks were due to many officers and staff who had not been assigned to the investigation, as they had to keep all other routine work going at a time of great pressure. Nicola and I hope our presence showed our deep gratitude to all caught up in the frenzied intensity of the operation. Despite the frustrations, points of conflict and media criticism of Operation Fincham, nothing will change the fact that everyone did their best.

At an informal reception after the ceremony, it became clear that many officers involved in our fight for justice had been deeply affected by the experience. Some told us of moments from the investigation that they know will be with them for the rest of their lives. It was a very humbling evening.

Also present at the awards was the detective who led the enquiry, Detective Chief Superintendent Chris Stevenson. Chris has become the third individual associated with the 'Soham murders' to be formally recognised. In the New Year Honour's list for 2005 he was awarded the Queen's Police Medal for distinguished service. I am sure he and his family must be very proud of his achievement. Chris accepted the award 'on behalf of every single member of the team who was involved in the investigation', and well done him.

The never-ending publicity led to a number of official enquiries. During the middle of March, a copy of Sir Michael Bichard's final report summarising progress on the reconvened Inquiry dropped through my letter box. Sir Michael's covering letter made it clear that there is still much to do, in addition his earlier recommendations. I am heartened by his assurance that he will remain a 'concerned observer' in the future – a future that will involve much hard work by all the agencies that deal with children.

Three weeks later Nicola and I received a contact letter from the new Home Secretary, Charles Clarke, confirming the government's intentions to continue and advance the work. It is clear from Mr Clarke's formal reply to Sir Michael that he will not allow any sense of complacency to develop; and like Mr Blunkett before him, Mr Clarke seems to be a tough, no-nonsense type. If further proof were needed, he has pledged to provide a further composite report to parliament and the public in October this year, and again in March 2006. It really does appear that significant changes which should benefit countless children and families will take place in the not too distant future. As Holly's parents, we are grateful and relieved that something positive and permanent will emerge from our loss.

Sir Michael's original recommendations included the establishment of a National Police Intelligence Service, so regional forces can share information more easily. Most of his report seemed intelligent, with a good dose of common sense, proposing improvements to the database kept by Social Services (why is the British government so bloody awful with computer systems?) and increased emphasis on vetting. He concluded that those recruiting for jobs that involve access to children need to be made to understand just how important it is to vet applicants thoroughly. It all sounds pretty straightforward and obvious to me: but there's been some resistance, for all the Home Office promises of 'rapid action'.

I'm sorry to say that much of this resistance has come from the National Union of Teachers. They've opposed the suggestion that fingerprints should be taken from new teachers, on the grounds of privacy. I've heard that though new teachers are vetted more intensely since the report, those who've been in post for many years are still not being vetted. So far, the task of making absolutely certain – there's no margin for doubt or error here, as Huntley's case shows – that no teacher poses any identifiable threat to children is one that has not been achieved yet. I can understand the logistical difficulties, but they seem to me to be irrelevant compared to learning from what happened. As Holly's dad I would rest much easier if the 'Spirit of the Bichard Inquiry' were taken as seriously as the new legislative guidelines.

In response to what was supposed to be Sir Michael's final report, the Home Secretary confirmed that 'the initial work of coordinating the implementation programme has been led by the Home Office in conjunction with the relevant government departments and national stakeholders. Having received Sir Michael's final report, the work is now effectively in the second delivery phase of the programme.' Let's hope the government sees it through.

But maybe priorities have changed. For two years, Holly and Jessica were always in the headlines, staring out from the front page – I've written about how difficult and strange that was for us. Now, in 2005, the media flavour of the month seems to be the notion that our children are out of control, with packs of little monsters in their 'hoodies' just waiting for a chance to mug their parents. You read of children as young as 8 being slapped with Anti-Social Behaviour Orders, as though adults need protection from virtual toddlers, and not the other way round. While I don't deny that the young commit a lot of petty – and occasionally serious – crimes in this country, I hope that somewhere, in the belly of bureaucracy, there's an understanding that children will always be more at risk from adults than vice versa. I hope most of all that those who shape policy never forget what happened when suspicions about Huntley lay lost in the files.

Holly is mentioned in our home most days and remains a constant presence in our thoughts. In a few months' time, she would have been fourteen years old, with a wonderful future ahead of her. Every so often, despite our strong appearances and agreed positive outlook, we can't escape the sense of loss. Sometimes it rolls in, as a gradual mist that makes for sad, reflective days; sometimes it descends as thick fog, a blanket of pain and confusion. We accept that these feelings will be with us for the rest of our lives.

Over a long period of time, friends and family members alike have slowly shared their feelings about our tragic loss, speaking of the impact it had on them and their children. Hopefully our 'plan' to embrace the rest of life in a positive fashion can lend a small example to those we care for, as they have been our support and salvation. This passage of our lives has also allowed us to add new friends and acquaintances, including some fine upstanding police officers! The Family Liaison Officers and their coordinator, namely Trudie, Chris, Stewart and Gary, will always feature in our lives. As they go about their business, moving home, welcoming new officers and mapping out their careers, Nicola and I will remain in touch. We both know we are fortunate to have so many wonderful friends.

We all still await one final piece of news. Although Ian Huntley has been given two life sentences, no tariff has been set. It has been nearly eighteen months since the verdict, and to be kept waiting so long for this crucial decision is almost unforgivable. It may yet turn out that the legal system, so contorted in its representation of the accused throughout the trial, will disappoint two families forced into this longest of journeys, at the very final furlong. I can only pray to the bottom of my boots that common sense prevails, and 'life' will mean life for Huntley. They must never let him out.

We accept that Soham will crop up in the news for many years to come – though as time goes by, it will appear further and further away from the front pages. These days, as I said before, the press no longer calls us for a comment when there's news about Huntley or Carr. But just a few days ago, on Tuesday 31 May, the *Daily Mail* reported that the Chief Constable of Cambridgeshire, Tom Lloyd, had set a less than brilliant example for his officers when he became 'extremely drunk' at a function! Mr Lloyd admitted 'inappropriately' addressing a female official, and the dreaded words 'sexual harassment' soon cropped up in all the tabloids. We knew the story would be big, and before long the phone was ringing off the hook again, with journalists asking Nicola and me to comment. We declined, as this development had nothing to do with Holly or Operation Fincham, and we felt it would be wrong for us to say anything. We do not consider ourselves to be guardians of public or police morality. We are just parents who became recognisable trying to cope with the murder of our daughter in the full glare of publicity.

In the end, on 7 June, Tom Lloyd resigned 'in order to safeguard the reputation of the Cambridgeshire Constabulary'. Can there be a positive result from this development? Perhaps there can. With Mr Lloyd now gone, the new chief constable, whoever he or she may be, will have an opportunity to start afresh, personally untouched by the criticisms levelled at the force throughout Operation Fincham and its aftermath. The new chief won't have to be defensive, and it will be easier for them to learn the lessons of the past few years. Nicola and I welcome the new appointment for that reason alone.

So, with a new set of ladders I return to start my window-cleaning round anew. Hopefully, with a few years' work, it will grow to resemble the business I once had. I know this return to my old line of work is the right move for me and my family. None of us harbour delusions of grandeur from our time in the public eye. All we want is a chance to pick up the life we used to know and enjoy so much. Nicola has kept her job, and her quiet, unassuming loyalty to her boss, even when she was facing extraordinarily difficult circumstances, testifies to her great strength of character. Nicola has always been the family organiser and linchpin, quietly insisting on high standards throughout our home and family life. Yes, our lives are back on track, and Nicola's rock-solid courage greatly accelerated the process of healing. I believe we have come through this terrible passage of our lives and survived, together, as a family. There is no better sentence for me to finish with.

Further information

The following addresses may be useful to some readers:

- *Grief Encounter Project* is at PO Box 49701, London N20 8XJ (telephone 0208 4467452).
- *Childhood Bereavement Network* is at 8 Wakeley Street, London ECIV 7QE (telephone 0207 8436309).

ACKNOWLEDGEMENTS

- Copy editor: Reuben Cohen
- Original jacket cover: Ian Hughes
- Maps: Sophie Clausen and Leia Berryman
- Psychology News Press who published the original hardback wish to thank Sonia Land and her company, Sheil Land Associates Ltd, for all their assistance, and also wish to thank Media Publishing Services for their help.

VIDEO

The video, *Our Daughter Holly*, mentioned in the text is available from Psychology News Ltd at 56 Britton Street, London ECIM 5NA (email *psychologynews@hotmail.com*).

Index